ADULT LEARNERS, ADULT EDU
AND THE COMMUNITY

STEPHEN BROOKFIELD

Adult Learners, Adult Education and the Community

Teachers College, Columbia University

New York and London   1984

Simultaneously published in the U.S.A. by Teachers College Press,
1234 Amsterdam Avenue, New York, N.Y. 10027, and in Great Britain by
Open University Press, Milton Keynes, England

LC 83-51118

ISBN 0-8077-2702-4

Text design by W.A.P.

Manufactured in Great Britain

89   88   87   86   85   84   1   2   3   4   5   6

Library of Congress Cataloguing in Publication Data

Brookfield, Stephen.
  Adult learners, adult education, and the community.

  Bibliography: p.
  Includes index.
  1. Adult education.   I.   Title.
LC5215.B67   1984   374   83-1832 0

ISBN 0-8077-2702-4

This book is dedicated to my parents, David and Sybil Brookfield

Contents

page

Acknowledgements   x

Chapter 1   **Introduction:**
An Overview of Concepts and Research   1

The ubiquity of adult learning; adult learning groups in the community; researching adult learning in the community: community adult education: redefining adult education in terms of group and community transactions; adult learning in the community — a conceptual analysis; experiential learning

PART I   **ADULT LEARNERS IN THE COMMUNITY: THE INDIVIDUAL MODE**

Chapter 2   **Independent Adult Learning: A Conceptual Analysis**   22

Independent learning and correspondence study; independence in learning; self-teaching; self-directed learning; autonomous learning; independent learning as the aim of education; voluntary learning

Chapter 3   **The Adult Learning Iceberg**   34

The inquiring mind; the work of Allen Tough; other research reports; researching the adult learning iceberg: a methodological critique; successful independent learning

PART II ADULT LEARNERS IN THE COMMUNITY: THE GROUP MODE

Chapter 4 **Community Adult Education**   60

The concept of community; the neighbourhood community; liberal and liberating models of community adult education; institutional implementations of community education — community schools and village colleges; contemporary community education provision in the United States and Britain; programme and process in community education; the educative community; a typology of the community practice of adult education

Chapter 5 **Adult Learning Groups, Community Development and Community Action**   90

Autonomous adult learning groups in the eighteenth and nineteenth centuries; radio listening and study discussion groups; community learning; community problem solving; community action and adult learning; community development — the educational component; the Antigonish movement, the Highlander folk school, the Liverpool EPA project

PART III SUPPORTING ADULT LEARNERS IN THE COMMUNITY

Chapter 6 **Identifying and Researching Adult Learners in the Community**   128

Assessing the needs of a community; the community survey; informal assessment methods; qualitative and quantitative modes of research; interviewing adult learners in community settings; grounded theory; participatory research; researching adult learning in the community — an example

Chapter 7 **Supporting Adult Learners in the Community: The Individual Mode**   149

Principles of adult learning; facilitating learning — the helping relationship; learning how to learn — mathetics and learning contracts; information, counselling and brokering services; public libraries and independent learners; learning exchanges; experiential learning

Chapter 8 **Supporting Adult Learners in the Community: The Group Mode** 173

Social change as an educational aim; community roles for adult educators; free universities; study circles; supporting adult learners in the community — a case study; training community adult educators

Chapter 9 **Conclusion: A Personal Postscript** 198

Value choices and contextual variables; accepting ambiguity — the limbo of the informal educator

References 204

Index 222

Acknowledgements

In keeping with the international character of this book I have special thanks to give to a Briton, a Canadian and an American. To Arthur Jones, past Professor of Adult Education at the University of Leicester, for showing me just how effectively qualities of intellectual challenge and humanistic concern can be combined; to Allen Tough, of the Ontario Institute for Studies in Education, for awakening and then nurturing my interest in informal adult learning; and to Jean Lesher for encouragement and informed criticism throughout the preparation of this manuscript.

For the emotional and aesthetic sustenance essential to the completion of this project I have to thank, in particular, Richard Thompson, Ashley Hutchings, Simon Nicol, Dave Swarbrick, Dave Pegg and Dave Mattacks.

For their personal support during the writing of this book I would like to thank Andrew Brookfield and Pam Howlett.

I am grateful to the National Institute of Adult Education (England and Wales) for permission to excerpt and paraphrase some material which appeared previously in *Adult Education* Volume 54 and in *Studies in Adult Education* Volume 13. (Further information on these periodicals is available from the NIAE at 19B de Montfort Street, Leicester, LE1 7GE.) I am also grateful to *Community Education Journal* (the quarterly publication of the National Community Education Association, Washington D.C.) which published another version of passages in this book.

ONE

Introduction: An overview
of concepts and research

The Ubiquity of Adult Learning

To declare that adult learning is ubiquitous is to assert a simple and self-evident truth. Learning occurs throughout the developmental stages of adulthood and in a variety of settings, only some of which can be designated educational in terms of formal adult education provision. In this sense, the much invoked term 'lifelong learning' can be said to describe an empirical reality rather than summarizing an adult education philosophy or representing a political strategy. We do not need to advocate the introduction of lifelong learning since this already exists; adults are continually acquiring new skills and knowledge in familial, recreational and occupational settings. A comparative symposium of views from Europe and North America on *Strategies for Lifelong Learning* (Himmelstrup *et al.* 1981) is, therefore, mistitled. What these authors regard as lifelong *learning* — 'the opportunity for individuals to engage in purposeful and systematic learning during the periods of their lives when this opportunity is most relevant' (p. 6) — is lifelong *education* as conceptualized by UNESCO (Lengrand 1975). What the contributors to this symposium are really advocating is that adults should enjoy a greater degree of flexibility and support with regard to their use of educational institutions, opportunities and facilities at different times in their lives. The assumption underlying this advocacy is that purposeful and systematic learning is possible only if the adult participates in formally sponsored adult education programmes. It is the contention of this writer, however, that there is no need to argue for lifelong learning as if it were a privilege to be bestowed upon a deserving clientele. Adults cannot help but acquire new skills and knowledge as they proceed through life and it would be a highly perverse individual who managed to shield himself or herself from all those circumstances and life changes which necessitate the development of new competencies.

Of course, merely to assert that learning is an ever-present feature of adult human existence is to make no judgement regarding the quality or effectiveness of such learning. It may be, as several authorities have claimed, that learning which occurs without the continued supervision of a professional adult educator is often chaotic, serendipitous, and ineffective. In an historic text issued by the then fledgling Adult Education Association of America the verdict of adult education professors was that 'the educational setting constructed by an external agent to make systematic achievement possible is still required in most cases for an individual to accomplish the needed learning' (Verner 1964, p. 31). The desirability of inculcating independent learning skills in learners is probably the most frequently cited purpose of education. However, the assumption of respected learning theorists such as R. M. Gagné is that 'according to experience as currently appraised, developing a student into a truly independent learner takes years. That is why organised programs of instruction exist — to fill these years with learning' (Gagné 1975, p. 120). Little has also opined that learning which is not under the control of a teacher or instructional agent 'does not attain the systematic achievement present in the formal instructional setting' (Little 1979, p. 8). Given this conceptual and theoretical stance, it is not surprising that the National Advisory Council for Adult Education (USA) should offer a definition of an adult learner which is orientated towards the pursuit of institutional recognition and accreditation of learning. To them, an adult learner is 'an adult who is enrolled in any course of study, whether special or regular, to develop new skills or qualifications, or improve existing skills and qualifications' (National Advisory Council on Adult Education 1980, p. 3).

The value-orientations underlying the foregoing definitions and arguments are clear; learning undertaken by adults outside formal education is inherently inferior in its design and execution to that occurring in institutional settings. Those individuals and groups which undertake to plan and conduct their own learning will invariably come to grief and this will cause them to enter professionally designed and controlled instructional settings. However potentially accurate such observations may be, they are generally made without reference to supportive empirical evidence. One purpose of this book is to assess the empirical veracity of these assertions through a review of research into that learning which occurs outside formal educational institutions.

Declarations regarding the existence of adult learning in non-formal and informal settings are commonplace in the literature of adult education. In his historical analysis of self-learning, Kulich points out that 'up to fairly recent times, when most nations accepted a goal of widespread and readily available schooling for everybody, self-education was the prime way for man to cope with the world around him' (Kulich 1978, p.

310). A recent review of British adult education contains the assertion that 'most adult learning goes on outside the classroom and always will. It is such a mundane and familiar activity that it is easy to overlook how deliberately and constantly many millions of adults are seeking to learn something new' (Rogers and Groombridge 1976, p. 58).

The massive survey of American adult education in the 1960s estimated nine million adults to be engaged in independent study and acknowledged that 'self-instruction is probably the most overlooked avenue of activity in the whole field of adult education' (Johnstone and Rivera 1965, p. 37). Again, the Alexander report on Scottish adult education declared that...

> There are many adults in all walks of life who have acquired the capacity to maintain the process of self-education through reading and discussion, through selective viewing and listening, through travel and by many other means, without the need to participate in any form of organised educational programs. (Scottish Education Department 1975, p. 49)

We may agree with Kathy Penfield, then, that 'we know that most of adult learning takes place informally and that adults learn all the time — but we know little of how well they learn, what resources they use and how effectively they work, or where there are areas of need that are totally unmet' (Penfield 1975, p. 43).

Despite recognizing that most adult learning takes place outside educational institutions, most adult education researchers choose to concentrate their attention and research energies on the minority of adults who actually participate in formal classes. This is partly a result of methodological considerations. After all, it is much easier to analyse the characteristics and activities of a readily identifiable sample engaged in classifiable activities than it is to survey the diversity of learning occurring outside classrooms. Also, since the survival of the service and its continued funding depend on attracting ever-increasing numbers of adult students on to courses, researchers may feel that their efforts ought to result in an increased clientele for adult education. From this point of view, any proof that adults can conduct learning projects in an effective manner without the supervision of professional educators is threatening to the service's continued existence.

Nonetheless, research into adult learning in the community has become increasingly common in the last two decades. In 1964 the American Commission of Professors suggested that 'research into self-education might be a fruitful area of investigation for adult educators' (Verner 1964, p. 31). The subsequent sixteen years have witnessed a host of studies, inspired primarily by the Canadian researcher Allen Tough (1978), which have considered the nature and extent of independent adult learning. In 1973 the American Commission on Non-Traditional Study estimated that over five million adults were engaged in 'self-study' — a total of 16.9 per cent of all adult learners (Gould 1973). More recently, an OECD survey contained information submitted by the US Department of Health, Education and Welfare which indicated that 'the major planner of adult learning...is the learner himself. Self-planned and self-initiated learning accounts for approximately two-thirds of the total learning efforts of adults' (Organisation for Economic Cooperation and Development 1979, p. 20).

Adult Learning Groups in the Community

Aside from the body of evidence amassed regarding independent, self-directed learning, the last twenty years have also seen a growth in adult educators' appreciation of the learning occurring within informal community groups. The writings of deschoolers such as Illich (1971) and Reimer (1971) have focused attention on the development of learning networks based on neighbourhood groups and local skill models. Freire's work (1972) with peasant illiterates in Latin America has provided inspirational support and a practical role model for educators seeking to develop problem-solving and problem-posing skills amongst such groups. The major British post-war report on adult education acknowledged the importance of voluntary community groups and societies in providing settings for educational discussion outside the formal adult education sector...

> The strength of these voluntary organisations lies in their relative informality, their ability to encourage a sense of loyalty to a movement, and their skill in promoting adult education in a satisfying social setting. (Her Majesty's Stationery Office, para. 119)

Indeed, before the onset of mass education in industrial societies, voluntaryism was at the heart of adult education rather than being a peripheral element. In the major studies of the history of adult education in Great Britain and North America authored by Kelly (1970) and Knowles (1977) respectively, we can see that working mens' reading groups, agricultural societies, coffee houses, mechanics' institutes and lyceums were exemplifying the self-help and mutual exchange philosophies advocated today by deschoolers and those opposing mandatory continuing education. To radical and progressive educators the following contemporary (1838) account of lyceums in action must sound remarkably familiar...

> Lyceums are associations formed for the mutual improvement of their members and the common benefit of society. Their members meet on frank, cordial, and

equal grounds. All declare, by joining a lyceum, that they wish to extend their knowledge; and from the manner in which they associate each may become, by turns, a learner and a teacher. All unnecessary formalities, as well as expenses, are to be avoided, that the way of learning be rendered as free as possible. (Barnard 1838, p. 40)

Thus, besides adopting the principle of pooling community educational resources for mutual self-improvement, the lyceum constituted an early example of an andragogical, open learning system. It was financially open and there was no prescribed curriculum. As Shawen has pointed out . . .

> The lyceum was a learner-centred operation . . . the members themselves determined the content of learning sessions. Learning outcomes were deliberately open-ended . . . a given member would become a teacher if he possessed some particular knowledge which was judged of benefit to others. This type of experience-sharing as a means of realising individualised learning goals is at the heart of modern adult learning theory. (Shawen 1979, p. 27)

The 'Anyone Can Teach — Anyone Can Learn' slogan of the American Free University movement can be seen as a contemporary equivalent of the 'by turns a learner and a teacher' lyceum philosophy recorded by Barnard. The lyceum movement is sometimes seen as a reflection or remnant of the pioneer, frontier mentality of the eighteenth and nineteenth centuries. As the 1948 Handbook of Adult Education in America recorded throughout the pioneer period natural groupings of individuals banded together to explore any subject matter which interested them. "Study groups" existed before that name for them was invented (Rogers 1948). However, the spirit underlying the formation of autonomous learning groups cannot be consigned to the nineteenth century. Indeed, it might astonish some contemporary advocates of self-help groups and open learning systems to learn that the 1930s and 1940s saw a number of national experiments in the creation and support of autonomous adult learning groups. The Learning Box schemes at the Universities of Western Australia and Sydney, partially funded by the Carnegie corporation, ran throughout the 1930s with the purpose of facilitating learning through self-help groups among scattered rural populations (Watts 1978). During the 1940s the Canadian Broadcasting Corporation (CBC), the Canadian Federation of Agriculture and the Canadian Association of Adult Education (CAAE) combined to create the *Farm Forum* series of radio programmes. The function of these broadcasts was 'to give farmers a new incentive to group action and neighbourliness, and to stimulate thought and understanding among rural listeners' (Conger 1978, pp. 224–5). The motto of the scheme was 'Read, Listen, Discuss, Act' and the medium for this early implementation of a Friereian 'praxis' was the self-help study group. In the 1950s the 'Great Conversation' entered into by adults in the American *Great Books* programme was conducted through the medium of locally-organized, study–discussion groups.

These experiments were not grounded in clearly-expressed grass roots political or educational demand. They served to stimulate and foster such a spirit but were initially the creation of 'passionate educators' (to use Faris's term) (Faris 1975) in the broadcasting networks. More recent ventures in the tradition of creating local, semi-autonomous adult learning groups are the *Living Room Learning* scheme sponsored by the University of British Columbia in the 1960s and the *People Talking Back* programmes of the CBC in the 1970s. Although not exhibiting the same political animation function as the *People Talking Back* experiment, the British Open University's attempt to encourage the formation of local self-help study groups as a central feature of its teaching–learning arrangements can also be placed in this tradition. Thus, to declare a role for adult educators in initiating and supporting local study groups outside the formal adult education structure is not to argue for some bold new initiative; rather, it is to continue a tradition which has been dear to the hearts of generations of adult educators.

Researching Adult Learning in the Community

As I suggested earlier, one of the reasons why university library shelves are not filled with titles on adult learning in the community is that such learning does not easily lend itself to investigation through the classic, scientific method. Based on the model of investigation said to be used by natural scientists, particularly physicists, the scientific method has several identifiable steps; (1) Identify the problem to be solved; (2) Develop a tentative hypothesis or explanation; (3) Operationalize the testing of the hypothesis or explanatory proposition by designing an experiment and specifying admissable evidence; (4) Collect the relevant data; (5) Confirm, refute, or modify the hypothesis. The method is characterized by apparent objectivity and detachment on the part of the investigator and results are represented with clarity and precision.

Such a procedure is well suited to studies where control and experimental groups are readily available, where accurate instruments exist for pre- and post test measurement, and where the parameters of the study are clearly drawn. In the investigation of that learning which occurs primarily in a natural societal setting (in families, community groups voluntary societies etc.) rather than within academic institutions or classrooms, such precision is hard to obtain. Students of adult learning in the community are entering largely uncharted research waters. They cannot enjoy the luxury of working with established research paradigms and, given the paucity of theoretical frameworks in this field, they are unlikely to be able to devote their energies to verifying or modifying any previously proposed explanatory hypotheses.

Faced with the aforementioned difficulties, the response of adult education researchers interested in adult learning in the community is often to abandon the elegance, precision and clarity afforded by established 'scientific' modes of enquiry in favour of qualitative or participatory research methods. This can, however, place a promising academic career in jeopardy, place a researcher in isolation, and require a measure of professional courage. In a revealing set of essays on the personal odysseys of young social science researchers, one contributor describes his abandoning of academic expectations concerning the scientific method in his study of farm workers. . .

> What I now realise, with the benefit of hindsight, is that the positivist paradigm of problem formulation, hypothesis, operationalisation and testing is not so much misleading as personally inoperable. Had I not possessed the initial interest in farm workers, irrespective of a professional interest qua sociologist, then I would never have been able to devote five years of my life to studying their social situation with all the boredom, tedium, depression and sheer physical effort that it entailed. (Newby 1977, p. 108)

This kind of identification with, and commitment to, the subjects of one's research is one of the characteristics of participatory research as proposed by the International Council for Adult Education. Participatory researchers argue that a full appreciation of adult learning in the community, especially that which occurs within the context of community action, community development, and within disadvantaged groups such as adult non-readers, can only be obtained if the researcher abandons the traditional canons of scientific methodology. This theoretical position has been argued strongly by ethnomethodologists (Garfinkel 1967) and advocates of grounded theory. It has seen its most large-scale implementation in national studies of adult basic education in America (Mezirow *et al.* 1975) and the United Kingdom (Jones & Charnley 1978), both of which used a grounded theory approach to the analysis of data.

Community Adult Education

As I have already indicated, the history of adult education contains many examples of attempts by animateurs and educators to foster the development of self-help study groups existing outside formal educational institutions. These groups were established for avowedly educational purposes and with clearly defined educational aims in mind. However, if we are to consider the full range of adult learning in the community, then we must also examine that learning which occurs in groups whose aim is not primarily educational — tenants' associations, citizen participation groups, neighbourhood improvement councils, co-operative societies and other community based groups. Chapter 4 presents a conceptual typology of community adult education and considers the relationship between education, development and action. Although development and action may be conceptually distinct from education, nonetheless there is an educative component in most developmental and activist initiatives.

The literature of community education and community development offers a rich source of confirmatory evidence for any researcher seeking to illustrate the neologistic perversity of academics. A host of differing meanings have been ascribed to the concepts of 'community', 'education', 'development' and 'action', and the discussion of these is bedevilled by terminological ambiguity. The term 'community education', in particular, is heavily culturally loaded. As Kirkwood (1978), Lotz (1977), and Roberts (1979) have all pointed out, the concepts of community education and community development have their roots in the colonial era of the British empire. In the United States community education has traditionally been associated with the efforts of the Mott Foundation. As expounded by Berridge (1973) and Seay (1977), it is school based and centres on the twin notions of using school resources for individual and community improvement and on using the community as a teaching aid or learning resource. American adult educators such as Hiemstra have adopted elements of this perspective and talk of the 'educative community' as a 'living learning laboratory' (Hiemstra 1972, p. 28) linking the family, school and community. In one of its earliest publications, the Adult Education Association of America also accepted the Mott view of the community as a learning laboratory or learning resource (Hallenbeck *et al.* 1962). A recent implementation of this philosophy has been introduced at the Northwest Regional Educational Laboratory in the state of Oregon which has produced various resource packs for teachers on *How To Make The Community Your Classroom* (Mclure *et al.* 1977).

British community adult educators however, draw a distinction between the *liberal* and *liberating* notions of community adult education. The liberal notion of community education regards communities as organic harmonious entities. Advocates of this philosophy and procedure argue that it is possible to serve the needs of all members of a community at any one time. Such a belief is exemplified by the definition of community education offered by the professors of adult and community education in an American 'delphi' study: 'the process of identification of community needs so that the community and its members can grow through social and educational programs' (Fellenz & Coker 1980, p. 319). Most British community educators subscribe to the alternative 'liberating' concept of community education. This acknowledges that communities are groupings rent by inequalities of class, status and power, and that in choosing to meet the needs of one sector (for example, tenants' associations) the educator must ignore or even oppose the needs of another (for example, landlords). To these writers, education is the arm of radical social action aimed at promoting the collective advancement of the working class and disadvantaged or minority groups. Community education assumes a political significance and the processes of community education, community development, and community action are seen as intertwined and allied to the pursuit of social justice.

The British advocates of this radical concept of community education look to North America in the 1930s for their role models citing such initiatives as the Antigonish co-operative movement and establishment of credit unions in Nova Scotia, and the Highlander Folk School's work in union education in Tennessee.

Canadian practitioners of community adult education also emphasize the activist and developmental aspects of their work looking to the radical heritage represented by Jimmy Tompkins and Moses Coady's fostering of credit unions and community action groups in Nova Scotia in the 1920s and 1930s. These efforts were based on St Francis Xavier university in the town of Antigonish and the notion of the educator as 'animateur', so much a part of the French Canadian perspective on the field, can be traced directly back to the activism of Tompkins and Coady.

Many of the activities of developers and activists are not overtly educational, in fact they are generally orientated towards achieving social and political change. Such change may be in the physical fabric of the community, as, for example, when a group of mothers campaigns successfully for the introduction of a pedestrian crossing near a busy interchange, or a refuge for battered wives is built as a result of pressure from womens' groups in the locality. Change may also be reflected in constitutional re-arrangements (for example, the establishing of neighbourhood councils), enshrined in law (the introduction of community legal aid) or simply reflected in altered attitudes (on, for example, the rights of gypsies). In all of these instances, however, those seeking to achieve change will have been required to develop new skills and to acquire new knowledge. In this respect, most development and activist initiatives have a strong educational component in that their protagonists engage in the deliberate and purposeful acquisition of specified skills and knowledge, as well as learning 'experientially'. Both of these kinds of learning will be reviewed within this volume.

Redefining Adult Education in Terms of Group and Community Transactions

The American Adult Education Association in the post-war era has adopted the practice of issuing a handbook of adult education on a decennial basis. For the current decade the 'handbook' has been extended to eight volumes covering theory and practice in the field, one of which attempts to conceptualize adult education practice in terms of three transactional modes. In *Redefining the Discipline of Adult Education* the authors argue that adult education transactions occur in individual, group and community modes. These modes are outlined as follows:

1. The individual transactional mode — refers to independent study courses or other situations where students learn by themselves.
2. The group transaction mode — where individuals meet together in a group to explore some mutual concern or problem.
3. The community transactional mode — where citizens collaborate to resolve a problem facing their community.

(Boyd & Apps 1980)

The authors do admit to similarities between the group and community modes of enquiry. Both focus on groups and are concerned about exchanges among members of groups. However, a basic conceptual distinction is drawn in that transactions in the group mode are solely intragroup, whilst those in the community mode are intergroup. Thus, the community group is outward looking and concerned about problems created by individuals or institutions outside the group. It seeks to influence persons and agencies external to the group.

From this writer's point of view, this classification appears to raise problems in that the adult learning covered in this volume moves across the three transactional modes. Each mode refers to a learning situation; whether the learner is working independently, in a group, or as a community member. The principle underlying this typology is that recognized by Aristotle as endemic to all classificatory schema; that is, the mutually exclusive nature of its constitutent categories. My own research and reflection, however, would suggest that this is not the case. Certainly self-directed learning cannot be regarded as equivalent to isolated learning since Tough (1979a) and Brookfield (1981a) have both attested to the importance of assistants and learning groups to self-teaching and independent learning projects. Knowles has also pointed out that self-directed learning 'usually takes place in association with various kinds of helpers, such as teachers, tutors, mentors, resource people and peers. There is a lot of mutuality among a group of self-directed learners' (Knowles 1975, p. 18).

In my own research into learning in local community groups and voluntary societies in the United Kingdom (Brookfield 1980a) it is apparent that adults whom Boyd and Apps would regard as independent learners in the individual transactional mode regard local hobbyists' groups and enthusiasts' societies as their most important learning resource. Reviewing a little known aspect of adult education history in America, Seller has outlined the parallel educational universe represented by immigrant self-help dyads and groups in the post World War One era. . .

> The Finnish boarding house, the Greek or American coffee house, the local candy store, the ubiquitous corner saloon — these and similar natural gathering places served as informal classrooms where 'old timers' taught newcomers a few basic English words, how to get a job, where to find help in case of illness or other crises, what local politicians could be relied on for various services, and which American laws were enforced and which could be broken with impunity. The night school taught American ideals; the saloon keeper taught American realities
>
> (Seller 1978, p. 89)

In this informal equivalent to the world of immigrant education as recounted in the fictional experiences of Leo Rosten's Hyman Kaplan, all three transactional modes are present. In community transactional terms the curriculum of such activities would certainly be determined by wider societal factors. However, intragroup communication would also be crucial in terms of the development of self-esteem and of immigrants retaining their indigenous cultural identity in an alien 'host' society. Finally, skills and knowledge would be learned from individual mentors as well as in groups. It is the contention of this book, then, that adult learning in the community cannot be compressed into one or other of the three transactional modes outlined earlier. In the studies documented in the following pages there are many examples of individual learning projects which make substantial use of groups as learning resources, which regard intragroup forces as important supports to individual learning, and which are oriented towards community development or community action. The activities of working class adults in London's East End as outlined in Young and Willmott's studies of Bethnal Green and Stepney (1962) constitute an excellent example of a multi-transactional educational venture. Disregarding the statutory welfare, housing and employment agencies these adults organized their own informal programme of instruction in health care, home maintenance, and child-rearing skills. These can be seen, then, as community orientated learning activities executed within dyad and larger group settings.

Adult Learning in the Community — A Conceptual Analysis

We need now to examine more closely the nature of the adult learning which will be the focus of attention in the succeeding pages of this book.

Learning is defined by psychologists in a number of ways, but two features seem to be central to most definitions; that learning involves change, and that such change is permanent in that it leads to altered behaviour. The contexts in which such learning, such permanent behavioural change, can occur are, as we have seen, many and varied — homes, schools, voluntary societies, community groups, workplaces, churches, even adult education classes. In whatever setting learning occurs, however, the permanent behavioural change is usually identified in terms of newly developed skills. These skills may be psychomotor (such as being able to play tennis) or cognitive (such as being able to understand developments in the economic life of the country). Often there will be a blend of both types of skill (as in wiring a house) when the adult will need to have a full knowledge and understanding of a field of interest before attempting to perform some operation new to him or her.

When we come to consider the settings in which such learning can occur we need to recognize the distinction made by Jensen (1964) between learning in the natural societal setting and learning in the formal instructional setting. This distinction has been adopted by Verner (1964), Clark (1973), Dickinson (1979), and Little (1979) among many others and it has important implications for our discussion.

Natural Societal Setting
This is the day to day world of individual experience represented by family interactions, recreational pursuits, and occupational life, and the learning occurring therein is often regarded as incidental. Apps (1978) has bemoaned the fact that 'unfortunately our society has not recognised the importance of incidental learning' and that 'even worse, many persons believe that unless learning opportunities are offered by some institution, the learning somehow is of lower quality or maybe is not learning at all' (p. 6). In a major British text on adult learning, Lovell has also recognized that. . .

> Besides the formal learning that adults undertake there is an even greater amount of learning of an incidental kind that comes about as a consequence of a person's everyday experiences. There are innumerable ways in which we learn and amass new ideas, facts, attitudes and skills as the result of our day to day interaction with our environment. (Lovell 1980, p. 10)

In the foregoing quotations, both Apps and Lovell seem to be arguing unequivocally for the value of incidental learning yet, clearly, they do not regard 'incidental', as equivalent to 'accidental'. Although learning occurring outside schools, colleges and universities may sometimes be unplanned and accidental, there must be much that is purposeful and deliberate. As the discussion on experiential learning later in this chapter shows, the circumstances occasioning learning may often be outside the individual's control; for example an enforced job change, childbirth, conscription.

However, the individual who decides that the acquisition of certain skills and knowledge is essential to managing such crises and changes successfully is behaving in a highly purposeful manner. Thus, the examples Lovell quotes as 'incidental learning' — work, parenthood, social and technological change, do-it-yourself — are not incidental (in the sense of being fortuitous) at all. They are attempts intentionally to 'amass new ideas, facts, attitudes and skills' (to use Lovell's words) in order that adults may better understand and control their social and occupational environment. The fact that such attempts occur outside classrooms does not make them 'incidental'. Although these learning efforts may be characterized by some writers as chaotic and incomplete, there is ample evidence from researchers in America, Canada, and Britain that much adult learning in the community is deliberate and purposeful.

To the British philospher of adult education, Kenneth Lawson, learning in the natural societal setting has no place within the concerns and practice of adult educators. He dismisses the idea of a learning situation, which he regards as 'so general as to be of little or no value as a guide to educational practice or as an indicator of the kind of situation that is educationally relevant' (Lawson 1979, p. 30). He argues also that it is only when a teacher 'engineers' situations in which exercises, problem-solving, experiments, analyses of performance, and criticism are present that adult education occurs. Both Verner and Little share this view, indeed Little regards attention to learning in the natural societal setting as socially dubious as well as philosophically inadmissible. He writes...

> Both fortuitous and intentional learning in the natural societal setting are inefficient and uncertain. Generally, neither a society nor an individual can rely solely on learning in the natural societal setting as the means of achieving the knowledge and skills necessary for survival in a rapidly changing world. (Little 1979, p. 8)

Dickinson, too, believes that learning in the natural societal setting is 'an inefficient way of learning which may even be harmful to the learner since no one is guiding the activity' (Dickinson 1979, p. 4). The implication within all these assertions is clear enough; adult learners themselves do not possess sufficient skills and judgement to conduct their own learning effectively and must consult those designated as 'professionals' in this sphere.

Formal Instructional Setting
The formal instructional setting comprises situations where an educational agent assumes responsibility for planning and managing instruction so that the learner achieves previously specified objectives. The advantage of the formal instructional setting is that 'learning is not left to chance but is planned to occur in a systematic ordered milieu' (Little 1979, p. 8). The

formal setting need not be restricted to classrooms, or even educational institutions. Factories, offices, community groups, pubs, churches and private homes are all settings for formal instruction. As Dickinson maintains...

> although the places where guided learning can occur are many and varied, the element common to all formal instructional settings is that someone is responsible for arranging the external conditions of learning to increase the probability that learning will occur. (Dickinson 1979, p. 4)

In which of these two settings for learning does adult learning in the community, as conceived in this book, occur? At first glance, the non-institutional, non-formal character of the natural societal setting seems the more relevant. The fact that such learning constitutes a deliberate, intentional pursuit of skills and knowledge, however, serves to suggest that 'formal instructional' should be the designated category. The learning may occur in natural societal settings — churches, enthusiasts' groups, living rooms, hobbyists' societies, tenants' associations — but it is characterised by the degree of pre-planning endemic to the formal instructional setting.

However, although the features of deliberation and intention place this learning within the category of the formal instructional setting, the term 'formal instructional' does seem oddly inappropriate. After all, this learning is outside the formal educational system and it does not exhibit the narrowly vocational quality suggested by the term 'instructional'. It is purposeful and planned, but is is likely to exhibit false starts, unproductive avenues of enquiry and a staccato rate of progress. The instructional role may be performed by different individuals at different times and in the case of self-directed learning, teaching and learning roles will be performed by the same individual. Again, just because learning is purposeful and deliberate does not mean it will be successful. For these reasons 'natural societal' rather than 'formal instructional' seems a more suitable term. In general, however, it is evident that the Jensen distinction fails neatly to consign adult learning in the community to one of its two categories.

One feature which is common to all writers who distinguish between the natural societal and formal instructional settings for learning is the equating of deliberation and intention in learning with the pursuit of previously specified objectives. In this book I propose to argue that there is much adult learning occurring outside formal educational institutions which is not oriented towards the attainment of previously specified objectives, but which can, nonetheless, be considered purposeful. I have outlined my thoughts on this point elsewhere (Brookfield 1980b). At this point it is enough to say that many adults are engaged in what is for them a lifelong exploration of a field of knowledge or area of interest without the assistance provided by adult education class membership. Their activities are prompted by the innate fascination a field holds for them and their chief reinforcement is the intrinsic pleasure gained from study. They offend against the insistence that observable, previously specified goals are a necessary condition of learning in that their 'goal' consists merely of wanting to know as much as possible about their chosen area of interest. These adults will frequently be unable to specify target cognitive or psychomotor skills at the outset of their learning project. In a struggle with an unfamiliar subject area in which no accredited expert is available to guide the learner it is inevitable that only the vaguest learning goals can be specified. A classical music enthusiast fired by a desire to know more of the work of composers who have granted him such pleasure can only develop an appreciation of the merits and subtleties of such music when his or her efforts result in an acquaintance with the 'grammar' of the activity (Peters 1965); that is, the standards and operations deemed intrinsic to the subject itself. Once this grammar is acquired, and the breadth and internal nuances of a field are recognized, then the learner can begin to set specific goals for short-term pursuance which can be sequentially organized.

The reader may, at this point, cry 'enough of this tortuous chain of reasoning' and demand an unequivocal statement of the features of adult learning in the community. This request is justified and the measured response to such a request is that such learning exhibits the following features:

1. It is deliberate and purposeful in that the adults concerned are seeking to acquire knowledge and skills.
2. Such purpose and intention may not, however, always be marked by closely specified goals. Learning may be apparently haphazard and therefore unsuccessful at times. A tenants' group faced with a massive increase in rents may spend much time engaged in unprofitable and inappropriate enquiries as they are initially unable to specify the terminal skills and knowledge they require to achieve their broad objective.
3. It occurs outside of classrooms and designated educational institutions and does not follow the strict timetable of the academic year.
4. It receives no institutional accreditation or validation.
5. It is voluntary, self-motivated and self-generating. Adults choose to engage in this learning, although the circumstances occasioning that choice may be external to the learner's control (as in the example in point 2).
6. Acknowledging that the term 'learning' is a gerund — a word which can stand as a noun or verb — it is used throughout this book in its active sense. Thus, learning refers to the *process* of acquiring skills and knowledge, rather than an internal change of consciousness.

Experiential Learning

Writers in the field of experiential learning use the term in two contrasting senses. On the one hand, experiential learning is used to describe the kind of learning undertaken by students who are given a chance to acquire and apply skills and knowledge in an immediate, relevant and meaningful setting. Experiential learning, therefore, 'involves direct encounter with the phenomena being studied, rather than merely thinking about the encounter, or only considering the possibility of doing something about it' (Borzak 1981, p. 9). It is learning in which the learner participates and is directly in touch with the realities that are studied. Those teacher training programmes which require students to spend their first few weeks actually teaching in schools, and which then use that experience as the basis for an inductive derivation of pedagogic principles, are examples of experiential education. This kind of experiential learning is sponsored by an institution and is designed to give students more direct experience in integrating and applying knowledge through internships, service activities, and other field study programmes.

The second type of experiential learning, and the one with which we are chiefly concerned, is also, in Houle's words, 'the education that occurs as a result of direct participation in the events of life' (Houle 1980, p. 221). However, such direct participation is not sponsored by an educational agency and the learning which results is referred to variously as learning through life, prior learning, or experiential learning. As Boydell (1976) remarks, this is the way that most people in fact do most of their learning. However, relatively little thought seems to have been given to the way in which we learn from everyday experiences, or to developing methods for helping us to learn more effectively.

The assessment of experiential learning causes problems for educational institutions when they come to consider the academic suitability of an adult without formal educational qualifications who wishes to enrol for a higher degree. Gartner (1976) has argued that in the eyes of credentialling agencies, those adults who can cite only experiential learning in support of their applications (rather than those whose learning is marked by the award of certificates, grades and diplomas) are effectively 'disenfranchised' when it comes to admission to higher education. In these terms, 'the disenfranchised are the non-young, non-middle and upper class, non-full time, and to a considerable extent, the non-male students' (p. 38). However, attitudes regarding the suitability of these adults for academic study are changing, partly as a result of the greater acceptance of philosophies of recurrent education, but chiefly because demographic change means that institutions of higher education can no longer count on an unending supply of suitable 18-year-olds presenting themselves as candidates for university and college entry. A major concern of colleges and universities is to develop new clienteles of adult students (Moon and Hawes 1980) which involves the recognition of, and development of accreditation and assessment procedures for, experiential learning. As the director of the US Fund for the Improvement of Secondary Education has commented: 'As colleges have become more serious about recruiting and serving adults, it has become clear that some of the precollege activities of these older students look very much like the incollege activities of others' (Smith 1976, p. xi).

Among many adult educators, then, the advocacy of a considered appraisal and recognition of the value of experiential learning has become something of a *cause célèbre*. Typical of such advocacy is Jacobson's statement that . . .

> The élitist attitude that knowledge can only be disseminated in certain classrooms by designated data/culture purveyors limits our educational horizons and denies the reality of media (television, radio, newspapers and magazines), work, and community experience as educative. (Jacobson 1976, p. 98)

Cyril Houle has also argued that 'we must cultivate a new spirit that accepts the educative value and worth of all experience, not merely that which is devoted to scholarly study or which is guided at every step by professors' (Houle 1976, p. 33).

Experiential learning does, of course, contain two components — experience and learning. Experience on its own has no intrinsic educative merit since one can experience any number of emotions, situations or crises yet exert no purposeful desire to acquire knowledge and skill. Experiencing a broken leg or blindness does not in itself constitute learning, unless learning be equivalent to the enlarging of the scope and intensity of emotions experienced by the individual. However, if one acquires new competencies in order to adjust to this new situation then that acquisition must be counted as experiential learning. Kirkwood argues that the learning component of experiential learning 'must be neither so esoteric as to defy description nor so mundane as to caricature the academic process' and that 'if such learning is to be creditable in academic terms, it cannot be random' (1976, p. 151).

This, surely, is the crucial feature of the learning component of experiential learning. The event occasioning learning may have been accidental but the learning which arises out of this changed circumstance is rooted in the adult's desire to adjust to a new situation. Unemployment is a case in point; a person may experience unemployment and if the resultant alienation and bitterness lead only to an apathetic resignation then the experience has no learning component. If, however, the adult takes steps either to cope with the mental, physical and financial shock of the prospects of long-term unemployment, or if he or she determines to acquire what are seen as new and more marketable skills, then experience has resulted in intentional, purposeful learning.

As experiential learning and learning in the natural societal setting can be considered to be roughly equivalent, the criticism voiced against the latter can be applied to the former. Proponents of the validity of experiential learning should be wary that in the vigour of their advocacy they do not exclude learning within the formal instructional setting or portray it as somehow intrinsically less rich, less multi-faceted, and less meaningful. In one of the few attempts to compare experiential and classroom learning, Coleman (1976) has identified the following characteristics of experiential learning...

1. It is ncn-mediatory: there is no adoption of a symbolic medium (of concepts, abstract ideas, theories, or propositions) but only action and observation of consequences resulting from that action. As Coleman comments, 'a typical observation of someone who has learned something through this process is that he cannot verbalise it, but he can do it'. (p. 56)
2. Motivation is intrinsic: because action occurs at the beginning of a sequence that results in satisfaction and unanticipated consequences, the subjective need for learning exists at the outset. This means that 'motivation is seldom a problem with experiential learning, while teachers often see it as the major problem of learning in the classroom'. (p. 57)
3. It is retentive: its non-symbolic nature ensures retention in that affective and cognitive aspects are linked. Thus, 'the associations that embed it in memory are linked with concrete actions and events to which affect was attached, and are not merely associations with abstract symbols or general principles expressed in abstract symbols', (p. 58)

The chief problem with experiential learning, Coleman argues, is the problem of induction. Experiential learning which is highly specific and associated with an individual event does not easily give rise to generally applicable principles. Whereas classroom instruction performs a mediatory, symbolic function in identifying the generalizable, transferable skills which are contained within events and operations, in experiential learning events have to be repeated many times before inductive generalization occurs. Experiential learning can be a very time-consuming process and this is why in some circumstances it will be more sensible to use instruction to achieve desired ends and inculcate required skills and knowledge.

It is the contention of this book, however, that experiential learning need not always be brought within classrooms for it to be effective. Indeed, a major debate in American adult education at present concerns the extent to which the pressure for credentialling leads to adults feeling inadequate, (Ohliger 1974), the perpetration of academic fraud, (McGee 1981) and a narrowing of the fundamental liberalizing purpose of adult education. Perhaps an equally profitable approach is to take that learning which results from events and experiences outside the classroom and seek to improve its quality as, when, and where it occurs. This may be achieved through the development of self-directed learning skills, through what Boydell (1976) calls self-actualization characteristics/abilities to be derived from learning to learn programs, or in a number of other ways. Some of these techniques will be considered later in this work.

PART I

Adult Learners in the Community: The Individual Mode

TWO

Independent Adult Learning: A Conceptual Analysis

One of the most serious barriers to the advancement of understanding in any field of study must be the existence of conceptual ambiguity and terminological confusion. The newcomer scrutinizing the various forms of informal adult learning in the individual mode soon comes to realize that the field is plagued by a plethora of definitions. Hence, the same act of learning (such as a mother scanning the library shelves for material on child psychology) can be variously described as self-directed learning, self-teaching, autodidactic activity, autonomous learning and individualized learning. Again, the single term 'independent learning' can be used by different writers to refer to such dissimilar activities as the completion of a closely prescribed correspondence course or a tropical fish enthusiast experimenting with different methods for diagnosing piscine disease: this, despite the fact that the decisions regarding the subject matter to be considered by the correspondence student, the reading list to be consulted, and the rate of learner progress, all rest with the correspondence teaching institution.

Clarification of the notion of independent learning is particularly necessary in view of the frequency with which correspondence study and independent learning are held to be equivalent. Driscoll's paper on 'New developments and changes in independent study' provides a good example of this...

> The three years that have elapsed since the last international conference have been important ones for independent study in the United States. Probably at no time since the correspondence study movement began in this country has there been so much activity and so much promise for the future.
>
> (Driscoll 1972, p. 26)

Similarly, Frank Brown's book subtitled *New Approaches to Independent Study* reveals itself as a cookbook of techniques for implementing individualized instruction (Brown 1968). Again, a journal article on 'Independent study:

three reports from Asia' (*Convergence* 1972) concerns itself solely with innovations in correspondence education systems.

Independent Learning and Correspondence Study

The use of the adjective 'independent' to describe the learning behaviours of correspondence students seems extraordinarily obtuse and perverse when we realize that the techniques of correspondence education (and other media of individualized instruction) tend to be rigidly prescriptive. One of the few writers to attempt to untangle this substantive and conceptual knot is Michael Moore who has presented what he calls 'a tentative theory of independent study' (Moore 1977, p. 6). His efforts are based on a fusion of research into self-directed learning with that into mediated instruction. Moore classifies educational programmes in terms of the autonomy they exhibit (the extent to which the learner conducts the planning and execution of learning) and their distance. Distance, in turn, is a function of structure (the extent to which the goals and procedures of the teacher match those of the learner) and dialogue (the extent to which interaction between teacher and learner is possible).

In Moore's terms, correspondence education systems usually exhibit high structure and low dialogue. They encourage convergent and conventional thinking and foster relationships of dependence rather than the opposite. The chief skill developed by a correspondence student, in Harrison's opinion, is how 'to develop perfunctorily 'relevant' answers to the questions asked of him which are based wholly on the encapsulated knowledge of the course material' (Harrison 1974, p. 3). The founders of the correspondence movement, William Rainey Harper and William Lighty did, however, set a laudatory, rhetorical tone in their writings which lingers to this day. Hence, proponents of correspondence education declare that studying in this mode results in the learner acquiring the capacity to think critically, to set learning goals, to locate appropriate resources, and to assess progress.

These speculations remain, for the most part, untested by empirical investigation. We may agree with Holmberg that 'Students developing independence and capacity for critical study' (1977, p. 102) is indeed an important aim of correspondence instruction; or that developing in all learners the capacity to carry on self-directed learning (Wedemeyer 1971, p. 550) is one aspect of independent study. However we need to know more about two features; whether correspondence learners conduct their learning in the same manner as independent, self-directed learners, and the extent to which the skills acquired through engaging in distance education are equivalent to those developed during independent, self-directed learning.

This writer's own attempt to compare the learning activities of correspondence students and independent learners (Brookfield 1980a) revealed that the physical separation of teacher and student clearly did not grant cognitive independence to the latter. Comparing the behaviours of a sample of correspondence students with those of a sample of independent learners highlighted the heavy reliance of correspondence students on their lesson units. These students viewed such units as self-sufficient and did not attempt to consult any non-prescribed texts. Such a reliance can be viewed as a tribute to the abilities of course writers. It can also serve as a warning against implementing a teaching – learning approach, in preference to a learning – teaching approach, in the design of correspondence study materials. In the learning – teaching approach, as conceived by Moore, 'it is the teacher who responds to the learner and the learner is self-directing in his learning activities' (Moore 1973b, p. 32).

Independence in Learning

As R. M. Gagné has pointed out in a discussion of learner mediation processes (1971), there is a sense in which we are all independent learners. Even within the formal classroom, teacher messages and behaviours (the learner's external stimuli) are perceived and coded according to the learner's own idiosyncratic coding procedures. The learner's past experiences and the previous learning which has taken the nervous system to its current state will perform a mediatory function with regard to the reception of new stimuli. Mediation is thus regarded as an inferred process by means of which external stimuli are coded by the learner's system before being functionally connected, or associated by learning, with responses. All learners perceive and codify stimuli in an individual, idiosyncratic fashion and to that extent all learning activities are characterized by a degree of independence.

Equally, however, there is a sense in which totally independent learning is an impossibility. Cognitive activity which is anything other than contemplative introspection involves interaction with external stimuli. Since this implies change (no organism ever retains its exact previous state of equilibrium after interaction) all contact with non-human materials such as educational broadcasts, books and magazines, must alter the learning effort. Such non-human resources are, of course, devised by humans. Their contents are deliberately sequenced for ease of assimilation and they may contain messages and information which are intended to effect learner change. In fact, an eminent British philosopher of adult education maintains that it is possible to define the term 'teacher' in such a way as to include 'the author of a book or the producer of a film, record or tape which is either intended to induce learning by whoever wrote or produced it or which is used by the learner himself as an intentional aid to learning' (Lawson 1979, p. 27). The physical absence of a human presence does not mean that the solitary reader or viewer is unaffected by the unseen author or producer, since these individuals partly control the learner's cognitive operations. As Moore points out, therefore, the independent learner must not be thought of as 'an intellectual Robinson Crusoe, castaway and shut off in self-sufficiency' (Moore 1973a, p. 669).

If it is not the physical separation of teacher and student that is the characteristic of independent learning, how then can we judge whether or not an adult is learning independently? The key notion here is that of learner responsibility. As I have written elsewhere...

> Independent learning is that which takes place when the decisions about inter-mediate and terminal learning goals to be pursued, rate of student progress, evaluative procedures to be employed and sources of material to be consulted are in the hands of the learner. (Brookfield 1980b, p. 3)

This does not mean that independent learning occurs in an isolated social and intellectual vacuum. In particular, it does not mean that independent learners are excluded from association with fellow learners and with experts. The learner may engage in the temporary submission of authority to an accredited expert when, for example, a budgerigar breeder visits a specialist on disease diagnosis to learn how to detect and treat common bird ailments. The overall responsiblity for the learning activity rests with the breeder and when the expert has provided the specialist knowledge required, the learner reasserts control over the direction of future learning.

Independence, therefore, is signalled not by the physical context in which the student is working but by the degree of control exerted over the content and method of learning. To this extent the location of the student is irrelevant. Should a class member decide to diverge from a tutor's notions of acceptable source materials, appropriate mode of study, suitable rate of learning, or topics deemed worthy of attention, then he or she can be said to be learning independently. The price of such divergence is likely to be high, however, when measured in terms of exclusion from class membership and denial of institutional accreditation, and this is why independent learners are sometimes characterized as 'mavericks' flaunt-ing a static and uncreative educational establishment. Jourard (1967), for example, believes independent learning is the embodiment and implementation of imaginative fascination requiring courage of heroic proportion.

This is by no means the whole truth about independent adult learning, though, and many who develop their own idiosyncratic style of learning do so because the formal education system as it stands cannot accommodate the demands of their particular situation, rather than because they reject the notion of formalized education *per se*. Indeed, they may be envious of the opportunities afforded for uninterrupted reflection to those more educationally fortunate than themselves who have the time and money to benefit from expert instruction within a group of like-minded individuals.

In the sense in which the term independent learning is used in this book there is a second important dimension of independence which we have to consider. As I have argued, the independent learner exhibits an independence from external instructional direction; the learner decides what, when, and how to learn, and is responsible for judging progress. Assistance from experts may be incorporated into a learning project but the learner controls the direction and future of learning. The second dimension of independence centres on the fact that the learner is independent of any institutional connection. There is no institutional recognition or accreditation granted to such learning; no institutional certificate or diploma is awarded in acknowledgement of successfully conducted learning. Neither does the learner receive any institutional financial assistance — he or she bears the full cost of conducting the learning.

We can offer, then, the following definition of independent learning as conceived in this book: independent adult learning is that learning which occurs independently of the formal education system and which is characterized by learner responsibility for the direction and execution of learning. Independent learning is equivalent to adult learning in the community in the individual mode. It should be viewed as a portmanteau concept, a generic term which covers a group of learning behaviours and under which a range of activities can be subsumed. At this point in our discussion we should perhaps consider briefly some of the most common synonyms for independent learning and some of the most frequently used similar concepts.

Self-Teaching

A term coined by Allen Tough to describe the activities of an adult who, having determined to acquire some previously specified knowledge or skill, will then 'assume the primary responsibility for planning his strategy, maintaining his motivation, and making certain throughout his learning that everything necessary for success is done' (Tough 1966, p. 30). A self-teaching project occurs when an adult has spent at least eight hours over a period of twelve months pursuing some particular knowledge or skill, providing responsibility for planning, directing and conducting learning resides with the learner. Chapter 3 considers in more detail the features of these short-term, skill-orientated projects.

Self-Directed Learning

In the context of adult education, this term is most associated with Malcolm Knowles. It relates to his notion of andragogy as the mode of teaching and learning most appropriate to adult education and its constituent features are outlined in his guide for self-directed learners and teachers. Self-directed learning is...

> a process in which individuals take the initiative, with or without the help of others, in diagnosing their learning needs, formulating learning goals, identifying human and material resources for learning, choosing and implementing appropriate learning strategies, and evaluating learning outcomes. (Knowles 1975, p. 18).

It is noticeable that the settings for self-directed learning which Knowles envisages are within the formal adult education system. A self-help study group in an Open University degree course would be a form of self-directed learning as conceptualized by Knowles. Other examples would be Free University seminars (Draves 1980), the negotiation of learning contracts within higher education (Berte 1975), or degree courses using independent study arrangements (Percy & Ramsden 1980). The Presidentially appointed American National Advisory Council on Adult Education has broadly adopted Knowles' definition in its outline of adult learning terminology (NACAE 1980). As Griffin (1978) has pointed out, Knowles' handbook has provided a *modus operandi* for many adult educators who are seeking to reverse the accepted teaching–learning relationship based upon a one-way transmission of information and teacher direction. Knowles, she believes, 'is giving us a label, a hope, some specific ideas for implementing that hope. He is helping us focus our energies...(and)... he is having a significant impact' (Griffin 1978, p. 6).

Autonomous Learning

Autonomous learning, as it is usually defined, is interchangeable with the concept of independent learning as discussed within these pages. The reason why 'independent' is preferred is rooted in the semantics of colloquial discourse. To this writer, the word 'independent' as generally used implies an absence of institutional affiliation or connection — the learner is independent of institutional recognition. 'Autonomous' carries with it the sense of learner control but it also implies separateness from fellow learners, as well as from institutional recognition. It suggests that the learner operates in a social and intellectual vacuum with no contact with fellow learners.

The term has been used by (amongst others) Miller (1964), Strong (1977), and Moore (1980). Moore defines an autonomous learner as one who can identify learning needs, generate learning goals and objectives, and evolve evaluative criteria. Autonomy and independence are held by Moore to be equivalent. Strong, also, emphasizes the primacy of learner control in her definition of autonomous learning in which the learner is the prime agent in planning objectives, setting standards, and devising learning methods. Autonomous learning, therefore, represents freedom — 'the freedom to choose what to learn, when, how and from whom, to choose from all that is logically, mentally and physically possible' (Strong 1977, p. i). The inculcation of the skills and self-confidence to use such freedom creatively is one of the most frequently-cited objectives of university teachers as revealed in surveys of professors in the United States (Chamberlain 1960) and Britain (Beard 1972).

Independent Learning as the Aim of Education

The desirability of encouraging learners' ability independently to conceive and execute learning projects also finds frequent expression in the literature of adult education. As Kidd writes, 'it has often been said that the purpose of adult education, or of any kind of education, is to make of the subject a continuing "inner-directed", self-operating learner' (Kidd 1973, p. 47). Gardner views the ultimate aim of instruction as being 'to shift to the individual the burden of pursuing his own education' (Gardner 1963, p. 12) and Dressel and Thompson declare that 'the ability to carry on independent study alone or with peers should be a major goal of education' (1973, p. 2). The capacity to think independently is seen as socially necessary by Keuscher (1970) who believes that the quickening pace of technological change requires citizens who are capable of independent action and self-directed learning.

This feature of the accelerating pace of societal change has also prompted Carl Rogers to support the placing of a greater emphasis on the development of an affective disposition towards independent learning . . .

> The aim of education must be to develop individuals who are open to change. Only such persons can constructively meet the perplexities of a world in which problems spawn much faster than their answers. The goal of education must be to develop a society in which people can live more comfortably with change than with rigidity. (Rogers 1969, p. 304)

Given this catalogue of arguments for the social and educational desirability of encouraging independent learning, it might be wondered that any teachers still bother to use traditional classroom methods. In fact, as one advocate for teaching independent skills points out, 'it would seem that it is not the central aim of by any means all teachers: for were it so, courses and methods of assessment would give additional credit to the capacity for independent study and thinking' (Beard 1972, p. 184).

Voluntary Learning

The voluntary attendance of adults at classes has often been taken as the distinguishing characteristic of adult education as a field of study and practice. Because the adult voluntarily enters into some kind of educational transaction with a teacher, the nature of the subsequent encounter is fundamentally different from that which pertains in school-based education. Such a distinction was explicitly acknowledged in the title of the massive survey during the 1960s of adult education participants — *Volunteers For Learning* (Johnstone & Rivera 1965). In Britain the spirit of voluntaryism permeates the world of adult education. Indeed, one of the chief providing agencies, the Workers Educational Association (WEA), functions only because of local networks of voluntary staff.

This British emphasis on voluntaryism is partly a result of the historical accident of remit and classification which led to the major reports on adult education of 1919 and 1973 concerning themselves solely with non-vocational adult education. Consequently, adult education was conceived as being limited within certain well-defined curricular boundaries. Adult education students followed courses in the social sciences (sociology, psychology, economics, politics), in the liberal arts (history, English literature, music), or in the creative arts (painting, pottery). The fields of industrial training or retraining, of continuing professional education, of in-service training programmes, indeed of all forms of education or training within the business or industrial spheres, were considered to be outside the scope of adult education. This was not to deny their importance, merely to declare that whatever else they were, their work-related, vocational, and occasionally compulsory nature meant they were *not* adult education. The creation in 1977 of a national Advisory Council for Adult and *Continuing* Education, which included within its scope such fields as industrial training, suggests that this tradition may be weakening.

In North America these distinctions do not obtain to anything approaching the extent that they exist in Britain. A period of professional adult education training in Britain would see the fledgling adult educator studying the historical and philosophical traditions underpinning the field and any honing of practical instructional or programming skills would be set within the context of liberal, non-vocational adult education. In a North American University department of adult education, however, the curriculum of programme planning, evaluation, and instructional methods is designed with the needs of programme coordinators in mind, including those working in business and industry. The composition of the student body on graduate adult education training courses would likely reflect this spread of professional concern.

The wide range of activities which it is currently considered practically and philosophically appropriate to subsume under the general category of adult education in North America, inevitably engenders certain tensions. In North American terms, adult education could probably be rephrased as the education and training of adults without too many objections being raised by the majority of those who see themselves as professional adult and continuing educators. This inversion and extension of the term 'adult education' means that within the field of professional adult education practice can be included military education, the Great Books initiative, continuing professional training, recreational education, and the Free University Network. Indeed, attendance at any national or regional conference will confirm this diversity and breadth of providing agencies, funding arrangements and curricular areas. It is against this background of a plurality of agencies and curricular concerns that we can set the debate on mandatory continuing education (hereafter MCE) and voluntary learning.

A major development in the field of adult and continuing education in the 1970s was the development of MCE procedures in certain states and professions. MCE can be summarized as 'the tendency of certain states and professional associations to require the members of certain vocations and professions to fulfill certain obligations in order to retain or renew their licences to practice' (Cross 1981, p. 40). As Cross points out, 45 states now require continuing education for optometrists and 42 require nursing home administrators to attend continuing education courses. A bill recently passed in the Iowa legislature requires all 23 professional licensing boards to introduce continuing education programmes as a condition of licensure. It is salutary to note, however, that an extensive review of the literature of MCE concluded that 'there is no evidence now available that there is any correlation between Mandatory continuing professional education and improved practice' (Cunningham and Hawking 1980, p. 17).

There is obviously a great deal of merit in ensuring that professionals are aware of new developments in research insights and in technological improvements in their field of practice. To any colleagues who have witnessed adult education teachers exhibiting a slavish adherence to pedagogic procedures and curricular concerns which they acquired twenty or thirty years previously, the notion of a periodic enforced updating of skills is immensely appealing. However, although it may be in the profession's own self-interest to embrace the idea and practice of MCE with enthusiasm, a substantial body of committed professionals have mounted a sustained and vigorous critique of this initiative.

This critique has found its chief forum of expression in the recently formed National Association for Voluntary Learning (hereafter NAVL) and the magazine *Second Thoughts*. A task force on voluntary learning was convened in 1979 under the aegis of the AEA/USA and the controversy found expression between the pages of the 1980 *Handbooks of Adult Education* series issued by the AEA/USA (Kreitlow *et al.* 1981). Since adult learning in the community appears to exhibit many of the characteristics of voluntary adult learning, it is appropriate at this point to consider in more detail the debate surrounding MCE and voluntary learning.

The late Roby Kidd, sometime Professor of Adult Education at the Ontario Institute for Studies in Education and Secretary General of the International Council for Adult Education (ICAE), criticized the enthusiasm with which some adult educators embraced the principles and practice of MCE. In a keynote address to the 1977 AEA/USA conference in Detroit he noted that MCE legislation had been accepted 'with approval or glee' and bemoaned the fact that 'we are pathetically pleased to be wanted, to be recognised even for the wrong reason, and we have been quick to see that in the short run there may be money to be made by offering programs to people who are legally compelled to attend some activities'.

The concern of NAVL members centres not so much on the requirement that professionals be made aware of new developments in their field, but that the spirit of MCE for specified professional groups will infuse the whole field of adult education. Of course, according to philosophers such as Paterson and Lawson, this is logically inadmissable since removing the voluntary component from attendance at adult classes would mean that whatever transpired would not be adult education. Adults might be involved but the ensuing activity would have to be described by some other term.

Let us now consider in more detail some of the chief objections to MCE as proposed by the AEA Task Force on Voluntary Learnng . . .

1. Making adult education compulsory is incompatible with the ideals of social democracy; it represents the extension of monolithic forces in society.
2. MCE bestows on professionals a badge of competence which is in reality often undeserved.
3. MCE, through its imposition of minimum standards, endangers free and spontaneous learning.
4. MCE works against the spirit of self-directed learning and encourages dependence on teachers and institutions.

As is apparent from the above, opposition to MCE is based not so much on an empirical research foundation as on fundamental ethical and philosophical objections. Indeed, the authors of the above statements acknowledge that 'the question concerning the value of MCE cannot be solved by research alone. The issue does not hinge on the empirical question of effectiveness, but on ethical and philosophical questions crucial to the practice of adult education' (Heaney 1980, p. 3).

Michael Day has condemned compulsory adult education as 'a repulsive idea... antithetical to the ideals which the early American adult education movement cherished' (Day 1980, p. 5). As he points out, and as Chapter 1 has already made clear, voluntary learning was held to be central to adult education by revered philosphers and visionaries in the field. Lyman Bryson, for example, felt that 'we are helped toward an understanding of the spirit of the movement if we think of all adult education as voluntary. Self-direction is its most characteristic quality' (Bryson 1936, p. 4). Similarly, Lindeman declared that 'Adult education , happily, requires neither entrance nor exit examinations', that 'adult learners attend classes voluntarily', and that 'what they learn converges upon life, not upon commencement and diploma' (Lindeman 1926, p. 114).

The ethical objections to MCE have been given vigourous expression by Kathleen Rockhill who feels that MCE limits individual freedom, turns education into an agent of societal control and places efficiency above ethical considerations (Rockhill 1981, p. 62). She calls for a network of voluntary learning settings based on individual learner needs and stimulated by a learning facilitator whose job 'would not be to teach but to catalyse, advocate, and encourage the design and execution of learning plans on the part of individuals and groups'. (p. 69).

What implications does the debate on MCE and voluntary learning have for our discussion of adult learning in the community? In particular, in what senses are these two forms of learning equivalent or, at least, connected? Firstly, it should be clear that adult learning in the community, in both the individual and group mode, is voluntary. It is in no sense mandated or compulsorily required by some credentialling agency. The circumstances occasioning that learning may not be of the learner's own making (as with the already quoted example of sudden unemployment) but the decision to acquire new and appropriate skills or knowledge does arise from the learner's consciousness.

Secondly, adult learning in the community is often conducted without any reference to providing agencies, and in that way it can be considered to be non-institutional. However, non-institutional is not equivalent to anti-institutional and to regard adult learning in the community as being so by definition is fundamentally misconceived. It is not that independent learners seek deliberately to flaunt the formal system, merely that the idea of using that system does not occur to them. As we shall see in the next chapter, it is simply much more convenient for many adults who seek to explore some new fields of interest, or to acquire particular skills, to decide to conduct their own learning projects. That decision does not imply some once-and-for-all rejection of any kind of institutional accreditation or assistance; indeed, we shall see that experts, mentors and a whole range of helpers are consulted during the course of learning.

Thirdly, adult learning in the community, like voluntary learning, is likely to flourish, and to be more effective, in a democracy. Such learning depends, after all, on a free flow of information, on the ready formation of autonomous special interest and enthusiasts' groups, and on easy access to any individuals who appear to possess the specialist expertise required by the new learners. It is unlikely that these conditions would obtain in a rigidly stratified, monolithic society, which placed a strong emphasis on accrediting all those entitled to help others to learn. Indeed, such a state of affairs is probably inconceivable; even in the most closed societies, underground networks and alternative sub-cultures transmitting knowledge and skills develop. Also, given the ubiquitous nature of adult learning it will never be possible to stop adults acquiring new competencies. A situation in which no learning occurs is equivalent to an intellectual catatonic state, and it is hard to imagine any society surviving in which a majority of members were actively discouraged from learning.

Finally, we can say that independent learning shares with voluntary learning an emphasis on learner control over the direction of learning. The adult who chooses to enrol in a class in order to expand aesthetic awareness, or to gain some practical skills, engages in a limited but voluntary submission of his or her individuality to the control of an expert teacher. This feature of temporary voluntary submission of personal autonomy to an accredited expert can also characterize what this book regards as adult learning in the community. In essence, both these contracts are voluntary. Of course, the adult enrolled in a formal class lasting two or more semesters grants control to the teacher in a more sustained manner than the independent learner who is more likely to obtain small amounts of help from a number of different assistants. However, the adult in the more formal setting has the option constantly available of being able to withdraw from the class if this is considered desirable. There will be no sanctions employed as punitive retribution if the student decides to leave the class. It is this kind of voluntaryism which also informs the learning transactions between adult learners in the community.

THREE

The Adult Learning Iceberg

The title of this chapter is derived from an analogy used by the Canadian researcher, Allen Tough, to describe the submerged dimension of learning activities which is beyond the purview of professional adult educators. Tough advises that we regard the adult's learning efforts as an iceberg, and that the attention of professional adult educators has mostly been focused on the one-fifth of the iceberg — professionally guided learning — which has been visible. Hence, research, theory, and practice have been concerned with the provision of courses, classes, workshops, apprenticeships, correspondence study, educational broadcasting, programmed instruction and other forms of organized adult education. Tough proposes that the massive bulk of the iceberg, up to 80 per cent of an adult's learning efforts, consists chiefly of self-planned learning and is ignored by professionals in the field.

The purpose of this chapter is to examine the research foundations for this belief through a review of research conducted to date into that adult learning within the community which falls within the individual mode; that is, all the forms of independent, self-planned and self-directed adult learning not guided by a professional. As well as presenting the results of these surveys, the chapter discusses some methodological and conceptual criticisms which have been offered regarding this stream of research and theory. We have already seen, however, that investigating the learning activities of adults who operate outside formal classes does raise particular and peculiar problems and may prompt some researchers to opt for a field in which their sample is more identifiable and clearly delimited. Visible indices of independent learning activities (book purchasing, library usage, hobbyists' society membership) are difficult to locate and to explore with any degree of precision. It will also be the case that many independent learners are unused to thinking of themselves as such and will find it difficult to reflect on their past learning, or even to identify their activities as any form of planned and purposeful learning.

I have written elsewhere that 'if one of the criteria for assessing the intellectual weight of a research effort is the number of confirmatory and follow-up studies it inspires, then the work of the Canadian researcher, Allen Tough, must constitute one of the most significant research endeavours of the past two decades' (Brookfield 1981c, p. 110). Measuring the importance of this research solely in quantitative terms reveals that a host of studies have appeared in Britain, America, Canada, Ghana, Jamaica, and New Zealand, all of which served broadly to confirm the accuracy of his speculations regarding the form of the adult learning iceberg. As you read these words there is most probably a graduate student diligently replicating one of Tough's interview schedules within a post-graduate adult education research programme.

As we have already seen, before Tough initiated his own lifelong research project into the phenomenon of self-planned adult learning, there were any number of declarations regarding the existence of such learning, but little empirical evidence to confirm the veracity of such assertions. Tough has now established an accepted research paradigm — an assemblage of methodologies, concepts and typologies — which can be adapted by researchers to a variety of settings. The following paragraphs document the results arising from Tough's own research efforts and the applications of his methodology by other researchers.

The Inquiring Mind

The text which is probably the most identifiable precursor of Tough's work is Cyril Houle's classic study of twenty two continuing learners *The Inquiring Mind* (Houle 1961). Houle spent a sabbatical year at the University of Wisconsin during which time he conducted lengthy open ended interviews with twenty-two continuing learners. These were adults identified by colleagues and friends to Professor Houle as continuing participants in adult education courses over a number of years. A typology of motivational orientation to learning was constructed by the author comprising three categories:

1. Goal-oriented learners: these adults use education to achieve previously specified objectives. They do not function solely within formal instructional settings but are willing to use private reading and educative visits as well as enrolling in an adult education program.
2. Activity-oriented learners: these adults have an extrinsic, instrumental attitude to learning in that they attend classes chiefly for social contact. The subject matter of the course is secondary to the social benefits bestowed by participation.
3. Learning-oriented learners: these adults have an intrinsic commitment to learning and regard themselves as continuing learners. A constant engagement in some form of learning is a chief distinguishing characteristic of their lives.

Houle's text has inspired Boshier (1971) and others to develop and apply his typology to an analysis of reasons for attending adult education courses. However, it also explores a number of themes which are echoed in Tough's work. Two in particular deserve special mention; firstly, the readiness of continuing learners to blend informal and self-planned learning with participation in formal adult education classes, and to see these as mutually complementary elements in a learning project. Secondly, the importance of Houle's continuing learners as 'stimulators'; those who 'have such a contagious belief in the importance of education that they infect those around them' and those who 'go beyond unconscious influence to direct stimulation' (Houle 1961, p. 77). These stimulators, as conceived by Houle, also have a direct conceptual link to the 'skill models' of Reimer (1971) and the 'animateurs' of community education theory (Blondin 1971). Houle was one of Tough's professors at the University of Chicago in the early 1960s and it was he who prompted Tough's interest in self-teaching. In the opening statement of Tough's first monograph, *Learning Without a Teacher* (1967), this debt was acknowledged. Houle had presented to his graduate class his conceptualization of the fundamental steps of programme planning, later expanded and published in *The Design of Education* (1972). Tough was required to apply these stages to an educational programme and chose his own programme of self-instruction conducted while preparing for a Ph.D French examination. He was surprised to discover that most of Houle's stages of programme planning had been followed during his own intensive preparation for that examination. This experience provided him with a substantive area for research — adults' attempts to teach themselves new knowledge and skill — and a conceptual framework for the investigation of that topic.

The Work of Allen Tough

Self-Teaching

In *Learning Without a Teacher: a study of the tasks and assistance during adult self-teaching projects* (1967), Tough researched the self-teaching activities of a sample of forty graduates in the Toronto area. Through a survey of pedagogic literature, through an analysis of his own self-education experiences, through pilot exploratory interviews, and through conversations with other faculty colleagues, he derived a list of twelve common self-teaching tasks.

1. Deciding on a suitable place for learning.
2. Considering or obtaining money.
3. Deciding when to learn, and for how long.
4. Choosing the learning goal.

5. Deciding how to achieve the goal.
6. Obtaining or reaching people, books, and other resources.
7. Dealing with lack of desire for achieving the goal.
8. Dealing with dislike of necessary activities.
9. Dealing with doubts about success.
10. Estimating level of knowledge or skill.
11. Dealing with difficulty in understanding some part.
12. Deciding whether to continue after reaching some goal.

The forty adults had all spent at least eight hours in the year prior to interview pursuing some previously specified knowledge or skill, and this qualified them to be regarded as self-teachers provided they had retained control over their learning. All these adults were found to have performed at least six of these self-teaching tasks with the median number of tasks performed being nine. The least performed task was dealing with lack of desire (task 7), but even this was undertaken by 17 of the 40 subjects. Difficulties were typically experienced in performing three tasks with deciding how to achieve a learning goal (task 4) being the most time consuming. This was followed by locating resources (task 6) and dealing with difficulties (task 11). Overall, Tough concluded that 'many of the projects seemed to form an extremely important part of the subject's life and seemed to dominate his time and thought for weeks or even months' (Tough 1967, p. 43).

During their pursuit of self-teaching projects the adults surveyed were given assistance by an average of 10.6 individuals with every subject using at least four helpers. Acquaintances (work colleagues, neighbours) and intimates (family members, close friends) were the helpers most frequently consulted. Fellow learners and librarians were the categories of helpers least used. The majority of the self-teachers did say, however, that they would have liked more assistance in the execution of their projects than they had been able to secure.

The influence of guides and mentors — one person who was particularly important in assisting the adult with the self-teaching project — was an interesting feature of the study. These guides or mentors tended to be either spouses or fellow learners with whom the self-teacher practised some skill, or a tutor. The opinion was also expressed by several subjects that encountering smug, critical, obstructive and generally unpleasant reactions to their request for help only served to increase their determination.

Finally, Tough was interested to note that self-teachers' perceptions of their learning were such as to denigrate the quality of their achievements. They would report that they differed from the usual or 'ideal' pattern, but would be unable to say what form this pattern might take. At any rate, the self-deprecating nature of adults' perception of their learning meant that it was held to be vastly inferior to that resulting from classroom attendance and participation in full-time education. Despite the subsequent interview revealing to interviewees that their learning was extensive, it was as if the self-teachers had no confidence in learning unless it had somehow been certificated as effective by an accredited professional educator.

Reasons for Learning

In *Why Adults Learn* (1968) thirty-five adults, all of whom had completed at least six months of education after grade 12, were interviewed regarding the origins of their learning. These adults were asked about their learning projects, a learning project comprising a series of related learning episodes at which the person had spent at least seven hours. A learning episode, in turn, was 'a relatively uninterrupted period of time, usually between 10 minutes and four hours, in which the learner's *primary* intention is to gain certain knowledge and skill' (Tough 1968, p. 4).

Five different strong reasons and one weak reason were typically present when adults decided to begin or continue a learning project. The most common reason for learning was the anticipation of using the knowledge or skill to be acquired in some applied manner. This was usually seen in the learner being assigned an 'action goal'; for example, being asked to take on a committee chairperson's duties. A sense of puzzlement or curiosity was noted as a fairly common reason for learning. The thirty-five sample members were also found to have one more reason for continuing their learning projects than for beginning them. Since this additional reason was rated as being 'very strong', Tough concluded that 'for many learners, the total motivation for continuing is stronger than their original motivation for beginning' (page 9). The research team also noted that, based on their review of over 100 projects, it was relatively rare for a learner to consider discontinuing a learning project before that project had achieved fruition according to the learner's analysis.

The plurality of reasons elicited for learning prompted Tough to issue two warnings regarding the study of motives for learning. Firstly, it demonstrated the inappropriateness of offering broad generalizations as to why adults learn. He considered it absurd to ascribe some monocausal explanation to all adult learning. Secondly, he condemned the simpleminded nature of the mutually exclusive distinction often drawn between vocational, practical learning and liberal, avocational pursuits. Elements of both were displayed in many of the learning projects surveyed.

The Adult's Learning Projects

Tough's standard reference work to date is *The Adult's Learning Projects*, subtitled 'A Fresh Approach to Theory and Practice in Adult Learning' (1979a). This summarized the results of his work in the 1960s as well as including data from a new study of sixty-six individuals drawn from seven occupational groups. He broadened his focus to take in the whole range of adult learning; self-planned learning, classroom learning, programmed instruction, credit courses etc. The conceptual heart of this work was still the notion of a learning project, but this now included affective change as well as the development of psychomotor skills. The term 'major learning effort' was also introduced and used interchangeably with 'learning project'.

The minimum length of time conducting a learning project was still placed at seven hours, but the average time was estimated to be 100 hours per learning project. After reviewing all his research to date, Tough presented the following conclusions regarding adult learning projects:

1. Almost everyone undertakes one or two projects a year.
2. The median number of projects conducted annually is eight.
3. It is common for an adult to spend 700 hours a year engaged in learning projects.
4. Seventy per cent of projects are self-planned.

Even if we disregard those circumstances and forces which result in the kinds of experiential learning already discussed in Chapter 1, we are left with the conclusion that the non-learner, the disinterested and apathetic adult, is a statistical aberration. Tough closed the book with the prediction that by the 1990s the comprehensive study of learning projects would be a well-defined field of research and theory. We can argue that his prediction has been fulfilled by a much earlier date. He also foresaw a rise in the esteem in which self-planned learning was held (by learners and professionals) and an increase in the various forms of help available for the individual learner. The relative prescience of this assertion will be considered in Chapter 7.

Intentional Changes

In *Intentional Changes* subtitled 'A Fresh Approach to Helping People Change' (1982), Tough has widened his focus even further to encompass the entire range of intentional changes undertaken by adults. A team of researchers in Canada, the United States and Britain interviewed a total of 330 adults on the most important intentional changes they had recently implemented. 180 members of this sample were interviewed during the course of the interview schedule being developed and were not included in the final sample of adults to be studied. This final sample comprised 150 adults drawn chiefly from middle and upper-middle class backgrounds. As with earlier surveys, Tough declared that he was confident that 'the general picture will prove to be reasonably accurate for many populations, even though the particular figures will vary a little' (Tough 1982, p. 16).

The changes selected for study had to be deliberately and voluntarily chosen. The persons concerned were not to have been forced or coerced into change and neither were intentional responses to accidental circumstances (bereavement, illness) to be included. The two chief areas of change (each comprising 42 per cent of all adult intentional changes) were concerned with changes in activities (job change, recreational pursuits, volunteer work, etc.) and personal changes (for example developing understanding and awareness, changing one's behaviour). Sixteen per cent of changes were concerned with altering the person's environment.

The majority of changes (71 per cent) were deemed to be of 'fairly large' or 'enormous' importance by their actors. The proportion of the change estimated on average to be achieved was 80 per cent, and 93 per cent of those concerned believed the changes achieved to be of definite benefit. Just over half thought their changes to be of large or enormous benefit to themselves and 39 per cent felt their changes to have benefited others to a fairly large extent.

Two particular features of the research were particularly interesting to this writer, particularly since I had been one of the researchers for the book responsible for interviews with British intentional changers. Firstly, in specifying the range of sources the adults concerned had consulted when deciding on the form their change might take, it was friends and family which were emphasized rather than books or professionals. The help provided by such 'amateurs' was mostly in one to one interactions; much less help was received from counsellors, educators, doctors, social workers, personnel managers, therapists, growth group leaders and other helping professionals. This parallels the findings in my own research discussed later in this chapter.

Secondly, Tough recorded self-deprecation on the part of those interviewed regarding the nature of their change which paralleled the self-deprecation displayed by the self-teachers in his first research project. As in the case of the forty self-teachers, the self-deprecation displayed at the outset of the interview changed to a more positive appreciation of the size and importance of the change by the end of the encounter. Finally, as is the case with his other researches, Tough noted on the part of those interviewed a desire for additional help and competence. It is the form such assistance might take which will be explored further in Chapter 7.

Other Research Reports

As well as Tough's own contribution to demonstrating what Virginia Griffin has called the 'huge and heretofore unnoticed or undocumented phenomenon of adults planning and initiating their own learning projects'

(Griffin 1978, p. 7), a range of studies have provided confirmatory or complementary evidence regarding his assertions.

Tough's research has concerned itself chiefly with adults who are either graduates or in professional occupations, frequently both. An early study which surveyed a group of adults of a similar socio-economic status was McCatty's investigation into the patterns of learning projects conducted by professional men (McCatty 1973). These were found to conduct a mean of eleven projects each year which effort required 1,244 hours of study. Job-related projects were the most common projects (55 per cent of the total) with these involving the learner in keeping abreast of new technologies, professional advances and changing circumstances. The mean number of hours per project did vary according to the mode of learning adopted, with self-planned projects requiring on average 148 hours. One-to-one projects required 79 hours on average and group learning projects required 48 hours. McCatty also explored the reasons for choosing different planners of learning and found that self-planned learning was the favoured mode because this allowed for a highly individualized and focused subject matter. The adult wished to learn how to change a fuse rather than receive a discourse on the causes of electricity. The chief reason for choosing a group or one-to-one instructor was the known ability of the instructor.

Peters and Gordon's (1974) survey of learning projects among 466 adults in urban (Knoxville) and rural Tennessee also recorded a high level of learning which served to confirm Tough's speculations concerning the amount of learning typically conducted in adulthood. Nine-tenths of the adults surveyed were found to have conducted one or more projects in the year prior to interview. The highest numbers of projects were recreational or job-related, with other projects in the areas of family relationships, personal improvement and religious affairs.

In terms of providing confirmatory evidence for Tough's speculations on a national level, the most important work done to date is that conducted by Patrick Penland (1977). Penland assembled a national probability sample of 1501 adults across the United States, all of whom were interviewed for one hour on the projects they had pursued during the previous year. Adopting the measure of a minimum of seven hours for a learning project, over three-quarters (76.1 per cent) had conducted at least one self-planned learning project. The mean number of projects undertaken by adults was three and 155.8 hours was, on average, spent planning and conducting learning.

Penland asked his sample members to declare their most important reasons for deciding to learn independently of formal structures. The reasons most commonly cited were (in ranked order), 'desire to set my own learning pace', 'desire to use my own style of learning', 'wanted to keep the learning strategy flexible and easy to change' and 'desire to put my own structure on the learning project'. It is striking that these are all reasons connected with learners' positive perceptions concerning the self-planned learning mode. Of least importance as reasons for adopting a self-planned mode were the prohibitive cost of transportation and insufficient funds for tuition costs — both reasons which traditionally are cited as responsible for non-participation in adult education. Clearly, the conventional wisdom which holds that self-planned learning is conducted because of the financial or geographical inaccessibility of traditional classroom provision is called into question by Penland's findings.

With regard to the most favoured locations for learning the home was, not surprisingly, held to be most important by the adults interviewed. Work settings were next in order of importance. A high level of satisfaction with learning conducted in a self-planned mode was recorded in two-thirds of the interviews with respondents who declared themselves to be 'very enthusiastic' about the newly acquired knowledge or skill. As a result of his researches Penland concluded that 'self-initiated and self-planned learning is learning of a high order made so not only by its prevalence but by the care and deliberation taken in its development' (Penland 1979b; p. 538).

An interesting target group of potential independent learners was identified by Hiemstra who researched the learning projects conducted by older adults. He studied 214 Nebraskans aged 55 or over (with a mean age of 68) drawn from a range of social settings and residential institutions (Hiemstra 1976b). Using the interview methodology devised by Tough comprising probing questions with reminder sheets Hiemstra found that the adults concerned conducted an average of three projects a year involving 325 hours of study. The majority of these (55.15 per cent) were self-planned with approximately one-third being under the control of an external instructor — a significantly higher figure than that recorded for the younger professional groups surveyed by Tough.

The dominant reason for learning in over two-thirds of all projects was personal enjoyment with most projects falling in the category of self-fulfilment (the creative arts, recreational activity and the liberal arts). Again, this contrasts markedly with the adults interviewed by Tough who displayed a practical, 'action-goal' orientation to learning. A final difference with Tough's research noted by Hiemstra concerned the learners' usage of various sources of information. Intimates (a most important source of information for Tough's subjects) were of relatively little significance to the older adults in their range of sources most frequently consulted. Of far greater importance were books, newspapers and pamphlets, all of which were cited as major learning resources. Hiemstra summarized his research as indicating that a group of older adults were actively and frequently engaged in self-directed learning without a reliance on traditional sources of information.

The only British replication of Tough's research (using the conceptual framework and methodology of *Learning Without a Teacher*) is that conducted by Strong who surveyed 18 lecturers in colleges of further education in the urban and rural East Midlands of England (Strong 1977). The 18 autonomous learners (as Strong labelled them) demonstrated a higher level of performance of the twelve teaching tasks identified by Tough, than did the 40 Toronto graduates. All 18 identified a minimum of eight tasks they had performed (compared to the six in the Tough study) and a median of 10.5 tasks performed was recorded (compared to nine in the Tough study). Each task was performed by a minimum of 55 per cent of the sample (compared to 42 per cent in the Tough study). Intimates were the most favoured assistants and help was given for an average of seven of the ten tasks commonly performed.

The foregoing paragraphs constitute a selective review of some of the major studies which have adopted Tough's substantive concerns, conceptual frameworks and methodological techniques, and then applied these to the investigation of independent, self-planned learning within their own locales. There are many more that could have been cited — Tough himself lists some 50 follow-up surveys in his 1978 overview paper on '*Major learning efforts : recent research and future directions*' — and the whole research effort in this area represents a major activity of adult education researchers. Copeland and Grabowski (1971) in comparing American and British research noted that self-directed learning was the chief substantive area studied for its contribution to theory building irrespective of its relevance to professional adult education practice. In his text on *Lifelong Learning* Hiemstra (1976a) identified self-directed learning as one of the two major evolving theory areas in adult education. Finally, as we have already observed, the most recent attempt by the American Association for Adult and Continuing Education to develop a conceptual model for adult education identifies the 'individual transactional mode' (largely based on research into independent learning) as one of their three transactional modes of adult education (Boyd and Apps 1980).

Given that this body of research constitutes a unified whole, characterized by a common substantive core and a generally accepted and applied methodology, it is useful at this point to offer some comments regarding the conceptual and methodological shortcomings which have been voiced regarding this research effort.

Researching the Adult Learning Iceberg : A Methodological Critique

As W.S. Griffith has remarked (in a letter to this author) the adult's propensity to conduct independent learning is more or less the only human characteristic which seemingly does not exhibit a normal distribution amongst the population. Such an apparent statistical aberration means that the claims of those researchers who argue that learning is ubiquitous deserve close and critical attention. The nurturing of a critical scepticism is made particularly difficult by the fact that researchers in this area are likely (as I did) to come to respect and admire their subjects. A spirit of self-critical scrutiny is necessary in all developing fields of research, however, and the next few paragraphs attempt to identify methodological and substantive shortcomings in research into the adult learning iceberg.

Sample Composition

The first of these — the biased nature of the samples studied — has already been noted. The great majority of adults interviewed by Tough and his team of researchers over the years have attained an educational level which is well above average. To assert that the behaviours exhibited by this educationally advantaged collection of adults will be displayed by individuals from a range of social class and cultural backgrounds is questionable. In his overview of research Tough does cite studies of Jamaican adults in an adult literacy class, unemployed adults in New Jersey, and unemployed adults with low educational attainment in Toronto (Tough 1978). A great many more investigations of self-planned learning amongst working class and ethnic groups will be needed before we can say with a justified degree of confidence that *all* adults conduct a number of successful self-planned learning projects each year. The *Intentional Changes* research was a laudable attempt in this direction in that it constituted a genuine comparative adult education research effort. Rather than being a collection of studies from separate countries united by some broad conceptual and substantive focus, the *Intentional Changes* study used a standard interview schedule which was administered to subjects in the three countries concerned. The resultant conclusions and generalizations do, therefore, have a greater validity than attempts inductively to derive some broad statement concerning the extent of independent learning drawn from a number of separate country studies, all using distinctive methodologies.

It is also true that Tough's studies show a bias toward those self-teachers and independent learners who are in their mid-thirties to mid-forties, and that the extent and nature of independent learning amongst adults in older age groups remain unknown. Hiemstra's research (1976b) is, of course, a notable exception to this. My own research into successful independent learners in Britain was with a group of adults aged between 40 and 65, most of whom had left school between 14 and 16 years of age. Again, more studies of a wider age range than the young professionals researched by Tough and his team are needed before we can declare that the ways in which younger adults conduct self-planned learning hold true across the age spectrum. Hiemstra's research (1976b) already cited and discussed shows that older adults display quite significant differences in the ways they plan and conduct their learning.

Interview Procedures

In order that his studies can be replicated by researchers in a variety of settings and with a variety of populations, Tough has placed a reliance on structured interviews in his exploration of people's independent learning. The price to be paid for this ease of replication is that of the researcher/interviewer excluding from the central substantive concerns of the enquiry those themes which the subject feels to be of importance, but which are not explored because the researcher has not included questions relating to these in the interview schedule. In all of Tough's studies the exact wording of questions, the order and manner in which such questions are put, and the kinds of prompts offered to subjects to encourage a response, are closely prescribed.

Tough is quite ready to admit that his research procedures are closely prescribed and tightly organized. In a 1976 lecture he gave this revealing and fascinating account of his research team's procedures ...

> We came along, in a simple minded way, and interviewed people about all of their learning efforts. We found they couldn't remember them. So we developed probe sheets that suggested some things people learn about ... we really pushed, poked, probed, and helped the person recall. (Tough 1976; p. 61)

As Pedler has commented, ''From the account of the interviews it appears that a lot of prompting occurred so that gratuitous responses may have been recorded and the case overstated'' (1972; p. 89). Tough himself is aware of the dangers of excluding from his findings those concerns which the subject feels to be important but which the researcher has not considered. His *Intentional Changes* study reflects this concern in that the final interview schedule was devised only after being administered (and continually refined) with 180 subjects. The instructions to interviewers in that project also emphasized the need to make the encounter a mutually beneficial and interactive dialogue ... ''In order to get an accurate deep understanding of intentional change, it is essential that the interviews be sufficiently leisurely with plenty of probing and dialogue'' (Tough 1982; p. 163).

The Quality of Learning

To assert that adults spend approximately ten hours per week engaged in the deliberate pursuit of previously specified knowledge and skill is to make no implicit assumptions concerning the quality of this learning. Indeed, Tough has been careful to state that the learner's assuming a planning function implies no necessary superiority over externally planned learning. In the first major study he undertook in this field Tough freely admitted that the path the self-teacher planned was often haphazard and ineffective (Tough 1967; p. 60).

This lack of attention to the quality of learning — in terms of some external measure of its effectiveness and the learner's own perception of its usefulness — characterizes much research in this area. The *Learning Without a Teacher* study was more concerned to obtain a quantitative measure of the time spent in learning than in determining its quality. To ascertain the extent of independent learning — even to demonstrate that it constituted an important phenomenon — was a laudable and important first step in this stream of research. The emphasis on the amount rather than the effectiveness of independent learning has dominated the research in this field. It is now timely and appropriate, I would suggest, for more attention to be paid to the quality of independent adult learning.

Independent Learning in the Group Mode

The starting point of most of the research quoted in this chapter is the individual learner. The emphasis on a clear specification of predetermined learning goals, and of learner control over the planning and execution of learning, has meant that an almost atomistic emphasis has been placed on the individual and isolated aspects of the independent learner's activities. Although it is frequently acknowledged that independent learning depends on the assistance of fellow learners, mentors and intimates, it is assumed that such assistants have a subordinate stance within the learner's pursuit of the unique *meisterwork* of an individual learning project. Indeed, this feature of independent learning is almost self-defining: the concentration on learner control and on a close, individualized specification of learning goals has meant that the subsequent research findings would be framed in such a way as to present the learner as a creative, 'cordon bleu' chef of learning. Just as a master chef deliberately chooses certain ingredients and blends these into a highly distinctive, individual dish, so is the independent learner conceived. Like the creative master chef, the learner is viewed as locating materials, resources, and assistance to produce a highly individualized learning project.

This emphasis has meant that the social context of much independent learning has been neglected. Researchers have preferred to concentrate on the features of individual learner control and to ignore the role of learning networks and informal learning exchanges. Luikart's exploration of the independent learning projects of sixty-four young adults and the connections between the use of assistants and these learners' personal networks is one exception to this generalization (Luikart 1977). Farquharson (1975) has also surveyed the use of peers as helpers in self-help groups in metropolitan Toronto. Both these studies show the way in which the collaborative and co-operative features within individual learning projects can be studied. It is interesting to note that Tough himself has acknowledged the dimension of peer group learning as an important one for future research: . . .

> Detailed information could (also) be collected on peer learner groups and self-help groups such as local historical and scientific societies, Bible study groups, garden clubs, consciousness-raising groups, and committees that learn intensively about a problem before making a decision . . . another high priority need is for detailed studies of unmet needs concerning peer self-help groups. (Tough 1978; p. 259)

One purpose of the chapters in the following section is to repair this omission and to show that focusing on only the highly individualized aspects of learning projects is to neglect the all important dimension of adult learning in the community in the group mode.

Successful Independent Learning

One of the chief doubts voiced in the preceding methodological critique concerned the effectiveness of independent adult learning. It was argued that too many studies had concentrated on the quantity of adult learning, rather than assessing its quality. The concluding section of this chapter reviews two studies both of which examine in some detail the activities of adults who have attained positions of local or national eminence through their independent exploration of widely varying fields of interest.

Avocational Academics and Independent Scholars

In his capacity as the director of a national study of independent scholarship for the College Board in New York, Ron Gross (1982) has devoted a considerable amount of time to studying the careers of what he calls 'avocational academics' or 'independent scholars'. These are two terms used to describe the same kind of person — the adult who exhibits no affiliation to any accredited academic institution but who explores a field of interest to a recognizably acclaimed high level of competence. Although he eschews the carefully designed methodology adopted by those researchers seeking to replicate the work of Allen Tough, Gross's work is concerned with the same substantive field and shares many of the philosophical orientations of the 'learning projects' breed of research. Indeed, in 1972 Gross renounced his University diploma (obtained in 1956) declaring in his letter of renunciation that degrees, credentials and diplomas were not authentic evidence of intellectual attainment.

As Gross points out, and as I have argued at earlier points in this book, a concern with amateur scholarship is an honoured element in the American cultural tradition. In fact, the introduction of a system of mass education in the post-war era is in historical terms something of an aberration. To anyone who has explored the sociology of knowledge it is also evident that the impetus for advances in knowledge, for the introduction of new concepts, and for the urge for a paradigm shift in any of the major disciplines, has generally come from independent thinkers located outside the University system.

Tough, Gross and myself have all devised similar metaphors to describe the range of non-institutional adult learning which can be observed: the adult learning iceberg (Tough), the invisible university (Gross) and the parallel educational universe (Brookfield). The differentiating feature between the Tough stream of research and that of the latter two writers is that the subjects in the former had only to demonstrate that learning had occurred, irrespective of its quality. The two latter researchers are concerned chiefly with visibly successful learners. Examples of the kinds of learner surveyed by Gross in a series of case studies are psychohistorians, unicellular plant specialists, researchers into the Sioux language and ecologists. Although no typical pattern characterizing the activities of avocational academics can be identified, Gross has distinguished three common elements in independent scholarship. Firstly, the impetus for learning comes from an innate enthusiasm for the subject studied, rather than (as in the case of Tough's learners) from being assigned a specific, practical, action goal. Secondly, independent scholars show a reluctance to plan future learning too closely, preferring instead to let the study develop according to its own inherent logic. Thirdly, these adults often concentrate their energy on producing a written product of some kind, which also serves to win recognition for the independent scholars concerned.

Whilst recognizing that significant and valuable intellectual work can be undertaken outside the formal education system, Gross does not elevate this independent scholarship in any reified manner, nor does he regard it as innately superior to 'professional' scholarship. Rather, he views the amateur and professional wings of a discipline as integrated in a complementary manner. Independent scholars tend to be in the vanguard when it comes to establishing and exploring new academic disciplines (such as women's studies, future studies and ecology) which eventually enter the formal curriculum of University studies. Gross also notes with approval the recognition voiced by David Riesman and Robert Stebbings that amateurs can function as partners with professional academics in the exploration of fields of mutual interest. Gross points out (1981) that independent scholars constitute a promising pool of graduate students who could be drawn to advanced graduate study as a midlife avocational choice. They are already an important audience for scholarly works produced by academic writers.

Because they operate outside the confines of academe, independent scholars often face problems in locating resources (financial, human and material) needed to support their studies. Other resource needs identified by independent scholars are for research assistance, secretarial help, interaction with fellow learners, access to computer facilities and the chance to discuss one's findings with an informed and critical audience (at professional meetings, learned societies and through publication). In a vigorous piece on the 'passion and pitfalls' of independent scholarship Gross (1981) proposed six reforms which could be undertaken by those within the formal system to help independent scholars:

1. The provision by colleges of accommodation and access to institutional resources.
2. The incorporation of independent scholars into research programmes with a sufficient degree of flexibility being allowed so that the scholar can retain control over learning.
3. The use of independent scholars as adjunct faculty.
4. Greater attention by grant-awarding foundations to the needs of independent scholars.
5. The creation by professional groupings of a special category of membership for independent learners to allow them to enjoy the facilities afforded by such membership.
6. The extension of publication opportunities to amateur scholars.

Gross believes that such steps would require no enormous increase in funding, merely a sympathetic adaptation of existing facilities to the needs of independent scholars. The rationale behind such an initiative is that of a mutually beneficial symbiosis — 'new relationships between independent scholars and these institutions would be good for the independent scholars, good for higher education, and good for the intellectual health of American society' (1981, p. 56).

Successful Independent Learners

A sustained attempt to investigate the learning activities of a group of successful independent learners was undertaken by the present writer between 1977 and 1980 (Brookfield 1980a). The impetus for the study derived partly from a desire for more information on the quality of independent learning and partly from an admiration for successful independent learners which resulted in a desire to know more of the lifestyles and learning activities of these adults. Although it contradicted what are considered to be the twin canons of scientific methodology — objectivity and detachment — this admiration for independent learners turned out to be an important reinforcement at those times of apathy which occur for any researcher during a lengthy grounded theory study.

The Research Sample

Inclusion in the sample of twenty-five independent learners selected for study was based on two highly specific criteria. Firstly, the adults concerned had to have achieved such a high level of expertise in their particular fields of interest that it resulted in their being awarded the acclaim of fellow learners and enthusiasts at local or national level. Secondly, this eminence and expertise had to have been attained without participation in externally planned programmes of instruction (such as adult education classes, correspondence courses or professional training courses) in the subject area concerned. The learning of these adults exhibited, therefore, several dimensions of independence. It was independent of sustained external instructional direction, independent of institutional accreditation or support, and independent of institutional financial support.

The measure of peer acclaim was used to judge whether or not the adults concerned had truly achieved a high level of expertise in their subject areas. If the majority of the members of a local hobbyists' society agreed that a particular individual was the local expert on dog breeding, botany, or ornithology, then this was taken as the best obtainable objective index of an individual's attaining a high level of ability. The adults in the Tough studies were chosen at random, not because of any identifiable expertise in independent learning. In the study under discussion, the adults had been previously identified as visibly successful in conducting independent learning projects.

The particular interests and fields of expertise of these adults are shown in Table 1 'Research Sample of Successful Independent Learners'. All twenty-five were resident in and around a town in the rural West Midlands of England where I had been employed as a community adult educator for six years. Just over a third of the sample came to my attention through the network of local contacts that all community educators must develop if their programmes are to be well grounded in the needs, circumstances and concerns of their local communities. A content analysis of local newspapers proved another invaluable source of suitable sample members who had achieved local notoriety or reputation for their success in learning. A local beekeeper was brought to my attention through reading a feature in a local paper on his recent authorship of a book on managing bee swarms. The use of informal contact networks and of local media within the context of a community survey will be discussed in Chapter 6.

The final source of contact for the independent learners comprised local hobbyists' clubs and enthusiasts' societies. Letters were sent to the

Table 1

Research Sample of Successful Independent Learners

Learning Activity	Duration of Learning (No. of years)
Organic Gardening	8
Chess	15
Drama Production	4
Freshwater Fishing	8
Fitness Techniques	22
Bridge	14
Horticulture	46
Philosophy	16
Tropical Fish Breeding	14
Philately	12
Narrow Guage Railways	19
Record Collecting	13
Budgerigar (Parakeet) Breeding	15
Antiques Collecting	5
Classical Music	29
Antique China	39
Botany	48
Ornithology	30
Steam Traction Engines	29
Pigeon Racing	12
Beekeeping	50
Aero-Modelling	15
Railway Management and Modelling	48
Rabbit Breeding	16
Pedigree Dog Breeding	20

Mean Length of Learning Activities: 22 years
Median Length of Learning Activities: 16 years
Mean Age: 45 years
Mean School Leaving Age: 16 years

secretaries of such groups who were asked to suggest individuals whose reputation for an outstanding ability in their field had been attained without the benefit of external instruction. A discussion of the methodology of the study is contained in Chapter 6. Briefly, the study was concerned to explore independent learners' perceptions of their learning activities, with particular reference to the way such activities were located within informal adult learning networks. The data collection technique used was that of open-ended interviewing and a grounded theory approach was adopted towards the coding of interviewee responses, to the generation of concepts and classifications, and to the identification of major substantive themes.

Origins of Learning

In his 1968 study of the origins of learning projects of thirty-five Toronto adults, Allen Tough elicited an astonishing variety of reasons for beginning a learning project. His results indicated that a single reason for initiating a learning project was uncommon and, typically, five strong reasons were present. Of the twenty-five independent learners interviewed in the study under discussion, fifteen revealed a perception of one overwhelming reason as being important to their learning. The other ten recalled two or three reasons, giving a median number of one.

This apparent discrepancy between Tough's work and my own may be partly explained by methodological differences. The Toronto study concentrated solely on reasons for starting and continuing a learning project. Additionally, interviewees were presented with a series of separate sheets giving alternative reasons for starting and continuing a project. In the English study the grounded theory approach meant that subjects were able to state their perceived reasons for learning as this theme occurred in natural conversation rather than having a number of specific alternatives presented to them. Additionally, the origin of learning was only one of several themes explored in the study.

The independent learners did experience difficulty in recalling exactly the events, people and feelings which prompted them to begin what would become lifelong learning projects. Their self-image was such that they would assert that they had 'always' been ornithologists, musicians, fitness enthusiasts or botanists. The influence of key individuals emerged as the most important factor with twelve respondents tracing the awakening of their interest back to parental or spouse encouragement. The role of the father was particularly noticeable here. Fellow learners were important reinforcers of developing interest but were rarely the direct instigators of learning.

Attitudes to Learning

Three characteristic and distinctive attitudes towards their learning were exhibited by the independent learners. Firstly, they regarded their exploration of their fields of interest as unending intellectual voyages. Over half of the subjects declared that they had no preconceived notion as to the terminal point of their learning. There was no sense of inadequacy about this; rather it was intimated that if the point of intellectual omniscience was reached the challenge, and thus the enjoyment, of their learning would disappear.

A second attitude displayed towards learning was a disregard for what would be considered clearly delineated subject boundaries by formally trained academics. There was a resistance to any kind of specialization within one field and a readiness to explore related areas of interest. The botanist, for example, was interested in birds, insects, moths and butterflies. The steam engine enthusiast had studied railways, paddle steamers and other forms of transport and had taken up photography to record his trips to exhibitions and engine fairs. In this regard the independent learners resembled Houle's 'learning oriented' adults discussed earlier in this chapter. The adults concerned displayed an openess to, and a readiness for, learning which was certainly reminiscent of the 'learning oriented' members of Houle's sample.

Finally, although these adults were pursuing what were highly specific and individualized learning projects, the idiosyncratic nature of their learning did not prevent them from seeing themselves as part of a larger learning community. Repeatedly, the independent learners declared that they belonged to a kind of fellowship of learning comprising fellow enthusiasts who shared the same concerns, pleasures and anxieties. Membership in this fellowship was expressed in a readiness to share knowledge and accumulated wisdom and this was all the more remarkable in that fellow enthusiasts were likely to be competitive adversaries in exhibitions, shows and competitions. As the horticulturalist remarked...

> Gardeners are, generally speaking, very charming people. They'll always give each other stuff and there are very few people that won't help you. If anybody asks me about something of mine, I'll always tell them. (Brookfield 1981a, p. 21)

Informal Learning Networks

As I remarked earlier in this chapter, a tendency of researchers in the field of independent learning has been to emphasize the isolated and individual aspects of such learning. The falsity of such an approach was demonstrated in the study of successful independent learners. These adults were gregarious in their learning; independence clearly did not mean isolation. The setting for the development of learning networks — groups of like minded enthusiasts who exchanged knowledge and skill — was usually a local hobbyists' club. Membership of such clubs or societies was mentioned by twenty independent learners and a total of sixty-five such societies was mentioned during the study. Twelve respondents belonged to two or more such groups and two were members of more than ten societies in their specialisms. Fifteen learners regarded these societies as crucial to the development of their expertise.

The most frequently attested benefit accruing from network membership was the exchange of information between individuals. Such exchanges occurred in an unprompted, spontaneous fashion: members would learn of each other's specialisms and exchange ideas on new techniques as well as offering advice on the solution of problems. The human resources of accumulated knowledge and experience contained within these clubs and societies were identified repeatedly as the most important sources of information to the independent learners, assuming far greater significance than the use of libraries or instructional magazines and pamphlets. The learning encounters between individual members were latent rather than manifest societal functions; that is, they took place in addition to, and separate from, the official business of the club or society. Despite their serendipitous nature, however, such apparently casual encounters and conversations were much more important than formal society lectures for the development of individual expertise. The crucial significance of human resources in this study confirms the emphasis on the use of intimates as assistants expressed by many adults in the Tough studies.

It is also interesting to record the similarity between this study and that conducted in Liverpool by Elsey (1974). Elsey surveyed twenty voluntary organizations in the district of Birkenhead and succeeded in prompting 350 members of such groups to complete a questionnaire on the educative aspects of their participation. The clubs and societies studied included the Women's Institute, the Townswomen's Guild, the Cage Bird Fanciers society, the Homing Pigeons society, Model Railway and Model Boat clubs, Choral societies, and the Photographic club. Elsey noted that formal society lectures were perceived as educative by members but that they also identified 'casual advice handed down by experienced and knowledgeable enthusiasts' (Elsey 1974, p. 393) as an important element in the development of their knowledge. In comparing the two modes of knowledge transmission and skill development Elsey concluded that 'On the basis of observation the latter method of "teaching" seems highly effective because of its immediacy and relevance' (p. 393). The predominance of an oral tradition in the transmission of knowledge and skill to independent learners noted by Tough, Elsey and myself is a rather surprising finding given the technological and self-instructional possibilities of the last two decades.

Another aspect of this oral tradition in the dissemination of skills and knowledge was represented in the consultancy duties assumed by the independent learners. Since one of the criteria for sample membership in my study was the local acknowledgement of the subjects concerned as expert in their particular field, it was not surprising that such fame resulted in unskilled newcomers to the field seeking out the experts concerned to request advice on the best ways to develop their talents. Relatively skilled enthusiasts were also prompted to contact the independent learners for the purpose of obtaining specific advice or specialist equipment. In this way the specially skilled learner came to serve as a resource consultant and skill model in the manner envisaged by deschoolers (Reimer 1971, Illich 1971).

Evaluating Independent Learning

As I have emphasized, the distinctive feature of this research was that it was concerned with a sample of visibly successful learners. Since I was a layman in most of the enthusiasms concerned, the expression of peer acclaim for the learner's expertise was the most objective measure of learning success I could imagine. A continuing concern of mine, however, was the ways in which the independent learners themselves came to assess their developing expertise.

Objective indices of evaluation were mentioned more frequently than their subjective equivalent. Such objective indices related mainly to peer recognition — hardly surprising given that the criterion for sample membership was peer acclaim of subjects' expertise. Success in independent learning was felt to be indicated by the bestowal of peer recognition and approval. Such acclaim was granted in six distinctive ways:

1. Requests from journals for articles and written contributions. (This recalls Gross's assertion that independent scholars frequently see the production of a written piece as the *raison d'être* of their activities.)
2. Requests from fellow enthusiasts for advice.
3. Selection as team members in tournaments and competitions.
4. Invitations to talk to other enthusiasts' clubs and societies.
5. Conferring of honorary society membership on the learner.
6. Election to the status of a judge.

In a few fields a convenient standard of measurement existed against which a learner's progress could be measured. The rabbit breeder, budgerigar breeder and tropical fish enthusiast could all judge their developing competence by the survival rate of the animals, birds and fish in their care. The fitness enthusiast guaged his increasing strength on the basis of the weights he was able to lift. Competitive success was also a highly quantifiable evaluative index and such success could become the central focus of an independent learning project. The angler expressed this competitive ethic most forcefully. It was not enough for him to hold a personal conviction regarding his abilities, these had to be acknowledged by his peers . . .

> I've got to actually go out and beat them. I've got to gain respect from them because I'm better than, or as good as, they are. So I think it's important — not only the fact that you are good, but that you're seen to be good. (Brookfield 1981a, p. 21)

It was very simple for an enthusiast to assess his success by the amount of money won in competitions, shows or exhibitions, or by the number of trophies gained, and a project's terminal point could certainly be translated into terms of competitive triumph. It is interesting to note that Elsey (1974, p. 393) also recorded an emphasis on competitive success in the pursuit of learning among his 350 members of voluntary organizations.

Subjective indices of evaluation were mentioned only in seven interviews. Such indices could be grouped together under the general category of 'developing critical confidence'; that is, the growing belief that one's knowledge was such that one could call into question the pronouncements of experts in the learner's field of interest. What had once been a respectful acknowledgement of superior expertise was replaced by a readiness to detect mistakes in revered texts, or by direct criticism of conventional wisdom . . .

> The world's top ichthyologist is H. A. I don't keep his books anymore because I disagree with a lot of his theories on tropical fish keeping. I didn't at first, I don't suppose I read anything else but A. and another American called W., but after a few years you start to realise that their idea of fish-keeping clashes with your own. Anybody who's a thinking person anyway.
>
> (Brookfield 1981a, p. 23)

Problems of Independent Learners
It is methodologically impossible to enter any grounded theory study with no preconceived notions as to possible and important substantive themes. When the research into independent learning was first conceived I had imagined that a significant part of the interviews would be concerned with the problems independent learners had encountered and overcome in the pursuit of their interest. As the interview programme progressed it became evident that the learners surveyed were unused to thinking of their activities in terms of problems to be resolved. Rather, the kinds of difficulties and perplexities which the learners had to face were regarded as enjoyable challenges or interesting diversions by these adults. To assume that learning problems would have the connotations of blockage, anxiety and obstruction was, on this writer's part, quite unjustified. The 'problem' of managing bee swarms more effectively was, for example, the central concern of the apiarist. It was not perceived as an anxiety-provoking difficulty preventing joyful learning, but rather as the absorbing focus of his activity and a source of continuing interest and enjoyment.

A Parallel Educational Universe
The twenty-five independent learners surveyed represent a submerged dimension of educational activity. It was as if the town in which these adults lived contained a parallel educational universe existing alongside, but unrecognized by, the formal adult education system. These learners

had devised sophisticated evaluative indices, they had evolved mechanisms for the exchange of information and they had erected frameworks of grades and awards of merit in the competitions to which they attached such importance. The intensity of feeling aroused whenever the topic of competition participation was raised in the interviews — either in subjects emphasizing the benefits of competition, or in stridently rejecting the competitive ethic — recalled to this writer the end of semester anxiety, pride and pain caused by the public display of examination results and class gradings.

The independent learners' use of more experienced colleagues in the same way as research students might use their supervisors, suggests a further parallel between the world of independent learning and that of the formal education system. Independent learners would turn to particular individuals for guidance and assistance and use them in the same way a student would use a research supervisor or study counsellor. The major difference between the two situations is, of course, that a research supervisor performs a more or less continuous directive function, whereas the experienced enthusiast would be consulted only at times of particular difficulty. Also, in the formal system the supervisor or counsellor would probably be in the position of granting some kind of certification or accreditation to the student, whereas the independent learner could afford to ignore the advice of his colleague without risking a public labelling of his efforts as inadequate or incompetent.

With this review of research into adult learning in the community in the individual mode we come to the end of the first section of this book. We have encountered evidence from a range of studies undertaken in a variety of settings which confirms what most people would assert as conventional wisdom — that a great deal of independent learning takes place in adulthood, that this can sometimes be of a very high order of expertise, and that the ability to conduct such learning holds fairly constant across class and cultural categories, as far as we have been able to ascertain. As suggested towards the end of the chapter, however, we do need to examine the learning which occurs within group settings, and which is of a collaborative and co-operative nature, if we are to come to some understanding of the range of adult learning in the community. It is the purpose of the next three chapters to shift the focus of attention to adult learning in the community in the group mode.

PART II

Adult Learners in the Community: The Group Mode

FOUR

Community Adult Education

The word 'community' is one which has the power to inspire a reverential suspension of critical judgement in the minds of adult educators, social workers and those within the caring and health professions. It is as if in invoking this term adult educators thereby imbue their practice with a humanistic concern and an almost self-righteous compassion which pre-empts any considered analysis of its central features. The term functions, therefore, as a premature ultimate; that is, as a word possessing such emotional potency that its invocation immediately precludes further debate. In this respect 'community' occupies a status in the adult education vocabulary similar to that of 'need'. As Wiltshire has pointed out (1973, p. 26) declaring that one is 'meeting the needs' of adult learners, or of one's community, has the effect of acting as a logical stop to analysis and critical scrutiny.

As a former community adult education organizer and head of a community adult education department I, too, have fallen into the semantic and conceptual trap of using the term 'community' adult education as a catch-all phrase to describe any adult education practice which I personally felt to be desirable. I have worn (and continue to wear) the badge of 'community adult educator' with some pride and have used it as a way of establishing my credentials as a concerned and responsible professional. I have also noted at many a conference and professional gathering the phenomenon recorded by Dennis whereby as soon as the term 'community' is voiced an expression of respect is visible on every countenance and all heads are bowed (Dennis 1968, p. 74). Maria Effrat, an American writer on community work, has commented that like motherhood and apple pie, community is considered synonymous with virtue and desirability (Effrat 1974, p. 2). Hence, attaching the label community to an adult education programme results in a mix of prescriptive and descriptive associations. To assert that one is practising 'community adult education' is to declare that one is doing something which is innately desirable, as well as to describe practice.

We can see, then, that phrases such as 'meeting the needs of the community' or 'meeting the needs of learners/clientele' are part of the adult educator's litany of venerated terms and concepts. Griffith has commented that 'meeting the needs of learners is probably the most persistent shibboleth in the rhetoric of adult education program planning' (Griffith 1978, p. 382). The problem with shibboleths and litanies is that they come to be revered as received wisdom. Hence, as Harrison has pointed out, in challenging the validity of their usage 'one runs the risk of being branded at best a cynic and at worst a heretic' (Harrison 1974, p. 50 – 1). In this chapter I hope to function as a loving critic (to use John Gardner's much invoked phrase) of the term 'community' and the phrase 'community adult education'. The chapter reviews the contrasting concepts of community (neighbourhood communities, communities of interest and of function) and considers the relevance of these to adult education. The distinction between liberal and liberating definitions of community adult education, already discussed briefly in Chapter 1, is further explored. Particular attention is paid to the influence of the Mott tradition in the United States and the Henry Morris Village College tradition in the United Kingdom. A typology of community adult education is offered consisting of the three categories of adult education for the community, adult education in the community, and adult education of the community.

The Concept of Community

'Community' is, in W. C. Fields immortal phrase, a 'euphonious appellation' which can be attached to almost any activity in an attempt to imbue such work with a sense of compassion and concern. As Stewart comments, the word 'consorts to an almost abandoned degree with a host of other words' (Stewart 1976, p. 69) without necessarily altering practice. Hence, we have community psychiatry, community adult education, community policing, community radio, community health and any number of other semantic marriages of a field of practice and the term 'community'. It is hard to resist the notion that such unions are primarily marriages of convenience and that any branch of the caring professions is seizing on the word community for fear of being thought of as somehow less than fully humanistic, or for fear of losing the chance of access to federal and state funds.

The popularity of the term cannot, however, be accounted for solely in terms of political expediency or as an instance of a current semantic fad. In a fascinating analysis of the meaning of the word Kirkwood has cogently summarized the reasons for its appeal in the following manner:

> The word community is popular, because through it people can express this yearning for a communion with each other. It is a yearning for social wholeness,

a mutuality and interrelatedness, as opposed to the alienated, fragmented, antagonistic social world of daily experience. Linked with this desire for warm relatedness is a desire for stability.

(Kirkwood 1978, p. 148-9).

To anyone familiar with the writings of nineteenth century sociologists this romantic and appealing vision of a pastoral togetherness calls to mind the distinction drawn by Tonnies between a pre-industrial *gemeinschaft* (community) and a mass urban *gesellschaft* (association) form of society. We can assume, then, that placing the term 'community' before a particular noun or verb (such as health or policing) implies that those involved as workers in that activity will be concerned to create a sense of shared identity, mutuality and common interest.

To talk of community in this *gemeinschaft* sense is to refer to a geographical locale in which people live and work, in which they develop relationships based on common concerns, and in which expressions of mutual assistance reflect the dominant social mores. Underpinning this sense of interrelatedness is the cohesion afforded by all members of the group subscribing to shared norms, moral codes, beliefs and attitudes. This subscription is enforced by the socialization process which ensures that new members to the group are initiated into its moral and behavioural codes.

In the western industrial societies of today, characterized as they are by social and geographical mobility and a plurality of ethnic, class, occupational, and interest groups, such cohesive groupings may be empirically unobservable. Their nearest equivalent may be some forms of total institutions (ships or boarding schools come to mind) or self-sufficient communes. Alternatively, the sense of common identity characteristic of community may be seen most frequently in what Danielson has called *The Politics of Exclusion* (Danielson 1976). The term refers to attempts by residents of affluent dormitory suburbs to maintain a sense of exclusive separateness. Although inhabitants of such locales will have a rigid separation between the occupational and domestic spheres in their lives, they will share a common concern to preserve what is seen as the 'quality' of their neighbourhood. This finds its most obvious expression in a desire to maintain property values, but will also include a mistrust of alternative lifestyles and 'deviant' sub-cultures. As Agnew points out:

Neighbourhood, then, comes to have an exclusionary rather than inclusionary significance: a means by which like-minded people can protect and enhance their private worlds from the threat of the different. (Agnew 1980, p. 30)

When confronted with a concept which apparently has little empirical relevance the natural responses are either to jettison that concept or to reinterpret it so as to make it refer to a more clearly observable phenomenon. Adult educators have, in general, followed the second course of action and chosen to talk of communities of interest (for example, jazz enthusiasts, vegetarians, or freshwater fishermen) or communities of function (for example, doctors or adult educators). In her analysis of community learning Joan Wright of North Carolina State University has defined community as 'a collection of people differentiated from the total population by a common interest' and declared that she is interested in 'the community of common interests, which supersedes other connections including that of geographical location' (Wright 1980, p. 101). Hayden Roberts of the University of Alberta has argued that it is no longer appropriate to insist upon stability and a distinct geographical locale as necessary conditions of community. He writes that:

> The community exists when a group of people perceives common needs and problems, acquires a sense of identity, and has a common sense of objectives. Thus a profession may be a community despite its lack of a physical locus.
>
> (Roberts 1979, p. 27)

The Neighbourhood Community

The notion of a locational neighbourhood basis underlying community is, in the sociological literature, most associated with MacIver and Page who viewed community as an area of social living marked by some degree of social coherence. The bases of community were held to be locality and community sentiment (MacIver and Page 1961, p. 9). The tradition of community studies as reflected in the North American and British literature certainly places a sense of geographical uniqueness at the centre of the concept of community. The earliest acknowledged American classic in the field, the Lynds' analysis of Middletown (in reality the town of Muncie) transferred the participant and non-participant observation techniques of nineteenth century anthropologists to urban America (Lynd and Lynd 1929).

In a follow-up study published in 1937 — *Middletown in Transition* — the descriptive detail of the first study was replaced by a greater theoretical sophistication and an attention to what would later become known as community power analysis. The Chicago school of urban community studies associated primarily with Robert Park comprised a collection of monographs investigating different ecological zones in the city, in particular the 'gold coast' (an affluent lakeside residential district) and the 'slum' area of Little Sicily (Zorbaugh 1929). Life in a small town in New England — *Yankee City* (Newburyport) — was the subject of five studies by Lloyd Warner and his colleagues (Warner and Lunt 1941). Warner was also director of the *Deep South* study of Natchez in Mississippi (Davis, Gardner & Gardner 1944). Other examples of small scale studies of town or neighbourhood communities are those of Bensman and Vidich (1958) in upstate New York, the study of the affluent Toronto suburb Crestwood Heights (Seeley, Sim and Loosley 1963) and Gans's analysis of an evolving New Jersey suburb (Gans 1967).

Perhaps the earliest British community study which assumed any pretensions to being a scientific or systematic analysis was Charles Booth's seventeen-volume survey of *The Life and Labour of the People of London* (Booth 1971) conducted at the turn of the century. Although this began as a statistically orientated account of poverty as measured by income levels and overcrowding it evolved over the course of the research to become an impressionistic observation of the inhabitants and their occupational, religious and recreational behaviour in well-defined neighbourhoods and streets. Lloyd Warner who, as we have seen, initiated studies of New England and Mississippi town life extended his interest in 1931 to Southern Ireland. After a visit by Warner two research workers on the Newburyport study were assigned as field workers and produced a study based on County Clare and Ennis known as *Family and Community in Ireland* (Arensberg and Kimball 1968). This emphasis on small-scale rural communities, which differed markedly from the Chicago school's attention to neighbourhoods within urban connurbations, was continued by Rees (1950) in Wales and Williams (1956) in Gosforth, England. However, two studies of small English towns conducted in the 1950s were sited in Glossop (Birch 1959) and Banbury (Stacey 1960). Finally, the establishment of the Institute of Community Studies in London afforded its joint directors — Michael Young and Peter Willmott — the opportunity to study changing patterns of working class life in Bethnal Green, an inner city neighbourhood in East London (Young and Willmott 1962). For excellent summaries of the empirical findings of these and other community studies readers are referred to four books; *The Eclipse of Community* (Stein 1964), *Community Studies* (Bell & Newby 1971), *Communities in Britain* (Frankenburg 1966) and *The Sociology of Community* (Bell and Newby 1974).

We can see, then, that the tradition of academic exploration known as community studies is predicated on the idea that communities have clearly delineated geographical boundaries. The American Commission of Professors of Adult Education inherited the conceptual basis of this intellectual tradition when, in one of their earliest publications, they declared the following:

> We accept these six elements as essential to a community: people, place, common concerns, organisation, morale, and government. We are dealing with that socio-geographic entity within which people live, work, and play, where things

get done, where personality is developed and where people have their places.
(Hallenbeck *et al.* 1962, p. vi)

The locational emphasis in community studies is still predominant in the minds of British community workers and community researchers. One of the most eminent of these, Colin Fletcher, has recently attempted to evolve a number of criteria by which the existence of 'community' can be determined. These criteria are divided into four sets of conditions — necessary conditions, sufficient conditions, historical conditions and emergent conditions. The most important of these — the necessary conditions which logically must be satisfied for community to exist — emphasize a sense of place. Hence, a distinctive name, a recognizable dialect, and the adoption of commonly agreed territorial boundaries are the three necessary conditions which, if met, grant to a collection of individuals and buildings the term 'community' (Fletcher 1980c).

This insistence on the neighbourhood basis for community is one shared by the present writer. It is true, of course, that the mere fact of neighbourhood habitation carries within it no inherent predisposition towards community. An area of two or three square miles in a city may contain an astonishingly diverse collection of groups, the membership and focus of which will shift over time. Also, as Riesman argued in *The Lonely Crowd* (1961), individuals can become so 'privatized' that their central life interests are centred exclusively on the nuclear family household. Nonetheless, the majority of public adult education activities draw their clientele and funding from a distinct and defined geographical area. Adult education programmers realize that classes, workshops and courses must be based on the circumstances, wants and concerns of adults within that vicinity. This is not to dismiss the concepts of communities of interest and communities of functions, both of which are valid and useful analytical constructs in that they refer to a discernible group of individuals united by interests and concerns other than geographical. However, adult learning in the community as discussed in this book is, broadly speaking, adult learning occurring within residential and locational settings — homes, hobbyists' clubs, neighbourhood groups etc.

It must be admitted, however, that the concept of neighbourhood community is one which still raises problems for this writer. For example, one role of the community worker, or the community adult educator, may be to create a sense of community where it clearly does not already exist. Hence, we must accept that such workers are not working within already constituted communities in that they do not meet the necessary and other conditions outlined by Fletcher. If a sense of common identity is absent in an inner city neighbourhood, a 'new' town or a public housing project, a community worker may be appointed to create networks, to develop community associations and to inculcate a sense of mutuality among local residents. Clearly, I do not wish to exclude such activities from the scope of this book by an insistence that only learning located within *gemeinschaft* type communities is admissible.

I would also accept that *gemeinschaft* type communities — small-scale groupings of individuals who share a sense of holistic identity and who follow broadly agreed moral and behavioural codes — may be empirically unobservable in many modern societies. However, I think it is possible to use the term 'community' in a way which removes many of the prescriptive and normative elements associated with *gemeinschaft* type communities. Some may argue that removal of these elements removes the emotive and analytical strength of the concept, leaving it to refer only to collections of individuals working or residing within certain, arbitrarily defined geographical areas. There is no doubt that, in operational terms, this latter sense is the one which many writers and speakers adopt when they talk of community. It is a favourite rhetorical trick of politicians to talk of the community when they mean nation or state, hoping thereby to imbue their policies and preferences with an impression of populism and broad support. Nonetheless, it seems to me that the available alternative terms such as area or geographical locale are inadequate or cumbersome. In the absence of any better alternative I prefer to talk of adult learning in the community and to use community in a residential, locational sense without the insistence that such collections of individuals always exhibit mutuality, interrelatedness, and a sense of common identity. This usage may not exemplify the semantic and logical impeccability so beloved of lingistic philosophers. I trust, however, that it is a usage acceptable to adult education practitioners and one which bears some relevance to their professional practice.

Liberal and Liberating Models of Community Adult Education

The purpose of this section is to demonstrate the plurality of practice and conceptual ambiguity which falls under the rubric of community education. Community is a value laden term which, like democracy, can be taken by different people as a description of, or justification for, widely differing activities. The breadth of interpretation and implementation possible within the category of community education is nicely summarized by Fletcher when he draws the distinction between liberal and liberating models of community education: 'liberal assumes that the person is "free" and should be yet freer and more enlightened whilst liberating assumes bondage and the setting free of whole classes of persons' (Fletcher 1980b, p. 69). The two notions of community education are, in fact, based on two separate visions of community: the liberal view is of a *gemeinschaft* type of community, an organic harmonious entity. The liberating view holds that communities are split by divisions and inequalities of an economic, political and ethnic nature.

Liberal Models of Community Education

The liberal model of community education is based on an assumption which, as adult and continuing education programmers will know from their own experience, is at best highly questionable and at worst practically inoperable. This assumption is that community education can comprise a programme which satisfies the needs of all members of a community at any one time. It is institution based in that it emphasizes delivery systems provided by some agency which exists to serve the needs of community members. Let us take three definitions of community education which exemplify the liberal model of community education. The first of these is that offered by professors of adult education and community education surveyed in an American 'delphi' study, a third of whom defined community education as:

> the process of identification of community needs and the marshalling of resources to meet those needs so that the community and all its members can grow through social and educational programs. (Fellenz and Coker 1980, p. 319)

A similar, though admittedly visionary definition, is that offered by Marcie Boucouvalas in her examination of the interface between lifelong learning and community education. Boucouvalas declares that:

> the ultimate goal of community education is the development of self-guiding, self-directed communities which are able to identify and satisfy the needs of all their community members through the coordination, cooperation, and collaboration of all community resources. (Boucouvalas 1979, p. 35)

Finally, a pamphlet written by a respected American community educator entitled *People Helping People*, which undertakes an overview of community education, includes this definition of the concept:

> Community education encourages the development of a comprehensive and coordinated delivery system for providing educational, recreational, social and cultural services for all people in a community. (Decker 1978, p. 4)

These definitions raise unanswered questions of great importance and contain within them a number of hidden assumptions and covert value judgements. The first two definitions, for example, emphasize the identification and satisfaction of community needs and of individual needs. These may, however, be in total contradiction as when a town council, as a group elected to express popular will, decides to introduce a shopping development in direct opposition to the wishes of a large number of local inhabitants. The concept of community needs is also highly questionable. What are usually offered as examples of community needs tend to be one person's (whether a community developer or local politician) prescription as to the kind of community change he or she considers desirable. To assert that community needs can somehow be synthesized from a number of individual felt needs is another familiar misconception. The best that one can hope for is that a community need as perceived by the educator reflects the majority preference of the inhabitants within an area.

A second problem with these three definitions is the way in which it is assumed that the needs of all members of a community can be met at any one time. This ignores the possibility that there will be times when the community worker or community educator is faced with requests for assistance from different groups whose interests are diametrically opposed. Fostering the 'growth' (to use the Fellenz and Coker term) of the members of a natural foods co-operative may be directly opposed to fostering the growth of members of the local chamber of commerce. The choice the worker or educator makes on how to use the time, money and other resources available will reflect the worker's personal value system or the norms of his or her employing body.

A case history described to me by one of my ex-graduate students at the University of British Columbia provides an apt example of the kinds of practical choices facing community workers which reflect deeper ethical dilemmas. This student was employed as a community worker in a suburb in which an application to erect a residential home for the mentally disturbed was being discussed. Several members of the local community asked him to assist them in opposing any application to build such an institution in their locale. According to the philosophical canons and practical injunctions contained in the three definitions previously quoted, the worker should have assisted the individuals concerned in their action. They had specified an action objective (preventing the granting of planning permission for the residential home) and were clearly expressing their need for the worker's help. In this instance, the individual concerned felt compelled to express his own support for the siting of the residential home and to refuse to 'meet the needs' of several members of the community. The ethical correctness of the worker's course of action is not at issue here; what is important is that it demonstrates that value free choices on the part of community workers are not always possible and may, indeed, be a relative rarity.

Liberating Models of Community Education
These models are usually associated with radical adult educators and political theorists such as Alinsky, Freire and Horton. They are based on a notion of community which emphasizes the existence of inequities in

terms of income, access to educational opportunity, and political power. Instead of acknowledging the existence of cohesive and harmonious elements in a community, writers in this tradition choose to concentrate on differences and disparities. Education, including adult education, comes to serve as a compensatory or readjustment mechanism concerned to promote the collective well-being of an identified disadvantaged or disenfranchised group. The community adult educator is seen as being forced to ignore the needs of one sector (for example, landlords) in order to serve the needs of another (for example, tenants' associations). Another feature of this school of theorists is the absence of clearly immutable distinctions drawn by such writers between education, development and action. Education becomes a political act and development and action are held to be interwoven and part of a broad movement to attain social justice. Thus, as a community adult educator identified with these views declares, 'in the most important sense success will depend on the extent to which adult education contributes to the process of social change' (Lovett 1971, p. 13).

As Lawson has pointed out (Lawson 1977) what Lovett means is that adult education is to be judged according to the extent to which it contributes to what he (Lovett) regards as *desirable* social change. If adult education is judged simply by the amount of social change it promotes — irrespective of the nature or form of such change — then the transition of an open, democratic society to a closed, hierarchical society would become a cause of celebration for adult educators. However, writers in the Lovett tradition are usually quite prepared to acknowledge that their practice is based explicitly on value systems. Again, the ethical merits of the value system chosen are, at present, irrelevant to our discussion. What is important is that there is a recognition that community educators are not functionaries, automatons, or dehumanized ciphers through whom in some mystical osmotic process are channelled the desires and wishes of a coherent community. Rather, educators are seen as political creatures who are faced constantly with the need to make choices regarding the allocation of resources and whose choices reflect personal biases or institutional preferences.

As already indicated, the criteria applied by liberating theorists to determining the success of a community adult education initiative appear to be political as much as educational. However, such writers would argue that this distinction is both artificial and untenable. To them the concept of a truly educated person is one which places political awareness and personal liberation at its core. There is, to these writers, a natural point of congruence between a raised political consciousness, a true perception of the inequities inherent in society, and a fully educated person. Such a person will be fully conscientized (to use the Freirean concept) and will express this in praxis; that is, in some form of social or political action.

Education is seen as the handmaiden of collective political action and the fully educated person is held to be one who realizes that an educative society can only be achieved through social change. Lovett remarks, for example, that 'what is required is an educational movement closely linked and committed to the existing community action movement' (Lovett 1978, p. 47) and allies himself with the historian R. H. Tawney who regarded successful adult education as linked to broader movements for social change.

The political basis of the liberating model of community education is well summarized by Lovett in an article in the international journal of adult education, *Convergence*. Writing as the director of a community action research and education project in Northern Ireland he argues that education is the arm of a community action movement which exists to promote the interests of working class adults. Although Lovett, like Freire,is careful to stress the dialogical process in education and the need to explore the private and public worlds of working class adults on their own terms, there is an implication that the end result of this dialogue will be left-wing, radical political change. Community education thus becomes 'a dynamic force in the community action movement' serving to indicate to adult educators the role of adult education in community action (Lovett 1978, p. 49).

Such a perspective is markedly in contrast to the emphasis within the liberal model of community education on the satisfaction of the needs of all members at any one time. It is also opposed to the notion that education — the planned initiation of learners into a body of knowledge or transmission of a set of skills — can be judged on its own terms, separate from its cultural context. Value-free education is, to writers in this school, a contradiction in terms. All education serves either to perpetuate the majority culture and to domesticate individuals or to develop a radical consciousness. If education develops in adults a perception of the world as divided into oppressors and oppressed then, to these writers, it can be considered real and authentic. The ethical or political correctness of these views is, of course, open to question and those wishing to consider well-thought-out critiques of this school of thought might like to read those of Griffith (1972), Lawson (1977), Paterson (1979) Apps (1979) and Elias and Merriam (1980). What is important for our present discussion is the realization by theorists of this school that practice reflects the value system and value preferences of the educator or sponsoring agency.

Institutional Implementations of Community Education — Community Schools and Village Colleges

The purpose of this section is to examine the institutional implementation of the liberal community education model in the United States and Britain as reflected in the C. S. Mott community school tradition and the Henry Morris influenced village college movement. Both these movements date from the 1920s and 1930s and the models of provision which developed at that time exercise a continuing influence on contemporary community education programmes.

The Mott tradition of the community school as the centre for community education provision and practice in a locality can be traced back to the efforts of Frank Manley in the 1930s. Manley was a physical education teacher in the town of Flint, Michigan at a time when the town was suffering from a number of social and economic problems which were the legacy of the great depression of 1929–31. The town had witnessed the collapse of the local auto industry and a sense of transience and instability infused the community. Unemployment levels were high, petty crime was rife and the educational system was severely underfinanced. Manley determined to revitalize the educational system through the introduction of the 'lighted schoolhouse' — opening school buildings in the evenings and at weekends so that youths and adults could use the classrooms, laboratories, gymnasiums and other resources during out of school hours.

As with so many other community education initiatives — the Antigonish movement in Nova Scotia, village colleges in rural England and the Highlander Folk School in Tennessee — the community school movement can thus be seen to have grown out of a response by one or two people to what they saw as a crisis facing the local community. To this extent the liberating theorists of community education can point to the way in which educational innovation was intertwined with the broader aims of community improvement and regeneration of the local physical and emotional fabric. In the case of Flint the town benefited from the patronage of Charles Stewart Mott, a local auto-industrialist who had been the town's mayor and who had established a charitable foundation devoted to community regeneration. Manley presented his ideas on the greater utilization of the facilities of Flint Public Schools to Mott who agreed to grant 6,000 dollars to fund the experiment.

The Mott Foundation has since established regional and university-based centers throughout the United States to encourage and develop community school provision. The Foundation has also extended support to community education initiatives in other countries. The Community Education Development Centre (CEDC) in Coventry, England, is funded partly by the Mott Foundation and in 1980 the Atlantic Canada Center for Community Education was opened in Halifax, Nova Scotia thanks to Mott finance. However, it would be inaccurate to portray the efforts of the Mott Foundation as constituting the sum total of community education initiatives over the last fifty years. The Mott influence has been, and continues to be, crucial but Mott does not exercise a hegemony in the field. The Kellog Foundation has also sponsored three community education programme initiatives in the form of the Michigan Community

School Service programme in the 1940s and 1950s (to relate community education to community development), the Cooperative Program in Educational Administration in the 1950s and 1960s (to train school administrators) and the Leadership Education programme for community colleges in the 1960s and 1970s.

In an important review of the contemporary relevance of community education Eric Midwinter, a veteran of the Educational Priority Area (EPA) project in Liverpool, has written that 'The village college, serving the many social and educational needs of a rural community, may be compared with the spasmodic growth of community schooling in the United States' (Midwinter 1973, p. 45). Both Midwinter in Britain and Hiemstra in the United States (Hiemstra 1972, p. 47) recognize that village colleges and community schools have their origins in rural communities or small towns, and that the concept will need to be reinterpreted (possibly on a neighbourhood school basis) for large urban connurbations. Nonetheless, both initiatives continue to exercise an important influence on the development of community education some fifty or sixty years after their genesis.

The concept of the village college can be traced directly to a pamphlet published in Cambridgeshire, England by Henry Morris in 1924 when Morris was secretary to the Cambridgeshire council. The pamphlet had the (hardly inspiring) title of *The Village College: Being a Memorandum on the Provision of Educational and Social Facilities for the Countryside with Special Reference to Cambridgeshire.* Cambridgeshire, like Flint, suffered from the problems of deprivation associated with poverty, as well as from increasing depopulation. Schools were poorly equipped and operated as one teacher, one room, all age schools, further ensuring that the most able younger members of rural communities migrated to the towns at the earliest possible opportunity. Indeed, when we consider the plight of contemporary urban city areas — poor educational facilities and opportunities, an ageing, low income population, high unemployment, and migration of the most able to more privileged areas — this is not so far from the conditions encountered by Morris in rural Cambridgeshire in the 1920s as first might be imagined.

The solution to the problems caused by a scattering of small, all age schools was to be the village college. Morris saw this college as implementing a model of lifelong education. In his eyes the village college would become the community centre for the neighbourhood and would be a visible demonstration in stone of the continuity and never-ceasingness of education (Morris 1924, p. 9). The college would include a nursery schoolroom (kindergarten) and infant welfare centre, a primary school for younger children, and a secondary school for the adolescent age range. The schools would offer facilities for crafts, domestic subjects and agriculture and would be sited close to the local village hall. School facilities would be open for adult use in the evenings, in the manner of Mott and Manley's 'lighted schoolhouse', and the adjacent village hall would function as an adult leisure centre as well as providing adjunct facilities (dining room, gymnasium etc.) for the school during the day. Rooms for use by local organizations and voluntary associations were available and the public library was to be sited adjacent to the college to serve as a resource for both the school and the adult community. The centralization of resources and facilities for use by all members of a community was based on the assumption that village colleges would serve a scattered rural population of approximately 10,000.

Morris held the post of Director of Education for Cambridgeshire until 1954 and was thus able to supervise the implementation of an idea which, in 1924, had seemed impossibly visionary. As Morris's biographer, Harry Rée points out (Rée 1973, p. 134) Morris's ideas were of such an innovatory nature that had they been left to any other chief education officer village colleges might never have been introduced. As it was, Morris had to canvass private industry, charitable trusts and individual donators for contributions towards the building of the first college at Sawston in 1930. Despite the depression of the early 1930s and the Second World War, Cambridgeshire continued to build colleges into the 1960s. The verdict of a renowned comparative adult educator is that 'they represent one of the most successful experiments in the recent history of adult education' (Lowe 1970, p. 69) while the foremost historian of British adult education regards them as unquestionably a tremendous success (Kelly 1970, p. 299).

Arthur Stock, the director of the United Kingdom National Institute of Adult Education, has identified three waves in the development of the community college idea. The first wave comprised their introduction in Cambridgeshire, the second can be seen in the efforts of other counties to adapt the village college model to small towns within their boundaries, and the third wave is the implementation of the village college model to an urban setting, either in the inner city or an 'overspill' public housing project. As Stock comments, 'in the attempt to meet the needs of urban size and complexity, the buildings have become large and complex; but the multi-age, multi-purpose principles remain the same, (Stock 1980, p. 13).

Contemporary Community Education Provision in the United States and Britain

A recent summary of *Community Education Developments: U.K. 1982* (CEDC 1982) published by the Community Education Development Centre (CEDC) in Coventry, England, lists sixty-two projects said to be representative of the contemporary state of community education. An eclecticism of practice and an all age clientele are the two features most immediately apparent in these initiatives. Target groups identified in different projects are the unemployed, the disabled, single parent families, gypsies, the 16–19 age group, school drop-outs, women, the working class, community groups, the 8–13 age group, the elderly, and ethnic minorities. Examples of community education practice include city farms, gipsy schools, literacy work, 'A' level work (grade 12), traditional crafts, drama, poetry, manual skills, developing community radio programmes, outdoor education, urban studies, community arts, and health education. Most of these activities are based on community schools and community colleges which designate a member of staff as 'community tutor' or 'community education organizer'. In Scotland and Northern Ireland independent centres and community development projects are more evident with a number of regional council sponsored projects in Scotland and community centres in Belfast, Northern Ireland.

Two features strike this writer regarding the relevance of these activities to the ideas of Morris. Firstly, the emphasis on all community provision urged by Morris does seem to be reflected in the practice in the 1980s. Secondly, the notion of the multi-purpose community college serving as the one centre for educational and recreational activities in a community has been adopted only sporadically. Community schools seem to be a much more popular model of provision. Such schools are usually based on existing primary (5–11 years of age) or secondary (11–18 years of age) schools and include a curricular emphasis on local community studies, a willingness to use people and plant in the community as learning resources for children, and an involvement with local community development initiatives. Encouraging the development of separate community primary schools and community secondary schools is directly opposed to the Morris notion of a single site, multi-purpose village college. There is also the risk (identified at the beginning of this chapter) that simply altering nomenclature from secondary school to community school will not reflect a permanent change in practice. Finally, it is interesting to note that with regard to the clientele served (the unemployed, ethnic minorities, gipsies, single parent families etc.) these contemporary community education initiatives do tend to exhibit the positive discrimination in favour of disadvantaged and minority groups often associated with the radical liberating model of community education discussed earlier in this chapter.

In an excellent recent anthology of readings on *Issues in Community Education* (Fletcher & Thompson 1980) the contributing authors submitted accounts of community education work in Northern Ireland, Liverpool, Sheffield, Manchester, Nottingham and Coventry. The study of work in Coventry centred upon the activities of the Sidney Stringer School and Community College which has gained a reputation for community education practice in England. Some brief mention of its work may serve to illustrate the kinds of difficulties which are encountered when philosophy is translated and reflected in practice. Other useful surveys of British implementations of community education ideas are contained in Jennings (1980), the appendix to Midwinter (1973) and the various issues of the *Community Education Journal.*

The Sidney Stringer School and Community College is located in a multi-ethnic, inner city area of Coventry, an industrial town in the West Midlands of England which suffered from heavy bombing in World War Two but which enjoyed an economic boom in the 1950s and 1960s based on the car industry. The Sidney Stringer school is an amalgam of two secondary modern schools (11–16 age range) and centres its curriculum on a compulsory two-year course in Social Studies which encourages students to understand their local community. Local adults are involved in framing the curriculum and acting as resources.

Several features of the Sidney Stringer experience deserve mention. Firstly, there is the head teacher's assessment that had a full, participatory decision-making democracy been allowed to operate with parents and staff, the reforms introduced such as abolition of corporal punishment and school uniform would have been reversed. The community use of school premises would also have been prevented (Jones 1980, p. 80). As it was, the few senior staff charged with introducing a community education mode were able to maintain their commitment to this only by adopting a paternalistic stance. Had they engaged in a problem-posing dialogue with colleagues and parents soon after the beginning of the project, there is little doubt that a reversion to traditional practices would have been urged. This frank acknowledgement of the way in which democratically impeccable procedures had to be ignored for fear of leading to authoritarian practice will be particularly refreshing to readers who tire of accounts of community work practice which reveal no tensions generated by a dysjunction of workers' ideals and clientele preferences.

The emphasis on community advisory councils in the Mott tradition was paralleled at Sidney Stringer in its creation of a Community Association which contained a council in which local parents, users, students and staff could vote on major issues. Again, Jones is refreshingly honest in his recognition that attempts to devolve power to 'the people' resulted only in the elevation of atypical individuals (in that they were used to committee procedures which many inner city residents had never encountered) to positions of responsibility. Many residents in the inner city area were confused about committee procedures and insecure regarding their rights (or abilities) to influence meetings. In the event, a strong staff presence was evident on the Community Association and council and the majority Asian ethnic group in the area was disproportionately under-represented (Jones 1980, p. 84). Despite this recognition of early problems and the ways in which well-meaning attempts at community participation could end up reinforcing traditional structures and practices, Jones did conclude that the school could function 'as a major instrument of community development and as an instrument for social change' (Jones 1980, p. 79).

In a seminal American work on community education published in the early 1970s, Jack Minzey and Clyde Le Tarte declared that community education was the concept and that the community school was the delivery system for that concept (Minzey & Le Tarte 1972, p. 11). There are now over 4,000 community schools in the United States the missions of which range from opening facilities to adult members of the community to serving as a catalyst for community development. Dickson has pointed out that public schools are permanent and politically neutral agencies in local communities (Dickson 1981) and that involving parents in 'soft' issues such as playground equipment and park development can lead to these citizens becoming involved in 'meatier, often politically charged issues' (p. 18).

Vasil M. Kerensky, Mott professor and director of the Community Education Center at Florida Atlantic University, has argued that 'community education is a much broader concept than simply opening the schools to the public' (Kerensky 1981, p. 10) and to assume that opening a school in the evening somehow turns it into a community school is a conceptual and practical *non-sequitur*. A school may have a substantial range of adult evening classes and a citizens' advisory council but the simple existence of such programmes and constitutional mechanisms does not automatically grant some kind of 'community pedigree' to that school. Kerensky believes, in fact, that school districts in California and Florida have citizens' advisory councils at schools which serve no community purpose in that they ignore community concerns and are merely administrative units. The notion that the school is only one educative agency in communities is reflected in the change of name of the American professional association in the 1970s from the National Community School Education Association to the National Community Education Association.

An analysis of community education provision in states on the east coast (Massachussetts) and west coast (California) will serve to illustrate the variety of practice and philosophy which is currently subsumed within the category of community education. The analysis of community education in Massachussetts is taken from a publication recently issued on behalf of the Massachussets Department of Education entitled *Community Education: An Action Handbook* (1979). The authors of this report identify six elements as endemic to a working definition of community education...

(a) Partnership between educational agencies and the community.
(b) Identifying community needs.

(c) Using all available resources.
(d) Democratizing educational decision-making.
(e) Recognizing learning as a lifelong activity.
(f) Encouraging full access to all facilities (cultural, recreational, educational) for all members of a community. (Massachussetts Dept of Education 1979, p. 4)

Six programmes were chosen to represent the range and variety of community education programmes in the state. One is based upon an existing adult education programme (Acton-Boxborough), one is run in co-operation with the public schools (Andover), one is entirely independent of the school system (Ashland), two are primarily community school programmes (Boston and Brockton), and one is a teacher-orientated, staff development programme (the SEED programme in Western Massachussetts). The concept of community education is seen as one which has come of age and which appears to be in the right place at the right time (Mass. Dept of Education 1979, p. 50).

Of particular note when considering the relevance of the legacy of Mott is the Boston community schools programme. This comprises eighteen sites serving over 30,000 people each week with each site being governed by a community school council. These councils are made up of locally-elected community members and their functions are to identify community needs and to devise appropriate programmes to suit changing community circumstances. The three schools mentioned in the analysis of provision in Boston all have particular emphases — on combining a community health centre and a public elementary school and serving as an advocacy centre for local Chinese (Quincy Community School), on providing facilities for senior citizens and teenagers (Ohrenberger Community School), and on providing family-orientated recreational and crafts activities (Lee Community School).

The state of California contains 160 community schools, 30 of which are in the San Diego area. As seen by Wayne Robins, the project director of the Schemes in Neighbourhood Action and Participation (SNAP) initiative for the Mott Foundation, these schools emphasize community development and an increased involvement of citizens in decision-making (Williams & Robins 1980, p. 59). In the city of San Diego itself, elementary schools form the basis of the community school system as these are seen as relating to local neighbourhoods more than are large public high schools. Each school is advised by a community council, much along the Mott lines, which assesses community needs and arranges programmes based upon this assessment. The San Diego community schools system was established only in 1973 and Williams and Robins note that a major problem which has developed is the unfamiliarity of many citizens with the idea of taking community leadership roles and becoming involved in decision-making. Local adults lack the process skills required to plan and arrange their own community education programs and attempts to transfer power to them can result in apathy or frustration (p. 61).

This last observation calls to mind the experience of the Sidney Stringer school in Coventry which was mentioned earlier. Even though the United States and Great Britain are two of the most politically literate, democratic societies in the world, it is still over-optimistic to assume that establishing mechanisms for devolved power-sharing will somehow induce the development of self-help, community leadership skills in community members. Because childhood and adolescent education has accustomed its recipients to externally imposed programmes and externally devised curricula, adults, particularly in inner city and other disadvantaged areas, will tend to assume that community education initiatives will conform to this pattern. The hardest of all transitions to make in community education (and its most important distinction) is that from programme to process. The conceptual and practical difference between these elements, and the ways in which movement from one to the other can be encouraged, has occupied the attention of a number of experienced American community educators. It is appropriate at this stage to consider their advice.

Programme and Process in Community Education

One of the ten myths regarding community education identified by Kerensky in a recent paper is that a good community school can be recognized by the existence of a large number of out of school hours programmes (1981, p. 11). This equating of the totality of community education with the provision of adult education programmes and out of hours access to school facilities, is one of the misconceptions most frequently and vigorously attacked by community educators. The basis of their villification is that a concentration on the provision of programmes neglects the whole dimension of 'process' in community education. The dangers of ignoring this dimension of human interaction have long been acknowledged by community development workers. In a classic of the field the Biddle's declared that. . .

> The essence of process does not consist in any fixed succession of events. . . but in the growth that occurs within individuals, within groups, and within the communities they serve. (Biddle & Biddle 1965, p. 79)

A process model of community development and its relation to adult education has also recently been elaborated by Roberts (1979, p. 34).

The origins of the current debate on programme and process can be traced to the publication of two books by Jack Minzey and Clyde Le

Tarte. In 1972 *Community Education: From Program to Process* first appeared, with its warning that the potency of community education could be diffused through an obsession with providing identifiable programmes as evidence that community education was occurring. A follow up work on *Community Education: From Program to Process to Practice* was published in 1979 examining 'The School's Role in a New Educational Society' (the book's subtitle). However, other community educators have been aware of the programme and process issue including Kerensky and Melby (1972), Lovett (1971, 1975) and Seay (1977). In 1972 a study of community educators in America commented that the acceptance of process as the distinctive feature of community education was commonly acknowledged by community educators (Weaver 1972). Such a perception is certainly reflected in the conceptual base underlying the practice already described in San Diego and Boston. In 1977 the Nevada Department of Education issued a report which also acknowledged that a cooperative community involvement process was at the heart of community education (Nevada State Dept. of Education 1977, p. 5). The discussion of process in the following paragraphs draws primarily on the work of Minzey and Le Tarte and on that of John Warden.

Minzey and Le Tarte regard the rationale of community education as being that of process. Hence, 'the ultimate goal of Community Education is to develop a process by which members of a community learn to work together to identify problems and to seek out solutions to these problems' (Minzey and Le Tarte 1979, p. 15). The ultimate expression of this process is, in Minzey and Le Tarte's adaptation of Maslow's hierarchy of individual human needs, the self-actualized community. However, the establishment of a general community education programme of courses, classes and activities tends to become the end of community education, instead of the first stage in an evolutionary process which takes the community towards self-actualization. A concentration on programme is unsatisfactory to Minzey and Le Tarte because some community members will have a mistrust of any formally-sponsored education programmes and because the generic nature of educational programmes means that many individual personal needs will not be addressed.

To qualify as an exemplar of community education a particular initiative must, in Minzey and Le Tarte's opinion, progress from the establishment of a general programme through several subsequent stages. Following the organization of a general programme (usually based on an analysis of programmes in similar neighbouring communities) will come a problem-based programme. This will consist of activities arising from individual community members' analyses of problems experienced in their lives. Once the problem-based programme stage has been reached, then the process stage begins. After scrutinizing his or her own motives the community education director will begin to develop a rapport with community members which will result in the formation of some kind of representative community group. This group will then assume responsibility for identifying problems for further examination. Once the problems for confrontation have been selected the group will move through the stages of discussion, organization, action and evaluation. This is, of course, a simplfied and simplistic representation of Minzey and Le Tarte's ideas. In particular, it makes little reference to the kinds of conflict created by special community groups pursuing their own sectional interests, or to the choices educators may have to make as process is evolved. In this sense, their model of community education is directly in the liberal mode discussed earlier in this chapter. Indeed, Minzey and Le Tarte acknowledge this in their definition of the community education concept as one 'which serves the entire community by providing for all of the educational needs of all its community members' (Minzey & Le Tarte 1979, p. 26–7).

John Warden's monograph on *Process Perspectives: Community Education as Process* (1979) is an impressive attempt to review the literature relating to the concept of process as reflected in the fields of community development, social work, sociology, anthropology and education. Warden also develops a fourfold process typology which covers the range of activities and perspectives included within community process orientations. The typology assumes the following form:

1. *Process as Procedure:* this aspect of process is seen in the attempt to achieve a specified aim in a limited time. An example of process as procedure would be an attempt by a development agency to engender public consultation and community participation in decisions regarding the form and function of a new recreation complex. It would emphasize the public inquiry process, user consultation procedures, and community forums.
2. *Process as Community Problem-Solving:* the function of the community educator in this context is to assist individual members and community groups in identifying problems and then developing phases in problem-solving.
3. *Process as Community Power:* this is associated particularly with the ideas of Alinsky (1971) and focuses on the notion of animating community action against identified adversaries. In realizing and then exercising power community groups come to develop a sense of self-reliance. Process as community power is seen in the activities of advocacy groups, citizens' action groups and other pressure groups.
4. *Process as Psychological and Social Development:* this is a humanistically orientated notion of process and centres on the development of self-actualized, fully functioning individuals.

In relating this typology to the field of community education Warden notes (1979, p. 37) that the fourth category is the one most favoured by community educators. This category does, of course, fit squarely into the liberal mode of community education. As Warden points out, the notion of the educative community as developed by Hiemstra (and discussed later in this chapter) is conceptually linked to process as a humanistic psychological and social development. Type 2, process as problem-solving, is the perspective which is seen by Warden as the next most familiar to community educators and examples he cites of this are the Minzey and Le Tarte approach, that of the Nevada State Department of Education, and the training materials of the Northwest Community Education Center in Oregon. Warden cites Berridge's (1971) analysis of procedures in initiating community school activity in Tipp City, Ohio, as an example of the type 1 process as procedure and also refers to an attempt by Berridge and Stark (1975) to outline specific procedures which need to be followed before introducing a community school programme. The category in the typology least favoured by community educators is, according to Warden, type 3 — process as power.

An endeavour of Warden's which merits special attention in the context of our discussion is his elaboration of twelve myths which serve to obscure clear discussion of the concept of process in community education. Two of these are worth mention here; the 'No Conflict' myth and the 'No Special Interest' myth. Both of these myths were identified, though not in these exact terms, earlier in this chapter in the discussion of the liberal model of community education. The 'No Conflict' myth assumes there will be a congruence of desires and perceived needs when community members are presented with an opportunity to articulate their preferences for community change. As Warden comments, conflict is bound to arise reflecting the different value systems held by groups and individuals and where no conflict of opinion is visible to community educators it is more than likely that educators and community groups are not addressing real community issues (Warden 1979, p. 50). The 'No Special Interest' myth is held by those who speak of process in terms solely of brotherhood and togetherness. Those who emphasize the process orientation in their community education work must recognize, however, that client groups will reflect particular ethnic, economic, social and political interests.

To some writers, notably Susan Baillie (1979), a preoccupation with process can betoken a neglect of the ends of community action and community education. The means of community education — process — assume the status of an end. Hence, involving individuals and community groups in forums and community councils or establishing a variety of consultative procedures becomes an end in itself requiring no broader justification. Baillie believes that 'Process is important but only in the context of the overall objective' (p. 72) and that community educators may neglect to address areas of critical community concern.

In a recent paper Warden has himself directly addressed the issues of the ultimate objectives and political dimensions of community education (Warden 1980). Recognizing that viewing community education as a political act may be a 'ghastly' thought for some, he argues that it can influence the way advantages and disadvantages are distributed among people and that one criterion of successful community education work which can be applied is 'the degree of success of political action and involvement that has been generated within the community' (p. 5). Ten ways in which community education has political implications are discussed by Warden including the encouragement it gives to democratic procedures, the assistance it provides in developing community leadership, and the manner in which it highlights the need for change. He also acknowledges that community education action can reflect political biases, particularly when the agency sponsoring community education views it as a form of public relations and is not committed to giving the power to groups and individuals to define and meet their own needs. Hence, for Warden, the process orientation within community education means that 'politics and political action will remain the fundamental business of community educators' (p. 10).

The Educative Community

In ending his discussion of process, Warden declares that those community educators who operate within this mode see 'the entire community with all its resources and people as an educational and community development enterprise' (Warden 1979, p. 59). This notion of the educative community is one dear to the hearts of most community educators and, as Boucouvalas has commented (Boucouvalas 1979, p. 35) even those community educators who do not use the term subscribe to the ideals contained therein. An adult educator who has spent some considerable time considering the educative community — both in developing its conceptual base and exploring modes of implementation with graduate students — is Roger Hiemstra, Professor of adult education at Syracuse University. His ideas on this are elaborated in a book and paper produced in the 1970s (Hiemstra 1972, 1975) and the following paragraphs draw chiefly from these two sources and from personal discussion with Hiemstra.

The educative community is both an ideal and a reality. In ideal terms it aims to use all community resources to develop individuals to their full potential. In actual terms it signifies that individuals are products of their environments, rather in the sense in which sociologists talk of socialization. The community functions as an educative influence in that 'it is the setting in which people's attitudes, talents, and behaviours are influenced' (Hiemstra 1972, p. 25). Hiemstra's work is concerned chiefly with the ways in which the ideal educative community can be achieved. Such a community would, in his words, become 'a living, learning, laboratory' (Hiemstra 1972, p. 28).

Hiemstra suggests several ways to promote what he calls 'activation' of the educative community, arguing that 'most persons and agencies in a community have a potential, if not actual capacity for being involved in the educational process' (Hiemstra 1972, p. 25). Some of these are the following:

1. Emphasize youth learning *from* the world rather than *about* the world.
2. Expand adult and continuing education to meet residents' needs.
3. Use the school as a centre for neighbourhood and community life.
4. Train teachers to work in community settings and not just classrooms.
5. Involve parents in determining curricula and supplementing school based education.
6. Make more use of educative agencies such as libraries, museums and the mass media.
7. Expand the role of community colleges.
8. Involve churches as sites for discussion on matters of familial and social concern.
9. Use a variety of community sites as learning resources for school and adult education — zoos, parks, galleries, YMCAs and YWCAs, and local industry.

An interesting account of an experiment in activating the educative community using graduate adult education students at the University of Nebraska is offered by Hiemstra in a 1975 paper. Students were asked to locate an agency, organization or individual not primarily identified as being involved in adult education and to approach the institutions or persons with proposals for adding an adult education component to their activities. Hiemstra records that forty of forty-five programmes offered were accepted and implemented and provides the following as examples of activating initiatives:

(1) A laundromat being the site of an exhibit on travel possibilities in the state
(2) Banks including book markers with details of local adult education organisations in their monthly statements sent to customers
(3) A dentist including preventive information in his monthly statements to patients
(4) Fire stations offering an open-house on a Saturday each month to increase awareness of safety precautions and procedures

(Hiemstra 1975, p. 84)

As Hiemstra acknowledges, the experiments cited above emphasize the adding of an educational component to already existing agency activities, or the increasing of community knowledge of existing adult education programmes. To this extent, they are only the first step in community activation and a prelude to using individuals as educational resources and to identifying educational needs. Hiemstra believes that adult educators need to be more than programme planners or teachers of adults and that needs diagnosis and resources location must become an essential element in the armoury of adult educators' skills. To him, 'perhaps the richest resources for teaching and learning are outside the walls of formal educational institutions' (Hiemstra 1975, p. 85).

The notion of the educative community as developed by Hiemstra exhibits many resemblances to the category of adult education in the community as outlined in the typology which follows. In both the emphasis is on recognizing the educational component in community settings and situations. There is also an agreement that formal adult education provision cannot in any sense be equated with the sum total of adult learning in the community. In recognizing that individuals and groups are engaging in self-planned educational activities, the role of the educator comes to exhibit supportive and facilitation dimensions, as well as those of initiation and planning.

A Typology of the Community Practice of Adult Education

As I remarked at the beginning of this chapter, the term community adult education is one which, in operational terms, is used to cover a range of contrasting and sometimes contradictory activities and behaviours. One way to reduce the conceptual ambiguity infusing discussion of community adult education is to isolate the adult education component in the term and to focus on the ways in which adult education practices can display a greater or lesser awareness of the structure and concerns of the community in which they are located. In this final part of the chapter a typology is presented in which three dimensions of the community practice of adult education are identified: adult education for the community, adult education in the community, and adult education of the community. As with Warden's process typology, this is not intended to be mutually exclusive and one adult education programme may contain elements which are located in more than one category of the typology. However, it is intended to show that many examples of what are blithely and generally called community adult education exhibit differences in intention and execution which mean they really need to be placed in different categories. In some of the practices identified in the following typology differences in kind as well as of degree are evident.

Adult Education for the Community
Adult education for the community covers the kinds of activities which are

regarded as the staple diet of adult education programme planning. As here conceived, it can be seen in standard programme planning texts such as those written by Knowles (1980a), Knox (1980) and Boyle (1981). Adult education for the community occurs when programmes are provided for adults which are based on some kind of needs assessment of the wishes and desires of adults within the locale of the providing centre. If a survey of felt and expressed needs reveals a desire for more courses in Transcendental Meditation, Do-It-Yourself, Understanding the Economy, or Keep Fit, then the programmer appoints instructors and publicizes courses. This appears to be a consumer-orientated approach to adult education in which the adult or continuing education programmer role is restricted almost to that of administrative functionary. It also suggests that the adult educator has removed from him or her the responsibility of exercising value judgements regarding the intrinsic merits of particular courses and activities. If the needs assessment reveals certain desires among the adult population, so the argument goes, the task of the educator is simply to produce programmes which satisfy those felt and expressed needs.

As all practising adult and continuing education programmers know, however, administrative and organizational life is never that simple. It is more than likely that a needs assessment will reveal a host of possible programmes and activities reflecting the desires and wants of sectional groups and particular individuals. Budgetary constraints or limitations on space may mean that all articulated needs cannot be met in terms of programme provision. Consequently, programmers will be forced to choose which courses, classes and workshops to run, and which to leave as latent and unfulfilled desires. In assessing the relative desirability of possible activities programmers will apply a number of criteria, all of which reflect the value systems of those individuals. Examples of such criteria are: (1) the ease with which appropriate instructors for suggested courses can be located; (2) the revenue which it is felt that programmes are likely to produce and the number of participants they will attract; (3) the status within the community of groups and individuals proposing particular programmes (this includes positive discrimination programmes); and (4) the programmer's personal judgement as to the intrinsic academic or aesthetic merit of various activities. Once again, it is apparent that adult and continuing education programmers never function solely as neutral, value-free automatons. Their decisions, choices and actions all reflect a personal or institutional ethic to which they subscribe.

Adult Education in the Community

The conduct of adult education in the community draws heavily on the notion of the educative community as propounded by Hiemstra and on the Mott tradition of using non-classroom community facilities and locations as educational resources. Outreach work, in which educators work with individuals and groups in natural societal settings, is also included in this category. Features of adult education practice which can be included within adult education in the community are the following:

1. The adult educator provides materials and expertise to support the submerged dimension of adult learning — the adult learning iceberg — identified in the previous chapter.
2. The learners retain the responsibility for setting learning goals and for deciding which advice and assistance to accept from professional educators.
3. The educator offers advice and assistance only after a period of initial immersion in a particular community.
4. The educator uses the community as a learning resource or laboratory.

In the exercise of activity 4 there will be times when condition 2 — the autonomy of learners in goal setting — may be contradicted. Hence, a community studies course sponsored by an adult education centre, which was conducted primarily in an experiential or field study mode, would be included as an example of adult education in the community. In such a course the tutor/instructor would probably decide the curriculum and the locations for learning — factories, transport centres, historical sites and so on. However, in its emphasis on using community settings as the location for learning it seems to me this can fall within no other category.

Adult education in the community differs from adult education for the community primarily in terms of the location of educative activity. There is also a difference in the relationship of educators to students. In adult education for the community the educator accepts the initial definition of needs expressed by community members as the prime determinant of which courses and activities to promote. However, once this decision is made most activities are cast within a certain institutional framework which circumscribes the extent to which educators can adopt an andragogical mode. In adult education in the community the students (or, more accurately, co-learners) usually exercise control over the content and conduct of learning and the adult educator becomes much more of a resource person. Although the selection of settings regarded as appropriate for the contribution of a 'professional' educator is a decision which rests with the educator, the rationale of this style of adult education is such that the educator then has to accept the learners' definitions of relevance. The educator may suggest particular alternatives but those suggestions should have no greater intrinsic validity just because they emanate from a 'professional' than suggestions from other members of the group. Indeed, the toughest professional requirement of this kind of adult education is the ability of the professional adult educator to keep silent. The greatest (and fatal) temptation for the professional is to suggest any number of courses of action — out of the most humanistic and admirable of motives — which only serves to emphasize the division between 'professional' and 'amateur' learners. In attempting to promote the learning of students the educator, by emphasizing superior powers of articulation or greater knowledge, comes to block that learning and to induce a feeling of inferiority among students.

The other dimension of adult education in the community — the use of the community as a learning resource or laboratory — is one for which it is hard to find documented examples in the literature of the field. In the school sector, community education is often equivalent to this activity; students are taken on field trips to industrial and ecological locations around the school and local experts are invited into the school to relate their experiences. We can assume that local history and archaeology classes include visits to local sites (this happened in several environmental studies courses I organized in my own centre) and that ESL tutors are also keen to ground their curriculum in community settings. However, the verdict offered in an early publication of the Commission of Professors — that 'the community is an ever present laboratory for adult education which is all too often neglected by adult educators' (Hallenbeck *et al.* 1962, p. 6) — still appears justified. Brock Whale has written a training module on *The Community as a Place to Learn* (Brock Whale 1976) for Canadian adult educators and Miller's classic text on *Teaching and Learning in Adult Education* (1964) included a proposal for a programme entitled 'The City as an Experience Context'. This integrated visits to neighbourhoods and interviews with local figures with analytic and interpretative discussion sessions in which the adult educator acted as a cognitive therapist encouraging reflection on the nature of these visits and interviews (Miller 1964, p. 233). Fletcher's recent paper on 'Community Studies as Practical Adult Education' (Fletcher 1980a) advocates using interviews and participant observation, the collection of life histories of local inhabitants, and visits to local businesses and factories, as part of a study course on the local community.

Adult Education of the Community

The third category of our typology, adult education of the community, carries an overt normative and prescriptive element not present in the first two categories. Adult education of the community cannot be shaped solely by the results of a needs assessment; rather, it rests at least partly on the educator's beliefs as to the kinds of features he or she thinks a community should exhibit. The educator possesses a vision of a healthy community — perhaps one characterized by a populace possessing self-help, problem-solving skills and leadership abilities, and one in which democratic behaviours and virtues are vigorously exercised. Perceiving that the community in which he or she is working is deficient in terms of the community infra-structure or pool of skills available, the educator concerned determines to move the community to a qualitatively improved state. This is a community based implementation of the central ideas of the British school of educational philosophy as exemplified by R. S. Peters (1965) in which education is conceived as the initiation of learners into worthwhile bodies of knowledge. Both adult education of the community and Peters' concept of education as initiation rest on the prescriptive judgement of an educator as to what constitutes an educated individual or community.

The realization that this aspect of adult education is avowedly prescriptive in no way denies its validity. Indeed, as I have argued throughout this chapter, all adult education practice reflects (implicitly or explicitly) a personal or institutional ethos. The only difference is that in adult education of the community the ethos is perhaps more readily discernible. This kind of adult education has many similarities with the tradition of citizenship training in which a democracy is seen to be dependent on its members acquiring a certain philosophical orientation and a set of civic virtues. In this kind of adult education the educator holds the community to be in a state of normative need (Monette 1977) and assumes a responsibility for transmitting values, skills and knowledge to members which will result in the community moving to a new qualitatively improved state. The features which an improved community should display cannot be determined by some kind of empirical study. This is what philosophers call a 'second order' question, since the sources of what constitutes a 'good' community are the educator's own preferences and values.

The most important difference between this form of community adult education and the preceding two in the typology is that in adult education of the community the educator holds a strong responsibility for determining the content and goals of the educational enterprise. Rarely does it happen that a single individual or team of workers can dictate exactly the features of a community they wish to introduce and then proceed to implement their predetermined master plan. However, the balance of determining such matters has certainly shifted from that equilibrium which is seen in adult education for the community and adult education in the community. In both of these categories the educator is largely responding to expressed needs and often grants to students a responsibility for setting the learning agenda. In adult education of the community educators have in mind a notion of the kind of community they wish to see and they do their best to ensure that this ensues.

Once again, it must be emphasized that acknowledging the normative, prescriptive base to adult education of the community does not mean that this is cast in some kind of authoritarian, dictatorial mode. In fact, most workers engaged in what I regard as adult education of the community would reject any suggestion that their practice exhibited any authoritarian aspects. They would hold that they were creating an open, democratic society, displaying virtues that were precisely the antithesis of those observable in a closed, authoritarian society. Nonetheless, these virtues are reflective of a particular prescriptive vision of what constitutes a good society. Again, for an adult educator to make moral or ethical judgements regarding what should be taught and what kind of society should be encouraged, is normal and inevitable. We may disagree seriously about the merit of the virtues which others hold dear, but we should not be surprised to find that they inform our practice.

The principles and practice of community development are closely linked to adult education of the community as here conceived. Compton and McClusky (1980) have explored this connection in a recent essay in which they argue that:

> Community education for development represents the how (practice and program) and the why (theory and principles) of teaching this social and behavioural technology to local groups for the sake of facilitating individual learning, group problem solving and community building. (Compton & McClusky 1980, p. 229)

The International Council for Adult Education (ICAE) has also produced a 'Design for Action' in which adult education is used in, and for, development in third world countries (Hall & Kidd 1978). The encouragement of self-help, leadership skills is also one of the tasks of the animateur as this role is conceptualized by Kidd (1971) and Blondin (1971). The animateur is seen as promoting an awareness of community deficiencies among community members and as developing in members the skills and knowledge necessary for them to take action. The ultimate objective is to heighten the motivation and capacity for self-direction in individuals and community groups. Education of the community and community development are equivalent to the extent that they are both based on preferences regarding the form of a good, healthy, fully-developed community.

This chapter has considered the concept of community education and surveyed its implementation in North America and Britain. I have tried to show the ethical and moral base endemic to much community adult education practice and to present a typology which introduces some conceptual order into what is at present an area characterized by conceptual confusion and practical contradictions. The next chapter considers the range and variety of adult learning which occurs in community groups, both those groups which are prompted and supported by adult educators and those which operate independently of the educational system.

FIVE

Adult Learning Groups, Community Development and Community Action

In our previous chapter we considered the philosophy and implementation of community education as both programme and process. The perspective adopted was, of necessity, institution bound, since the models of community schooling currently in vogue emphasize the initiating and directive functions adopted by institutional personnel. In this chapter the focus shifts back to the phenomenon of adult learning in much the same manner as this engaged our attention in Chapters 1 to 3. The purpose of this chapter is to review the kinds of adult learning which occur in community group settings. Some of this learning will be the result of action undertaken by groups orientated towards social, political, and economic objectives — credit unions, neighbourhood action schemes, tenants' associations, citizens' rights groups and mutual societies. Although these groups exist for other than educational ends, nonetheless their activities contain within them an active learning component. The chapter will also consider those adult groups established primarily for educational purposes — both those which arise from the desire and efforts of learners and those which are partly stimulated by educators — which exhibit a measure of autonomy. We begin with an historical overview of such autonomous adult learning groups and then examine more contemporary initiatives in community development and community action which contain within them a strong community education component.

Autonomous Adult Learning Groups in the Eighteenth and Nineteenth Centuries

Changes in nomenclature, as argued in the previous chapter, do not always signify the introduction of innovatory and dynamic practices. Equally, the introduction of academic terminology to describe a set of behaviours and activities does not mean that such phenomena did not exist prior to their legitimation through a terminological baptism. Although accepting the phenomenological assertion that in naming the world we create it, this does not mean that the behaviours we identify as self-directed learning and community education did not exist prior to the invention of those terms. As Kulich has pointed out 'The universal man of the Renaissance, the highly skilled guild craftsman of the Baroque period, are excellent examples of the self-learning adult' (Kulich 1978; p. 310). Alexander the Great, Julius Caesar, Marcus Aurelius, Alfred the Great, and Erasmus are all cited as examples of self-learners and Thomas Edison is regarded as 'perhaps the best known American example of the self-educated and self-learning adult' (p.311). Huey Long has also undertaken valuable work in the study of self-directed learning in Colonial America (Long 1976).

The development of American adult education as a field of practice and study exhibiting a self-conscious awareness of its particular and distinctive features is usually placed in the mid-1920s. It was in 1925 and 1926 that, at the instigation of Frederick Keppel, a series of regional conferences culminated in the establishing of the constitution of the American Association for Adult Education in Chicago in March 1926. However, the eighteenth and nineteenth centuries had witnessed the development of at least three models of community based, voluntary adult education, which still have a contemporary relevance and influence: the Junto, the Lyceum and Settlement Centers. In his exploration of the birth of a national adult education movement in the 1920s Stubblefield (1979) has pointed out that at least two of the intellectual bench marks which shaped the growth of the field — Lindeman's *The Meaning of Adult Education* (1926) and Hart's *Adult Education* (1927) — place adult education in a community based mode. As Stubblefield argues:

> Lindeman and Hart . . . took as their focus the community, a community that had ceased to be educational, that left the individual powerless, that was controlled by conflicting special interest groups and experts.
>
> (Stubblefield 1979, p. 189)

Present day readers of Lindeman will recognize that in the early part of this century he had anticipated current injunctions to 'start where the students are' and to use the 'teachable moments' of major personal changes in the adult life cycle. Lindeman believed that the curriculum of adult education should be grounded in students' immediate needs and concerns and that such education would take as its starting point those points in adult life when individuals were facing adjustments and changes in the spheres of work, family life, leisure and community life. The setting for adult education was to be the small discussion group and this was a mode uniquely suited to release collective energies to be devoted to creative community problem solving. Joseph Hart anticipated another major concept — that of the educative community — when he enjoined student teachers to study the community as an educational resource. To Hart, the whole community functioned as an educative agency and the establishment of educational centres (not unlike Morris's Village Colleges) in each community would serve to promote a spirit of continual intellectual exploration. The writings of both these luminaries did not, as sociologists of knowledge would immediately aver, develop in some kind of intellectual vacuum. The philosophical underpinnings and the institutional vehicles for the realization of these ideas can be seen to owe much to the community based and neighbourhood models of the junto, lyceum and settlement centre.

The Junto

The Junto was established in Philadelphia by Benjamin Franklin in 1727 as a discussion circle of twelve friends. The agenda for discussion was based on Cotton Mather's *Essays To Do Good* published in 1710 which served as the vehicle for the consideration of questions of morals, politics, and natural philosophy. The group met weekly on Friday evenings and members were regularly expected to read an essay on some topic of personal or social concern. The junto was an outgrowth of the neighbourhood society proposed by Mather and Stubblefield believes that it shows how 'early in America a form of adult learning emerged that centered on the study of the community, the conditions of its religious and civic health, and the actions that citizens should take' (Stubblefield 1981; p. 3). To Cremin, such activity illustrates the mutual education characteristic of the colonial era:

> Locally and regionally and informally, systematically and haphazardly, face to face and through correspondence, Americans instructed one another, in taverns and coffeehouses, in Masonic lodges and militia musters, and in tradesmen's associations and chambers of commerce, as well as in formal institutions and societies organised to advance and communicate one sort of knowledge or another. (Cremin 1970; p. 410)

The American Philosophical Society (founded in 1766) was the most evident successor to the junto with the junto itself falling in to decline in the 1750s. However, one contemporary remnant of Franklin's initiative is the Junto School in Philadelphia revived in 1941. Merriam estimates that this served over 15,000 adults annually in the 1940s, 1950s, and 1960s, during which time it also trained discussion leaders in the Great Books programme (Merriam 1979). In the 1970s the Junto became a clearing house for adult education, offering counselling on adult education opportunities in the Philadelphia area, assisting in the professional development of teachers and community leaders, and maintaining a referral service for groups and institutions wishing to employ experienced adult education teachers.

The Lyceum movement

As Chapter 1 has already noted, the lyceum movement exemplified many of the andragogical, student-centred principles currently in vogue in adult education. The origins of the lyceum movement can be traced to the publication in 1826 of an article by Josiah Holbrook arguing for the creation of an adult learning centre in each American town. The first study group was established by Holbrook in Millbury, Massachussetts, in 1826 and by 1835 over one hundred county lyceums, fifteen state lyceums, and three thousand town lyceums were in existence. Each town lyceum was to be, in Shawen's words, 'a pooling of community educational resources for mutual self-improvement' (Shawen 1979, p. 9) and the whole movement was conceived as 'a voluntary, locally-oriented federation of study groups' (Shawen 1979, p. 10). County lyceums would serve as clearing houses for equipment and curricula generated by town meetings.

Holbrook saw the lyceum as performing four important educational functions. Firstly, it would raise the general level of intellectual discourse in the community by generating interesting topics of conversation in families and neighbourhoods. Secondly, it would result in the increased patronage of libraries. Thirdly, it would improve the quality of schooling through serving as an information exchange forum for teachers. Fourthly, it would become a clearing house for community information as community members would be stimulated to study their local communities (Bode 1956). To Knowles, the most important legacy of the lyceum experiment was its establishment of the idea of an integrated national system of local study groups engaged in purposeful education (Knowles 1977, p. 18).

Settlement Centres

The third example of an autonomous adult learning group evident in the eighteenth and nineteenth centuries is the settlement or neighbourhood centre most associated with Jane Addams. Toynbee Hall in London was the first settlement center to be created (1884) with centers following in New York City (1886) and Chicago (1889). It is the last experiment — Hull House — which is the best documented and most famous example of this movement.

The settlements were sited in poor communities and staffed by college educated, middle-class workers who were to study the lives of the poor, to generate public awareness of their plight and to press for civic improvement. In terms of the typology of community adult education proposed in the previous chapter, the work of settlements as outlined by Addams (1910) constitutes an example of adult education of the community. Middle class educators were to apply the knowledge generated in universities to those locations — the depressed quarters of inner cities — where it was most needed. In the course of this the middle class would come to develop an understanding and appreciation of the life of poverty which would result in the design of new programmes closely related to the needs and circumstances of the poor.

This kind of civic regeneration has been criticized by Violas (1973) as an example of an objectionably paternalistic liberalism, in which Addams is seen as using the principles of mass psychology in the cause of effective social control. Directly opposed to this view is Cremin's belief that Addams' work constitutes an example of liberating education, rather than paternalistic authoritarianism. In their discussion of these contrasting perspectives Stubblefield and Hunt conclude that "adult education history is not served well by accommodation to one of these schools" (Stubblefield & Hunt 1982, p. 219) and that Addams' work needs an analysis from a distinctive adult education historical perspective. Whatever the covert ideological assumptions underlying the establishment of settlement centres, they seem to this writer to represent an early example of community-based adult education. In their emphasis on understanding the lifestyle and experience of the poor, on siting any resultant programmes in the neighbourhoods in which they were generated, and on mutual self-improvement among residents, the settlements anticipated many of the urban action and community work projects of the 1960s. Individual actions can only be understood within their cultural context and before judging the democratic impeccability of Addams' and others' efforts to change society through educational programmes we need to appreciate the social mores and predominant normative values shaping these individuals' *weltanschaung*. It is all too easy to fall victim to a form of political and intellectual ethnocentrism in which anything less than an apparently full-blooded commitment to the immediate implementation of an egalitarian society is seen as an example of some kind of moral and ethical bad faith. Within their cultural and temporal context the settlement centres were undoubtedly daringly radical even if, to some adult educators in the 1980s, they exhibit lamentable elements of paternalism.

Radio listening and study discussion groups

As I remarked in Chapter 1 in the white heat of the post-war technological era it is easy to assume that experiments such as the Open University, TEVEC, the University of Mid-America, and Athabasca University are implementing some daringly innovative rationale. In fact, whilst the technological hardware may have evolved to a degree unrecognized by the first 'passionate educators' (Faris 1975) who saw the educative potential of broadcasting, many of the practices and problems still remain. An historian of educational broadcasting might convincingly argue that the 1930s and 1940s was the golden era of this activity with listening group schemes in Britain, the United States, Canada, Australia and New Zealand which represented a break with tradition far more traumatic than that embodied in the 1970s with the development of various open learning systems and varieties of non-traditional provision.

Farm Forum and Living Room Learning
The operational principles and philosophical bases for the Canadian *Farm Forum* were framed by Ned Corbett, the director of the Canadian Association for Adult Education (CAAE) in 1935, but were rooted in the Antigonish experiment of the early 1930s (discussed later in this chapter). As with many of the community-based adult education initiatives discussed in this book, the *Farm Forum* experiment arose out of educators' perceptions of community disintegration and the unifying and regenerative potential of adult education. The *National Farm Radio Forum* (to give it its full title) was not intended to be engaged solely in the transmission of knowledge. Rather, the radio programmes were to be the catalyst of local small discussion groups in which the most valuable educational experiences would occur. These groups would not only increase an understanding of the principles and practice of agriculture among listeners, they would also stimulate neighbourhood action for community improvement. Corbett believed that 'to have continuing success, study groups not only have to study but should engage in some form of group enterprise, which would produce some immediate and visible effects within the local community' (Conger 1974, p. 11).

The *Farm Forum* was interactive in the sense that local groups submitted their reactions to the broadcasts and printed materials to the Farm Radio Forum National Office, and this interactive dimension was reflected in later Canadian broadcasting experiments such as *Living Room Learning* and *People Talking Back*. In his verdict on the contribution to adult education made by *Farm Forum*, Conger (1974) offers the following assessment: . . .

1. As with the Antigonish movement, *Farm Forum* encouraged social activism among farmers geared towards community improvement and economic advance.
2. *Farm Forum* demonstrated the adult educational potential of radio broadcasting.
3. *Farm Forum* showed that 'the farmer possessed no intrinsic desire for self-education' (p. 12) and that the study group and action goals were the setting and motivation needed to make adult education attractive to farmers.

This last contention deserves a critical scrutiny and is certainly open to question. It seems rather harsh to declare that *no* innate desire for self-education existed among farmers as a class. Indeed, as the first section of this book argued, there is considerable empirical evidence (as well as a widely-held prescriptive belief) that a sustained and deliberate disinterest in self-education is an empirical rarity. It may, of course, be true that educators who have what they see as the best interests of minority, disadvantaged, and other target groups at heart, become frustrated when clients exhibit a less than immediate and full hearted gratitude towards professional educators for their efforts. Whatever the effects of the programmes on individual members, in quantitative terms it was a major success with approximately 21,000 participants enrolled in 1,600 forums during the period 1949–51 (Faris 1975, p. 100). Kidd (1963) estimated 30,000 participants in the 1949–50 season.

The *Farm Forum* idea was proposed as a model of mass adult education ripe for replication in the Third World in a UNESCO collection of papers issued in 1954 (Sim 1954). In a major review of the field in the 1950s it was described as a challenging example of how a mass medium could strengthen face-to-face groups (Sheats *et al.* 1953, p. 57). Yet, as Ohliger wrily observed, 'with all this testimony to its success, the *Farm Forum* slipped quietly into oblivion on April 30, 1965' (Ohliger 1968, p. 176). The previous winter had seen approximately 230 groups in existence.

Ohliger (1968) cites three reasons for the Forum's decline. Firstly, the three supervisory institutions (the Canadian Broadcasting Corporation, the Canadian Association for Adult Education and the Canadian Federation of Agriculture) exhibited an ever-increasing divergence of functions and concerns. Secondly, the scheme failed to establish an organizational structure to support and maintain the network of local field groups. Finally, the listening groups proved unable to adapt to the increasing urbanization of Canadian society. Hence, 'the *Farm Forum* movement simply had not become a firm enough part of the basic Canadian social structure to make the change to urban atmosphere' (Ohliger 1968 p. 185).

An experiment in the stimulation of adult learning cast, unlike the activist oriented *Farm Forum* initiative, in a liberal education mode was the *Living Room Learning* scheme sponsored by the University of British Columbia (UBC) in the late 1950s and early 1960s. Financed initially by the Fund for Adult Education, the *Living Room Learning* scheme centred upon the activities of home-based study discussion groups which were stimulated by specially prepared printed and audio visual materials rather than by radio programmes. Groups were led by volunteers from the community, such volunteers attending discussion leader training workshops dealing with group processes and discussion management. The aims of the programme were partly to help adults to understand their own culture but, more importantly, to develop skills of critical thought, to encourage a tolerance of opinions and opposing ideas, and to improve communication skills. At its height in 1964 the scheme catered for over 1,500 adults in seventy seven (mostly remote) British Columbia communities (Buttedahl 1978) and the decision by UBC to discontinue its grant support to the experiment was met with 'community uproar' which was 'substantial' (p. 236). The programme supervisor responsible for running the programme noted, in particular, the importance of word of mouth recommendation and publicity with regard to attracting new participants to study groups. Hence, 'the neighbourhood coffee party became essential for introducing and launching *Living Room Learning* in a new community' (p. 240).

BBC Wireless Discussion Groups

From the inception of broadcasting in Britain a concern for the educational aspects and functions of this medium of communication has been apparent. The BBC, under the seminal early influence of Lord Reith, was charged with a tripartite function — to educate, to inform, and to entertain — and this same breadth of responsibilities was incorporated into the charter governing the creation of the Independent Broadcasting Authority. In 1928 a joint committee of inquiry of the BBC and the British Institute of Adult Education chaired by Sir Henry Madow reviewed the future role of broadcasting in adult education and in the subsequent year published a report entitled 'New Ventures in Broadcasting'. The committee recommended the formation of local discussion groups which would base their curricula on radio programmes, such a scheme to be coordinated by a Central Council for Adult Education and a number of area councils. Kelly records that the scheme was something of a failure and cites the absence of skilled group leaders as the chief reason for this (Kelly 1970, p. 319).

Perraton laments that 'what might have been a significant element in our patchwork system of adult education barely survived the outbreak of war' (Perraton 1978, p. 1) but he offers an aetiological analysis very different from that of Kelly. To Perraton the wireless discussion group movement failed to emulate the success of *Farm Forum* for five reasons: (1) there was inadequate co-operation between the BBC and other adult education agencies; (2) the educational experience of wireless listening was seen as innately inferior to that of tutorial class attendance; (3) the subject matter content of radio programmes was embarrassingly radical to BBC executives; (4) the most creative mind in educational broadcasting at that time, Mary Somerville, concerned herself wholly with schools programmes; (5) a lack of any activist element or goal orientation which would grant a sense of community purpose to discussion groups. A more favourable account of the listening group movement is given by Heywood

(1981) who records that in the seven month's from September 1931 to March 1932, 369 groups were in existence with approximately 4,000 participants. For a contemporary account of listening groups readers are referred to the work of Hill and Williams (1941).

The Great Books Programme

The mission of the *Great Books* programme was, in the words of one of its founders, to provide 'education to be human beings, education to make the most of our human powers, education for our responsibilities, education for freedom' (Hutchins 1959, p. v). This liberal education was in Hutchins' view 'the education that no American gets in an educational institution now' (ibid.) and yet it was vital for the development of community, for the creation of a free society, and for the survival of democracy. Hutchins believed that the major premise on which American democracy rested was 'that the people will be informed enough, intelligent enough, and interested enough to judge the policies proposed to them by those whom they have chosen, with information, intelligence, and interest, to represent them' (p. vi–vii). The individual's pursuit of a liberal education thus became a national democratic necessity as much as a private quest for enlightenment. The vehicle for this enlightenment was the *Great Books* programme.

The *Great Books* idea can be traced back to the Junto's reading and discussion of Mather's *Essays To Do Good*. Its twentieth century implementation came initially at the University of Chicago in 1945 when Mortimer Adler and Robert Hutchins devised a scheme of reading and discussion for adults in association with the public library. The following year the Great Books Foundation took over the responsibility for promoting the scheme and in the late 1940s and 1950s thousands of study discussion groups arose across the country. A variety of study discussion programmes using records, educational broadcasts and printed material developed at this time under the aegis of the Adult Education Experimental Discussion Project. Some 50,000 adults enrolled in 2,700 groups in the Great Books Foundation in 1959–60. In 1960 Bode reported that New York University's Division of General Education alone had 91 discussion groups with 1,500 students meeting in living rooms (Bode 1960).

The chief survey of the *Great Books* programme was that conducted in 1958 and 1959 by the National Opinion Research Centre which surveyed a national population sample of 172 *Great Books* groups comprising 1,909 individuals. The study was sponsored by the Fund for Adult Education and was concerned in particular to study retention and drop-out among *Great Books* participants. Members of discussion groups tended to be, according to the study, 'highly educated, upper middle class, young, married people' who were 'highly involved in their communities' and who 'come to the program seeking intellectual stimulation in the discussion rather than uplift or self-help' (Davis 1961, p. 212–3). Not surprisingly, groups with many active members were found to exhibit high levels of retention. Also, Davis and his research team hypothesized that 'in the discussion process and in the social relationships which it develops or reinforces, there is a powerful cement which binds the members together and provides a major gratification from participation' (p. 216). The programme was also felt to confirm the familiar adult education truism that participants exhibited an already developed interest in, and knowledge of, intellectual questions. All in all, the study concluded that 'those variables which seem to characterize the *Great Books* member also seem generally favourable for program retention' (p. 220). Hence, members were highly educated, active in their communities, of political diversity, and of a high social status. There was, however, a slight suggestion that the programme's official leadership style might have benefited from a greater flexibility of technique.

Community Learning

In the first part of this chapter we considered the activities of groups established for avowedly educational purposes where the acquisition of new skills and knowledge was of paramount importance. These groups exhibited a measure of autonomy in terms of curricular flexibility, geographical isolation or an absence of institutional affiliation, but their rationale was overtly educational. In the rest of this chapter our attention is directed towards those groups established for social, political and economic objectives. Such groups may not recognize an educational dimension to their work but they generally provide settings for learning and, in some instances, organize sophisticated instructional programmes. The educative component in community action and community development will be examined later in this chapter. At present, we turn our attention to the concept of community learning.

In the recent handbook on *Redefining the Discipline of Adult Education* (Boyd and Apps 1980) Joan Wright, Associate Professor of Adult Education at North Carolina State University (Raleigh) uses the term 'community learning' to refer to 'the learning that occurs when both the transactional mode and the client focus involve the community as a primary actor' (Wright 1980, p. 101). In simpler terms, 'community learning occurs when the focus of learning is the community and when the learning transaction requires participants to assume their community roles' (Wright 1982, p. 262). She argues that in the course of performing community roles adults are involved in situations which have great potential for learning. Community learning, therefore, is that learning which has as its focus community improvement and also that learning which occurs as adults perform community roles.

Three typical forms of community learning as suggested by Wright are:

1. The promotion of a special interest — Wright quotes the example of a Community Access Interest Group (CAIG) formed to increase public access to cable broadcasting. Participants in the CAIG had identified useful resources and potential allies, they had become acquainted with relevant conventions and structures and had become skilled at presenting their case to officials and other publics.
2. Implementation of a public policy — in determining a procedure for reviewing requests for funding from local community services, a committee of the Human Service Coalition (an amalgam of the United Way, Human Service agencies and local government representatives) were faced with three learning tasks. These involved devising an acceptable review process, informing potential applicants of its features, and evolving evaluative criteria to judge programmes subsequently submitted.
3. Expression of public preferences — exercising a democratic right to vote, joining and assisting the growth of pressure groups and responding to a survey of public interests are all examples of individual members of the general public making choices and judgements of community significance.

In her treatment of community learning Wright adopts a holistic approach which at times seems to reify community in such a manner that it assumes an identity above and beyond that represented by the sum total of individual abilities and interests. This almost mystical notion of community was characteristic of the founder of modern sociology, Emile Durkheim, who conceived of an holistic social consciousness existing superior to, and separate from, the sum total of individual consciousness. Hence, such apparently individualistic phenomena as mental breakdowns and suicide could be explained only in terms of community forces and currents. Wright refers to community adaptation to change in terms similar to Durkheim implying that the community can be regarded as a single, unified organism. She gives examples of communities learning to adapt to political changes such as alterations in federal law and to natural changes such as floods or fires, and speaks of the community's responsibility to maintain itself and provide for its citizens' needs.

Such a reification of the concept of community is a partial reflection of the liberal model of community education identified in Chapter 3 which views communities mostly as harmonious, cohesive entities. Liberating theorists would regard this conceptualization as one which ignores community power structures and the potentially divisive elements in communities represented by sectional interests. As well as attempting to conceptualize community learning Wright has suggested appropriate roles for adult educators in the recognition and support of such learning and these will be considered in Chapter 8.

To summarize, Wright views informal community learning as learning about the community which occurs in naturalistic settings as adults perform various community roles. The learning tasks centre on aspects of community improvement. In terms remarkably similar to those employed by Hutchins in his justification of the Great Books programme, Wright believes community learning to be 'a process essential to the maintenance and balance of individual and social freedom, and to the survival of a democratic society' (1980, p. 124). We need now to turn our attention to another thematic concern beloved of community educators — community problem-solving — to assess the adult learning component in this activity.

Community Problem-Solving

The attempt to encourage a community to recognize, confront, and then work towards a resolution of a problem is a theme of major necessity and urgency which recurs in the literature of community action and community development. As Warden's category 3 in his typology made clear (Warden 1979), and as it is implemented by Minzey and Le Tarte (1979), the community problem-solving focus is also crucial for those community educators who profess to adopt a process orientation. Once again, the distinction between liberal and liberating models of community education explored in Chapter 4 has particular relevance to our discussion. Those subscribing to the liberal model of community education, in which a harmonious and cohesive community is served by a community education programme meeting all individual and community needs, will emphasize problem-solving as an activity which unites individual community members and encourages a sharing of experience and expertise. To the liberating theorist of community education, however, which situations or behaviours are viewed as problems will be reflections of the political and moral stance of the definer. The introduction of a new shopping mall will not be a problem to store managers within that complex, but it will be perceived as such by residents who are faced with increased traffic volume or other disruptions resulting from such a development, and to small store owners in the vicinity who fear a loss of revenue. To take another example, difficulties in overcoming bureaucratic regulations to secure alterations in the zoning ordinances relating to a piece of land to allow commercial or residential building on that land will be a problem to a developer. To residents concerned with recreational facilities or ecological matters this situation may be a cause for celebration rather than anxiety.

As sociologists of deviance have long recognized, definitions of what constitute problems may tell us more about the definer's moral codes, economic status and social values, than they do about the constituent features of problems. To a drug addict the 'problem' is how to obtain sufficient funds to obtain supplies of the required yet illegal stimulant. To friends and family the 'problem' is how to wean the aberrant individual away from a dependence on the drug while concealing such dependence from employers or narcotics investigators. To law enforcement agencies the 'problem' becomes one of infiltrating user and dealer networks and obtaining sufficient evidence for conviction. To the medical fraternity the 'problem' is how to control and then reverse the addict's dependence through physical and psychotherapeutic means. In this community situation, familiar enough in most inner city areas, what constitutes the 'problem' to users, dealers, and manufacturers will be in direct opposition to what is the 'problem' for enforcement and medical agencies. The Freirean process of 'problematizing' (Freire 1970, p. 8) itself illustrates my point most aptly. To Freire, the problem is how to encourage the disenfranchized, powerless members of a society first to realize their situation and then to acquire sufficient self-confidence, political skills and organization to work for change. To governments who oppose the process of democratization, the problem is how to stop people engaging in 'problematizing'.

To readers who think this point has been laboured enough I would only add that we should be aware that definitions of problems tell us much about the structures and codes of a society or sub-culture. Problems are not physical phenomena which can be identified and classified according to some unambiguous, objective evidence. The ways in which certain situations or behaviours become labelled by some as problems, and the ways in which these labels and definitions then gain some kind of consensus or majority acceptance, is a crucial question for community educators as well as for sociologists of knowledge, power or deviance. In Chapter 4 I argued that even such an apparently neutral activity as adult education for the community involved the educator making decisions regarding programmes to be sponsored, which reflected institutional values or personal norms. Those community educators advocating community problem-solving as the rationale for community education should be aware that only rarely will they encounter situations in which all members of a neighbourhood community agree that a certain practice or occurrence constitutes a problem. What is far more likely to be the reality for community educators is that a number of conflicting, contradictory intra-community problems will emerge. Sectional interest groups will, in pursuing their cause, only arouse the opposition of others who will perceive the interests of those groups as threatening, anti-social or immoral. Community workers may find themselves acting as arbitrators, peacemakers, or instructors in the skills of negotiation of inter-group communication. However, there may be times when workers will be unable to avoid alliance with one particular group or interest. Indeed, were community workers never to experience ethical dilemmas and to feel no contradictory claims upon their loyalties, then these workers would most probably be little more than automata or functionaries.

The literature of community problem-solving as an educational activity owes much to the work of John Dewey who saw the survival of democracy and true education as existing in a symbiotic relationship. In his criticisms of subject-centred curricula and rote learning and his belief that education should be grounded in the child's exploration of real life concerns, Dewey pre-dates much of what is now mainstream adult education. As Elias and Merriam argue (1980, p. 55) Dewey recognized the importance of lifelong education even if he devoted much of his attention to schooling. Hence, the ideas of adult educators such as Knowles, Kidd and Miller regarding teachers and students as co-learners and the need to involve students in setting learning agendas are present in Dewey's thought. Griffith has also pointed out that the Freirean emphasis on adults' involvement in creating curricula based on real-life problems and concerns complies with the views of 'just about every other adult educator who has ever attempted to describe the conditions which are most conducive to adult learning' (Griffith 1972, p. 68). Campbell has seen Dewey's emphasis on the student's spontaneous activity and the educative value inherent in that activity as paralleling the process of community problem-solving. An attempt to solve a community problem offers the educator any number of opportunities to assist the learning of members (Campbell 1980).

Definitions of community problem-solving which concentrate on its general features or replicable processes tend to be somewhat opaque. It is in the descriptions of such activities that different writers' perceptions of community problem-solving become clear. Kaplan and Schwartz offer the following definition: 'Community problem solving through Community Education involves people in identifying problems and needs, searching for alternative solutions, and implementing those solutions" (Kaplan and Schwartz 1981, p. 22). Kaplan and Schwartz view the advisory council as the chief mechanism in such activities and council members will assist in needs identification and in publicizing and communicating resultant programmes to community members. Campbell takes a wider view of community problem-solving with a community council representing only one form of problem-solving group (Campbell 1980). Other examples would include spontaneous neighbourhood groups, groups engaged in planning community development, and groups affiliated to community organizations such as the Rotary or Lions. Hence, to Campbell, 'A community problem-solving group is a group of citizens who voluntarily attempt to solve a problem in their community' (Campbell 1980, p. 142). Hiemstra (1972) views community problem-solving as part of the process of activating the educative community while McCullough (1978) has outlined the andragogical elements in community problem-solving.

This last analysis by McCullough makes the point that just as individual self-planned learning in a natural societal setting can be inefficient, haphazard and incomplete, so 'Community problem-solving is also often engaged in by adults in an inefficient, haphazard, sometimes even counter-productive manner' (McCullough 1978, p. 8). McCullough argues that the adult educator as andragogue is a role which can be easily performed in community problem-solving groups. Since community problem-solving is an educational process, the adult educator can function as the process expert helping adults to take the steps necessary to the attainment of goals set by the community members. The educator will help identify appropriate resources, assist in needs identification and be the agent of change, the facilitator (p. 9). Working in such an andragogical mode as here conceived by McCullough, the educator is engaging in what I described in Chapter 4 as adult education in the community, particularly when community members retain the responsibility for goal setting. According to Campbell this form of adult education has advantages over other forms since organizing a group takes less time than that required for arranging a class, the participants are already motivated, the curriculum is relevant to participants' lives, and group activities address directly the needs of the adults concerned (Campbell 1980, p. 141–2).

The literature of community problem-solving and community development tends to emphasize procedural aspects and programme designs rather than the individual educational benefits to be derived from participation in such activities. One attempt to identify the potential for individual growth within community problem-solving is Coggins' (1980) analysis of the four categories of potential individual growth latent in group community problem-solving. These are:

1. Stance toward self — changes in one's self-awareness, sense of self-worth, and a commitment to self-development.
2. Stance toward others — understanding and appreciating others' strengths and weaknesses.
3. Stance toward life — development of a sense of commitment, a future orientation, and a willingness to take risks.
4. Stance toward knowledge — particularly an awareness and appreciation of problem-solving processes.

(Coggins 1980, p. 165)

The ways in which adult educators can encourage the kind of educative growth above will form the subject matter of Chapters 7 and 8.

Community Action and Adult Learning

Community action is the term within the general field of community work which is subject to perhaps the greatest misinterpretation. In one sense it is a semantic and conceptual nonsense. Quite literally, a community cannot act — only individuals or groups composed of individuals within a community can do that. To talk of a community taking action is to be guilty of the kind of conceptual holism and reification alluded to earlier in this chapter. Hence, most examples of community action discussed in the literature refer to small group pressure exerted for social and political change which will benefit members of that group. Only in the most extreme instance, and using the term community in its most limited sense (to refer, perhaps, to a total institution) can a community act with a unified purpose. Members of a community can associate to achieve some intra-community change such as altering the zoning ordinances governing certain pieces of land. More or less the only time a community, in the sense of a neighbourhood, does act is when it is faced with an external threat of some kind. For a time a village or suburb may unite to prevent an airport being built in the vicinity, or a freeway being routed through a residential area. Again, in times of warfare one can accept that communities will exhibit a sense of common identity and shared purpose so that one can talk of community action with some meaning. Adult educators, however, will generally be engaged in community-based activities which are less traumatic than warfare and less contentious than opposing city hall transport policy.

In their analysis of community work in the early 1970s the Community Work Group sponsored by the Gulbenkian Foundation identified two distinctive notions of community education prevalent in the United States and Britain respectively. To these academics the American notion of community action was deliberately broad and referred to 'action in the community, of whatever kind, action informed by a wide range of assumptions,' undertaken by all manner of groups, with a wide range of objectives' (Community Work Group 1973, p. 39). A more limited view of community action in Britain was offered by the Community Work Group in which fewer common characteristics of community action were identified — the collective nature of community action, the disadvantaged acting on their own behalf, a neighbourhood base to action, and empowerment of minority groups as the chief goal of community action (p. 40–41). Verner (1971), however, described the kinds of changes which were initiated and implemented by one section of the community as *social* action. Community action was reserved for those instances where a unified sense of purpose was exhibited by a whole community. To Verner "community action is a process of change conceived and carried out by a community acting as a discrete social unit" (Verner 1971, p. 422). Verner identified seven levels at which action (that is, planned change) could take place and he deemed that community action could only occur at level six, the community level.

To this writer, however, what Verner defines as social action — 'action programs leading to changes that affect a community and that are initiated and carried out by segments of the community' (p. 422) — seems to be an admirable working definition of community action, particularly if the word 'program' is omitted. I see no particular merit in calling such programmes examples of social action. Verner also drew a distinction between the educational process leading to action and the action itself. The learning process becomes part of community development and is conceptually separate from community action so that the adult educator is seen as having no part to play in the community action process, and neither is he or she involved directly in the action resulting from development. Verner sees the separate and distinctive role of the adult educator as follows:

> Adult education has an important role to play in the training of community-action leadership, but such leaders are not adult educators since their principal concern is the action process itself rather than the educational process that is prerequisite to action. (p. 427)

As conceived in this book the scope for adult educators to assist learning in the context of community action is much wider than that indicated by Verner. The educator has a role to play not only in transmitting skills and knowledge as a necessary prerequisite for action, but also in assisting adults to derive the maximum educational value from the community learning (to use Wright's term) which occurs in the course of community action. I would also disagree with Verner's insistence on a separation of animateur and educator functions and his belief that these two roles require two different kinds of training. As Chapter 8 makes clear, the animateur role is seen as having an educative dimension.

Community Development — The Educational Component

The notion of development, of communities just as much as of individuals, is prescriptive in nature. Lotz describes the term community development as 'a portmanteau word to cover a multitude of processes, projects, programmes and approaches in social change' (Lotz 1972, p. 79). This is undoubtedly true, but the unifying factor underpinning this multitude of activities is that development is equated with improvement and what constitutes improvement is a value judgement made by an agency or individual. Community development as prescriptive improvement tends to take one of the following two forms:

1. A change in the physical fabric of the community. Such changes could take the form of a new irrigation system, an altered transportation system, or the

introduction of a new recreational complex. The notion of what constitutes development (that is, desirable change) in these cases usually rests with an external agency.

2. The inculcation of a sense of community where one is conspicuously absent in, for example, 'twilight' inner city areas, scattered rural populations or 'new' towns. Here the community development worker creates networks and judges success by the resultant demand for community action by residents.

In their discussion of the educative dimensions of community development Grantham and Dyer (1981) regard the two versions of community development outlined above as examples of, alternatively, social planning and social action. To them community development is a process located in the middle ground between these two categories which seeks 'to alter human attitudes and behavioural patterns through education, exhortation, and other group methods for stimulating self-development and fulfillment' (Grantham & Dyer 1981, p. 15). Taken as read, this definition stands as an adequate definition of education *per se*, rather than of community development. Community development does attempt to alter attitudes and behaviour, and to stimulate fulfillment, but it rests on a normative preference, often of the development worker or agency rather than of community members, as to what are the desired behaviours or improved attitudes. Compton (1971) reduces the concept of community development to the simple phrase 'people participating in the improvement of their lot' (p. 384), a phrase which acknowledges the element of normative preference in community development.

Some general observations regarding the roles adult educators can play in community development, together with illustrative examples of such work, are contained in Chapter 8. For the present, three specific case studies of community development, and the educative dimensions therein, are presented in the rest of this chapter. The initiatives discussed are Canadian (the Antigonish movement), American (the Highlander Folk School) and British (the Liverpool Educational Priority Area project).

The Antigonish Movement

The Antigonish movement occupies within the history of Canadian adult education a position somewhat akin to that of the Workers Education movement in British adult education history. Both are cited by present day analysts as examples of a fine heritage of social commitment in the field of adult education within a democratic (rather than revolutionary) tradition. Both are also a cause for lamentation by present day adult educators in that their contemporary implementations appear now to have lost much of their innovatory and committed character and to have been assimilated by mainstream adult education. Hence, in his book on community development in Canada Jim Lotz observed that poverty and deprivation were still rife in Canso and Little Dover half a century after Tompkins began his work there, and that Father Gerry Rodgers now of the extension department of Saint Francis Xavier University and 'the living embodiment of the Antigonish Way' was 'a very lonely man' (Lotz 1977, p. 113).

History

The Antigonish movement was so named because the town in which the movement's headquarters were located (at the extension department of Saint Francis Xavier University) was that of Antigonish in eastern Nova Scotia. In the 1920s the three chief industries in the area were mining, farming and fishing and as in Flint, Michigan, the area was also suffering from rural depopulation as the young and ambitious left for the towns. Father Jimmy Tompkins was at this time Vice-President of the Saint Francis Xavier University. He was aware of the adult education efforts of the British Workers Education Association (WEA), the Danish Folk Schools, and the Swedish Study Discussion Circles and in 1921 published a pamphlet entitled 'Knowledge for the People — A call to Saint Francis Xavier University'. In 1922 he was removed by the University to a remote fishing village — Canso — where the inhabitants lived a crofter subsistence lifestyle of great hardship. Tompkins determined, in Lotz's words, 'to bridge the gap between book learning and real life, and to put knowledge into a form that the ordinary people could understand and use' (Lotz 1977, p. 105).

The initial opportunity for implementation of this principle was the assistance provided by Tompkins to the fishermen at Little Dover in establishing their own cannery. Tompkins provided study material and financial support and the cannery was completed in the winter of 1929–30. During 1927 and 1928 Tompkins was also instrumental in prompting the formation of a royal commission of inquiry (the Maclean Commission) which drew attention to the danger to fishermens' livelihood represented by large trawlers.

Lotz has commented that Tompkins can be regarded as the John the Baptist of the Antigonish movement, a lonely voice preaching in the wilderness. The Saviour of the moment, by this analogy, was Father Moses Coady, Tompkins' nephew. Coady was appointed Director of the Saint Francis Xavier Extension department in 1928 and immediately involved himself in setting up the United Maritime Fishermen to represent fishermens' groups in the maritime provinces. In 1933, after visits by Roy Bergengren the Director of the American Credit Union Association, the first credit unions were established and these were followed by the 'poultry pools' set up to improve poultry production. By 1939, 19,600 people in the maritimes were enrolled in 2,265 study clubs and 342 credit unions were in existence.

Methods

The governing principles of the Antigonish movement, as summarized by Laidlaw (1961) and Conger (1974) were:

1. The primacy of individual needs — such needs to be met and capacities to be developed in social contexts.
2. The root of social reform lies in education.
3. Individuals are most concerned with economic needs — therefore education must start with the economic dimension of life.
4. Group settings are those most suitable to education.
5. Social reform both causes, and is dependent on, basic change in social and economic institutions.
6. A fully self-actualized life for all in the community is the aim of the movement

Points 1 to 3 are nicely summarized in the following quote from Coady:

> We hold, therefore, as a fundamental principle, that an adult education programme, to produce results and affect the lives of the people must result, in the first instance, in economic action on their part ... this is good pedagogy. We must take the learner where he is. We build on the interests that are uppermost in his mind. (Coady 1979, p. 7)

The methods used to achieve a self-actualized community emphasized the importance of point 4 above, the use of study groups and discussion circles. As the worker entered a new community a mass meeting would be called at which the need for economic and social change was presented by workers to villagers. After the meeting a network of small study groups and radio listening groups would be established by people such as A.B. MacDonald (the Saint Paul of the movement according to Lotz) at which problems were identified and discussed and study materials examined. These groups were introduced as the prelude to direct action in the form of credit unions, co-operatives and other social or economic reforms. Conferences and training courses were also held at Saint Francis Xavier for volunteer workers and local leaders.

The movement constitutes an example of adult education of the community (although located in the community) according to the typology advanced in the previous chapter because it was based on a prescriptive notion held by a few committed individuals regarding the ways in which they felt communities should be changed for the better. As Lovett has recognized (Lovett 1980, p. 158) Coady did not believe merely in meeting felt needs, putting instead more emphasis on the creation of critical awareness. Where dissatisfaction with the existing order and a perception of inequity did not exist, Coady believed it was the community worker's responsibility to engender such a perspective. This paradigm shift or 'perspective transformation' (Mezirow 1977) was the first stage in a process of community action and self-help in the economic and political spheres.

Coady and Freire : a comparison

In a fascinating occasional paper Armstrong (1977) has compared the ideas regarding adult education of Moses Coady and Paulo Freire. As she observes, Nova Scotia in the 1920s and 1930s and North East Brazil in the 1950s and 1960s were regions characterized by poverty and by a lack of co-operative initiative. However, while Freire sees the solution to poverty and apathy as lying ultimately in the transformation of an oppressed society, Coady wished to see the farmers, fishermen and miners of the Maritimes play a more prominent role within existing society adjusted in some way to be more egalitarian. Coady was reformist in a social democratic tradition, rather than an advocate of large scale revolutionary change. As Lotz remarks, 'He wanted to help people to find a place in that system, not to replace it' (Lotz 1977, p. 113). On this point Armstrong makes the very valid point that 'Coady could remain a moderate, working within the system, because in his particular situation the system proved flexible enough' and that 'In the same way, Freire might well have remained a moderate reformer, given a social structure amenable to such reform' (Armstrong 1977, p. 6).

One of the clearest points of congruence in the thought of the two men is the emphasis on the interconnection of thought and action. To Freire such a link is enshrined in the notion of 'praxis'; to Coady the educative process is inseparable from a move towards economic change. However, the practical methods undertaken to initiate a process of critical reflection on the part of learners do differ. As we have seen, Coady would begin work in a new community with a mass meeting. Using uncharacteristically militaristic metaphors Coady wrote that 'intellectual dynamite' would be exploded at this meeting and that an 'intellectual bombing operation' would serve 'to blast these minds into some real thinking' (Coady 1939, p. 30–2). Freire advocates a more subtle process of community immersion in which the worker meets informally with individuals and talks to them about their daily lives. Having derived a sense of their outlook on the world Freire suggests that probing questions then be put by the workers to individuals or groups (culture circles) which illustrate contradictions in their outlook.

Armstrong, like Lovett, acknowledges the prescriptive basis underlying the philosophies of Coady and Freire. Neither claims to be neutral and both are fired with a vision of a new, more fully humane society, although the form of that society might differ. Hence, 'Both attempt to bring the learner toward a particular goal; neither would rejoice if that learner decided to ignore the process and remain unaware' (Armstrong 1977, p. 14). She concludes her analysis with the assessment that 'Overall, Freire and Coady are much more alike than they are different' (p. 20).

The Antigonish achievement
In a report on the fiftieth anniversary celebrations of the Antigonish movement (Kidd 1979) a Cape Breton woman offered her remembrances of attending a lecture given by Father Jimmy Tompkins as follows:

> He said the masses of the people have power and intelligence. He said 'Don't wait for some great statesman to come along and solve your problems. Get organized into study clubs and solve your own troubles yourselves. (Kidd 1979, p. 6)

Such a simple injunction to undertake community self-help was not new. What was new about Antigonish was the remarkably detailed programme of techniques used to achieve that end. Coady, Tompkins, A. B. MacDonald, Sister Marie Michael, Kay Desjardin and the others involved in the movement were not woolly-minded idealists. They organized mass meetings, study groups, discussion circles, training courses, kitchen meetings, community refresher courses, and they became extremely adept at obtaining funds to finance economic projects such as credit unions or processing plants. The overall focus of their programme was clearly economic and served to grant a direction and purpose to community action which is not always typical. As Laidlaw (1961), Lotz (1973) and Lovett (1980) have observed, the movement was highly organized to good educational and economic effect. Lovett assesses the Antigonish achievement thus:

> It did succeed in engaging large numbers of workers in relevant education linked to social action with methods and techniques which even today would be regarded as too radical for many educational institutions. It drew no barriers between social action and adult education and was engaged on a number of fronts linking one to the other   (p. 160)

The Highlander folk school

At several points in this chapter and the previous one we have seen how major community adult education movements have taken root in a particular historical era and economic setting. Flint (Michigan), Cambridgeshire, eastern Nova Scotia were all regions which, in the 1920s and 1930s, were characterized by economic depression, rural depopulation, and crippling poverty. In the attempts to combat such deprivation educative initiatives emerged as part of a community development process. The same combination of circumstances can be seen with the Highlander movement which was located in Grundy County, Tennessee, an area of mining and farming communities hit by the worst effects of the depression of 1929–31.

History

It was during the stock market crash of 1929 that Myles Horton, the founder of Highlander, arrived in New York to study at the Union Theological Seminary. Horton had been a student at Cumberland University and in the summer of 1927 had gone to Ozone, Tennessee, to organize bible classes. Instead of just teaching children interpretations of the scriptures, Horton invited parents to come and talk over their problems at the church in the evening. Their concerns were emphatically secular — how to find and keep a job, how to combat the denudation of the forests — and Horton spent his time identifying resources (mostly Ozone inhabitants) in the community to help in resolving these problems. It was the events of this summer which, according to his biographer Frank Adams, sowed the seed which was to flourish later as the Highlander folk school (Adams 1972, p. 498).

While in New York Horton fell under the influence of the radical theologian Rienhold Niebuhr and he also read Dewey, Lindeman and Hart as well as the sociologists of the time. Indeed, in 1930–31 he studied at Chicago with Robert Park during which time he frequently visited Jane Addams. The latter's intention of starting a rural settlement centre was, to Horton, remarkably similar to his idea of a mountain school in Ozone. The final element in Horton's early education was a visit to Denmark from the end of summer 1931 to January 1932 during which time he studied the Danish folk schools. Adams writes of the Danish trip:

> He saw more clearly the role he could play in a changing society. He became convinced that the people, no matter how poor or untutored, would know what they needed to learn, if he could only listen to them and to translate what he heard into an educational program. (Adams 1975, p. 23–4)

The Highlander folk school was eventually established in 1932 at Dr Lillian Johnson's house on Monteagle mountain, north-west of Chattanooga, in Grundy County. What Adams regards as the catalyst for Highlander was the strike by non-unionized miners in the town of Wilder against the local coal company. Horton visited Wilder and arranged for students and teachers from Highlander to join in support of the strikers and to write to newspapers appealing for food and clothing. Horton was arrested and charged with "coming here and getting information and going back and teaching it". Highlander students and teachers became radicalized by the strike so that the curriculum became allied to the promotion of social change and union workers came to figure strongly in the student clientele. As well as promoting a union education programme Highlander made concerted attempts to desegregate their student population. In the 1950s Highlander became involved in the civil rights movement after Horton had become disillusioned with the bureaucratization of the union movement. One particular reflection of this concern for civil rights was the establishing of a Citizenship school on Johns Island, South Carolina. This school was concerned to develop literacy skills amongst the black islanders to prepare them to take the voter registration test. Among its innovations were that work would have to be outside traditional school settings and that the curriculum and teaching materials should be based on adults' concerns and daily experiences. Horton spent six months visiting the island and immersing himself in the islanders' culture but he did not perform as a teacher. True to the notions of neighbourhood self-help principles he held all his life, he insisted that Citizenship schoolteachers be black. During the period 1957–63 Septima Clark, Director of Education at Highlander and the person responsible for the initial contact with Johns island, estimated that nearly 100,000 adults had learned to read and write because of the literacy programme (Adams 1972, p. 515).

Central Principles
Unlike Coady and Tompkins' work with fishermen, farmers and miners in eastern Nova Scotia, the work of Highlander was not based on a closely specified vision of community change. As Lovett has pointed out:

> It did not initiate programmes of social action, like Antigonish. Instead it concentrated on identifying and working closely with emerging social movements thrown up by the times and people, providing them with practical advice and assistance on the ground as well as educational support in the form of workshops at Highlander. (Lovett 1980, p. 161–2)

The fundamental and immutable axiom which underpinned the whole Highlander operation was 'learn from the people; start their education where they are' (Adams 1975, p. 206). The current Director of Highlander has identified five central concepts as providing the direction for Highlander (Clark 1978, p. 45–6).

1. A commitment to democratic education and decision-making.
2. An emphasis on working with groups.
3. An assumption that conflict is an inevitable element in society.
4. The use of short residential workshops to help others solve their problems.
5. Participant involvement in workshop discussions.

However, although residential workshops are the medium for problem-posing and resolution, there is no set curriculum nor a fixed catalogue of instructional techniques. The emphasis is on identifying the natural learning patterns of Highlander students and working to these. Adams summarizes this in the statement that 'Education, then, had to develop naturally from the people themselves, from the ways they could and would learn, and had to be reinforced constantly' (Adams 1975, p. 207). Workshops are 'vigourously nonacademic experiences' (p. 210) in which participants come together in a relaxed atmosphere to evolve collective solutions for common problems. There is a rejection of outside solutions and a belief that only those solutions devised by the victims of problems (and not by well-meaning outsiders) will succeed.

Two types of workshops have most commonly occurred at Highlander. When a movement is gaining strength, workshops are broad based experiences with no specific focus or curriculum. As a movement takes shape, however, so workshops become concerned with particular problems and techniques. The view of the learning process underlying either kind of workshop is that 'all learning is self-acquired and that people will learn, and put to effective use, only what they themselves determine is necessary' (Adams 1975, p. 213). Conti summarizes the Highlander philosophy:

> Highlander is an idea and a process. It is the idea that people have within themselves the potential to solve their own problems. It is the process by which individuals come to realise that their problems are shared by others, that problems can be solved collectively, that their individual problems are not solved until the common problem is eradicated for all. (Conti 1977, p. 38–9)

In this recognition of the connection between individual anxieties and collective problems the Highlander philosophy parallels the link made by C. Wright Mills between private troubles and public issues (Mills 1959).

Conti has undertaken a comparison of the thought of Horton and Freire much along the lines of Armstrong's analysis of Coady's and Freire's philosophies. On the whole, he identifies an even greater congruence of philosophy and practical injunctions between Horton and Freire than Armstrong did in her analysis of Coady and Freire's writings. Hence, Horton and Freire are seen to share:

1. A commitment to a populist (rather than representative) democracy.
2. A belief that education is used by a ruling establishment to oppress people into a culture of silence.
3. A recognition that education must be concerned with raising the consciousness of the oppressed so that they take action to solve their problems.
4. A belief that only in collective action can there lie a solution to individual problems.

5. An awareness that those seeking to raise consciousness should respect the values and culture of the oppressed and frame educational activities within their experience. (Conti 1977)

Conti summarizes his thoughts regarding the similarity between the two theorists as follows . . .

Using a learner-centered approach which emphasizes discussion, dialogue, and communication, they gear the curriculum to make use of (and to enhance) the life experiences of their learners . . . Both also encourage their clientele to test their learning in real life situations. (Conti 1977, p. 42)

Highlander: Contemporary Developments
The Highlander Research and Education Centre in Knoxville, Tennessee has assumed the mantle of radical community development work of the original folk school. It still concentrates on the eradication of poverty and inequality in Tennessee, primarily through the workshop training of groups and community leaders. In an interview in 1976 Horton declared 'We think education can be self-education' and that 'the experts are the poor people. Experts on black lung or coal mining are the people involved' (Kennedy 1981, p. 105). His notion of praxis was elaborated thus:

It's the action that counts, not talking. You can analyze later on. When people get over that action, then you need to talk about it, to internalize it, discuss it. You need to try to get people to understand the importance of it. It takes too long the other way. You do it and then talk about it. You don't talk first or you talk yourself out of it. (Kennedy 1981, p. 177)

A recent report of the Center summarized the prevailing philosophical rationale as follows:

It has, as a matter of course, chosen to work with leaders and groups who were ahead of their time, perhaps because they resisted prevailing trends. It had put into practice in its day to day programs an alternative educational perspective. Most importantly, it has been consumed with the notion that commonfolk can and should be their own leaders. (Highlander Research & Education Centre 1980, p. 1)

That the radical tradition of educative community development is still embodied in the centre's activities is illustrated by a news item in the report; 'Recent workshops at Highlander have reflected some of our current major concerns and our general and historic commitment to helping people deal collectively with community and workplace problems which reflect the maldistribution of power in society' (p. 4). A memorandum written by the Director of the centre and published in the international journal of adult education *Convergence* demonstrates the continuing concern 'to use education to help bring about social change' (Clark 1978, p. 52). Hence, Highlander's success is not measured by criteria derived from the educational experience of the workshop itself. Rather, it is the social change resulting from workshop participation which Highlander staff regard as the most readily identifiable, objective, index of evaluation.

The mechanics of a Highlander workshop, once considered so daringly radical, now seem to embody the mainstream andragogical principles of humanistic adult education. Consider the following passage:

> Staff can always set workshop topics, but participants bring their own personal agendas and these agendas have a way of becoming the real topic of discussion. This is natural and good, for it means that, in the long run, the participants, not the staff, control content. We must also remember that many serious and valuable discussions take place outside the workshop sessions so that one additional element to be considered in recruiting is a balance of individuals and groups who can benefit mutually from informal exchanges. (Clarke 1978, p. 49–50)

In the emphasis on students determining curricula and setting learning agendas, and on the informal aspects of workshop attendance, Highlander's methods are not far removed from many less controversial adult education initiatives. However, it is important to remember that such a philosophy has been implemented at Highlander from its inception in 1932 and that Lillian Johnson, who gave her home in Grundy County to be the Highlander folk school, was initially shocked by the lack of formal courses and a planned curriculum in evidence at Highlander.

The role of Highlander Center workshops in the community development process is well illustrated in a recent paper by Gaventa and Horton (1981). In 1977 a number of community groups in West Virginia combined into a coalition called the Appalachian Alliance. The Alliance established a Task Force to study land ownership and taxation issues and to challenge what were seen as failures in public policy by the Appalachian Regional Commission (ARC). The ARC was regarded by the Alliance groups as being too concerned with encouraging urbanization and with ignoring problems caused by land ownership patterns. Funding was obtained from the ARC to establish a Regional Land Ownership Task Force and this was to undertake the 'systematic, accurate collection of land ownership data, while facilitating maximum participation and potential for follow-up action' (Gaventa and Horton 1981, p. 33). Highlander was involved in various ways. Firstly, regional staff responsible for coordinating the Task Force research were based at Highlander Research and Education Center. Secondly, a training workshop for potential participants in the Task Force research project was held at Highlander at the beginning of the project in May 1979. The research methods to be adopted were decided at this workshop and participants were given some initial training in their use. Highlander also sponsored an evaluation workshop some two years after the beginning of the project. Other workshops held at Highlander, and growing out of the findings of the study, have been concerned with land reform, and with minerals leasing. Collaboration between the Alliance and Highlander has, in general, assisted in the creation of a network of groups and individuals concerned with rural land usage in Appalachia.

In comparison with most of the other initiatives discussed in this book, Highlander stands apart in that much of its own work is undertaken within an institutional format; that is, a residential workshop at Highlander. However, no discussion of community-based adult education, and of the ways in which adult learning in the community might be assisted, can ignore Horton's work. Firstly, Horton established the principles of short residential workshops only after a period of considerable immersion in the communities in which he was working (for example, St John's island) and after first hand experience of the Danish folk high schools. Secondly, the curricula of Highlander workshops have always been grounded in grass roots community concerns. Participants are encouraged to voice the problems and anxieties most pressing in their lives and the content of the workshop becomes the analysis of the cause of these problems and the exploration of possible solutions. Thirdly, Highlander judges its success not by criteria which are generated by and applied to workshop management or the effectiveness of instructional techniques. Instead, success is held to be reflected in positive community change, in individuals' and groups' realization that they possess resources which can be applied to community problem-solving, and in the growing recognition that externally-imposed programmes for change have no intrinsic superiority over those devised by local residents. The means for promoting community development may appear to be institution based but the substantive concerns of workshops and the criteria applied to determine Highlander's success are both strongly community based.

The Liverpool Educational Priority Area (EPA) project

The third initiative to be discussed in this comparative analysis of the adult educative component in community development was located in the City of Liverpool in the north-west of England between 1969 and 1972. Unlike the cases of Antigonish and Highlander, this work was located in an inner city area. Liverpool is a city the people of which are characterized by a gritty sense of humour born out of decades of adversity and economic depression. As I write these words Merseyside (the city of Liverpool together with its satellite towns) has one of the highest unemployment rates in the United Kingdom. It also has a history of exciting educational and artistic innovations some examples of which can be seen in the EPA project of the early 1970s.

Background

In 1968 the then Labour government in Britain designated a number of the most deprived inner city areas as Educational Priority Areas (EPAs). Liverpool was selected as one of these areas and the districts known as Liverpool 7 and Liverpool 8 received additional funds from the Department of Education and Science and an encouragement to explore alternative modes of provision suitable for an inner city area. Eric Midwinter, Director of the project (and a noted community education theorist) recognized the adult education component in any attempt at inner city regeneration. He also acknowledged that:

> Our adult education officer, Tom Lovett, had probably the most off-putting job of all of us. He had a study population of 170,000 and, where the other members of the team had schools and other institutions on which to base their efforts, Tom Lovett had little or nothing. His technique — the searching-out of non-formal groupings and the gradual extrapolation of problems for educational action — turned the usual practice of adult education on its head. The course came last. (Midwinter 1972, p. 155)

As Midwinter declared, Lovett's work in the EPA gave the project a truly lifelong dimension and this 'pioneering work was to be as meaningful in its ramifications as any other in the project' (Midwinter 1972, p. 70). Certainly Lovett's work had a great effect on other adult educators and his and Keith Jackson's early writings were, as Newman remarks, 'despatches from the front line' infused with 'an exhilaration just beneath the surface' (Newman 1979, p. 113) which had a great influence on community adult education work in the 1970s. The Russell Report's (HMSO 1973) concern with provision for the disadvantaged and the need for alternative models of provision and practice for such groups owes a debt to the work of those within the Liverpool EPA team and the influence of that three-year project is still crucial within British adult education. Fortunately for the world of adult education, Lovett is not only an innovative adult educator but also a prolific and interesting writer. The Liverpool experience has not, therefore, remained as the province of the few workers in the project but has been relayed to interested educators in Britain and North America.

Community roles for adult education

Fourteen months after beginning his work in central Liverpool Lovett published a personal report on work in progress in a major British journal,

Studies in Adult Education (Lovett 1971). His central thesis was expressed as follows:

> Adult education must be seen, not simply as classes and discussions for the adult members of the community, but rather as an integral part of a whole series of activities — sponsored by a government, the local authority, voluntary agencies, churches, residents' groups — which are community-based and concerned with the total community. (Lovett 1971, p. 2)

Six community roles for adult education were identified by Lovett, the first of which was adult education cum community development. Arguing that community development was the only appropriate course of action for adult educators with some communities Lovett described his work in assisting residents' groups, claimants' unions and credit unions to develop. A second role identified was that of adult education as a resource for community development. In this capacity the educator is restricted to offering assistance to an already established group as and when the occasion arises. As Lovett argues, "It is necessary, therefore, to attend meetings of residents to make oneself known and accepted so that when the occasion arises such assistance can be offered" (p. 5). Acting as an aid to parents and schools was a third role for adult education and the one which was initially seen by EPA leaders as the most profitable for adult education. However, in his early progress report Lovett averred that it had been the most difficult to perform. A fourth role, deemed extremely successful by Lovett, was that of adult education as a forum for discussing personal, moral and social problems. The performances of this role centred chiefly on Lovett's work with mothers' groups and he recounted his initiation of discussion sessions on 'The Community and the Outsider'. Other groups alternated discussion sessions with bingo or other social activities and Lovett deliberately underplayed any overtly educational component in these discussions. He also argued that the tutor's involvement with the group must extend beyond discussion to other activities connected with the group, for example helping with a pantomime or organizing a bazaar.

Adult education as an extension of recreation and entertainment was the penultimate role identified by Lovett and in the performance of this role Lovett sited discussion on *National Enquirer* or Sunday Mirror type issues (Naked Apes, Witchcraft, The Permissive Society) in public bars. Since the pub was the social focus of any working class community Lovett believed that any attempt at adult education in the community should use this setting for educative discussions. Finally, adult education was seen as having a counselling function within the community and Lovett argued that adult educators were in a unique position both to assist individuals in becoming aware of the educational opportunities open to them and to prepare educationally inexperienced adults for entry to intimidating institutional settings. The development of a network of counselling, information and advisory services in Britain during the 1970s and 1980s has illustrated the prescience of Lovett's perception.

Immersion in the Community

Lovett recognised that as an outsider coming to work in the EPA he needed to spend a period of time getting to know the area, its problems, and local residents. As he later wrote:

> This meant becoming involved in a number of community activities which, on the surface at least, bore no relationship to adult education. Social functions, community councils, residents' associations, summer play schemes, pubs, community centres, school open days — all provided an opportunity to make contact with local residents. (Lovett 1975, p. 31)

On his arrival in Liverpool he and his family found themselves living in two rooms in the heart of the EPA and this circumstance was turned to some professional advantage in that it enabled him to be perceived as a community member facing the kinds of accommodation problems experienced by many families in the area.

As part of this initial phase of community immersion and investigation three 'probes' were made to explore community members' perceptions of adult education. The first of these was in organizing a local history group for parents of children at a school in the dock area of the city. It soon became apparent that those few parents who did attend were regarded as 'headmaster's pets' by other parents. A second experiment, this time based on an adult education shop held in a large department store, attracted some 10,000 visitors who viewed the exhibition while shopping. However, Lovett admitted that attempts to start discussion groups based on some of the topics advertised at the exhibit were a total failure. The third exploratory project was a house-to-house survey of one particular locale — Earle Road — in which part-time interviewers tried to guage what people regarded as the important concerns in their lives. A general meeting was held in a Church Hall after this survey to which over 150 people who had expressed an interest in participation in some kind of informal discussion were invited. Thirty-one attended, despite an extensive publicity drive, who decided to form four groups (keep fit, hairdressing, domestic science and a general discussion group). As Midwinter commented with regard to this phase of community immersion and exploration: 'The Major feature of this exercise was the massive injection of energy and time it cost' (Midwinter 1972, p. 157). A committed team of adult educators had spent several weeks working full time wholly to create an adult educational programme for approximately forty people.

Adult Education and Community Development

Three often interrelated aspects of adult education for community development were identified by Lovett in the major book he published on his experience in Liverpool, *Adult Education, Community Development and the Working Class* (1975). The first of these concentrated on social action and self-help, in which the emphasis was placed on assessing and enhancing the educational component in the community development process. The second concerned discussion and group work with a range of informal groups not involved explicitly in community action within the EPA. Finally, theatre and local media were used to promote an awareness amongst local inhabitants of their class position and to encourage a critical scrutiny of institutions and power structures.

Into the social action and self-help category fell four particular experiments. Lovett assisted in the conversion of a local Handicraft Centre to a Community Centre initially by suggesting this conversion and then offering advice on how to deal with local planning authorities. Thereafter his role was subordinate and an independent centre committee was formed. After a successful application for urban grant aid had been made a more specifically educational role was undertaken which involved his organizing local courses and other educational activities. As Lovett acknowledged, performing a number of broad community work roles as well as adult educational ones at a time caused considerable strain.

A second opportunity for developmental work was presented by the formation of a summer play scheme for children of mothers living in high-rise tower blocks. One of the most interesting lessons of this experiment was that represented by a failure. Adult students at a local Teachers Training and Teacher Education College were drafted in to run the play scheme but these students proved unable to involve local adults in the project. Ultimately it was left to Lovett, some volunteers, and some parents to bring other parents more closely into the project.

A third opportunity for developmental work occurred when a local community council asked Lovett to chair a sub-committee considering the lack of educational opportunity for schoolchildren in the EPA. Taking this opportunity to offer a more systematic educational input he organized a six-week course on social problems and community councils. Finally, Lovett became involved in the Shelter Neighbourhood Action Project (SNAP) an initiative sponsored by SHELTER, a national housing action group. Despite the apparent opportunities afforded by this project for an educational input Lovett was critical of the SNAP team workers' approach which emphasized the need to meet deadlines for official planning purposes. The pace of learning and change was dictated by external circumstances and not the perceived needs of local residents.

The second community development component, that of group work and discussion, violated many of the traditional practices of adult education in the United Kingdom. The topics for discussion were sensationalist and popular, the venues were pubs or homes, and the role of the 'tutor' was that of impartial chairman. Examples of topics chosen were 'Naked Apes — Are We?', 'Life on other Planets — Is it Possible?', 'Permissive Society — Good or Bad?' and a specialist speaker began each discussion with a fifteen-minute presentation. Lovett acknowledged the blend of entertainment and education implicit in such discussions and experienced difficulties in his chairman's role. Assertions were countered by irrelevant statements, references to local events and personal, subjective interpretations. This personalized, anecdotal response to the introduction of abstract, conceptual elements in a discussion is one of the problems most frequently encountered by tutors working with educationally inexperienced adults seeking to resume their education. As I have written elsewhere in an analysis of adult study problems:

> This personalised response to formal, academic language and specialised terminology is particularly evident within the field of the Social Sciences and every tutor of adult classes must have a catalogue of instances in which the discussion of a concept or type of behaviour has degenerated into the exchange of often unrelated personal anecdotes. For adults whose everyday concerns are framed in familial and occupational terms, the appreciation of conceptual categories detached from individual experience has to be deliberately developed. (Brookfield 1979, p. 94)

The discussion management skills required of adult educators working with community groups will be discussed further in Chapter 8. Although acknowledging that there existed an element of showmanship in holding informal discussions in bars, Lovett believed that it was only by working in such settings that one could begin to develop students' understanding and to get them used to assessing evidence, formulating conclusions, and considering general principles rather than relating personal experience.

After the experience of working with formal discussion groups in public bars, three attempts to encourage such activity based on institutions were initiated; the Tuesday Club, the Smithdown Mothers Club and the Merlin Street Community Centre. The Tuesday Club comprised a group of coloured women, or white women married to coloured men, who met in a local school once a week. After six months working with the group a young female research assistant attached to the EPA team decided to introduce some more systematic education into the meetings with a series of discussions on social issues. The meetings continued for approximately two years though some difficulties were experienced with tutors pitching their discussion at too high a level. A similar experience occured with the Mothers Club where the tutor's refusal to discuss his own marriage aroused a certain amount of suspicion. However, some members of the group resolved long-standing marital problems and developed the self-confidence to apply for courses and jobs partly as a result of their association with the Mothers Club. Finally, at a local community centre a six-week course on local history was run by a tutor involved in the original pub discussions.

In all of the initiatives described in the preceeding paragraphs three points are of particular importance. Firstly, knowledge of the local area and a considerable time spent in listening to residents in order to ascertain their needs was a necessary prelude to any kind of educational intervention. As Lovett commented 'It was necessary to establish a close relationship with all the groups before constructive educational work could be undertaken' (Lovett 1975, p. 93). Secondly, this work required a paradigm-shift on the part of the worker concerning the traditional role expected of an adult educator. Thirdly, tutors working with the informal discussion groups had to recognize that therapeutic and purely educational aspects of these meetings were inextricably interwoven. Lovett remarked that this mix was 'unavoidable and probably necessary' (Lovett 1975, p. 95) and that educational work would have been impossible without the cathartic, therapeutic dimension afforded by an exchange of individual problems and experiences. To emphasize an earlier point, the crucial aspect of this work was that 'it was necessary to establish a personal relationship with the group concerned and to work through from a very informal social group work situation to one specifically educational' (Lovett 1975, p. 96).

The final element in the EPA community development work focused on the promotion of an awareness among local inhabitants of their class position and on the encouragement of a critical scrutiny of institutions and power structures. In the pursuit of this raising of consciousness two experiments were undertaken using, respectively, theatre and local radio. An 'Educational Darts' show was organized in a local community centre by a local community arts group in which the random throw of a dart — representing the accident of birth and class — was used to show the reality of structured educational inequality. The show was deemed a partial success in that it attracted large numbers but Lovett remarked that many in the audience reacted passively to an unfamiliar situation.

A more ambitious project was the production of a series of programmes on Radio Merseyside, the local radio station, entitled *Living Today*. Six programmes were made drawing upon the experiences of a number of local groups who were also to form the audience. The programmes comprised taped comments from local residents on themes such as 'The Family', 'The School' and 'The Neighbourhood', interspersed with popular songs and dramatic episodes. Follow-up programmes were arranged on the range of welfare services available in the area and the radio station arranged in-service training for community groups who wished to use the facilities of local radio. As Lovett pointed out, the cheapness of local radio, its accessibility to local residents, and the fact that a tape recorder could be taken into the most informal setting in an unobtrusive manner, made local radio a powerful tool in community development and adult education. Because programmes could be produced much more quickly than on television, local situations and demands could be presented and analysed as they arose and developed. Indeed, Lovett believed that in the production of programmes on social issues of concern to residents, which were linked to a network of local listening groups, lay the potential for a striking increase in working-class participation in adult education. Unanticipated by Lovett there has also been the recent boom in video taping and playback facilities which opens local TV channels to community group use.

Although the original Liverpool EPA team has largely dispersed (Lovett is now working in community education in Northern Ireland) the influence of their efforts is still felt within adult education. A relatively structured outcome of the work is the *Second Chance Education* programme now established at the Institute of Extension Studies in Liverpool University. This is sponsored by the WEA and is intended for adults with no formal educational qualifications, but with some evidence of union or community activism. The course organizers stress the personally liberatory effects of education and argue that the *Second Chance to Learn* programme is a potentially explosive awakener of personal potential (Filkin & Yarnit 1980). Students are encouraged to develop a critical class consciousness and to acquire the skills which will assist them to engage in purposive community action. The project has as its aim:

> To stimulate a critical consciousness of the way society works, to counter the view which presents the inner city areas of Liverpool and other cities as victims of circumstances, as regrettable accidents. We attempt instead to chart Liverpool's decline historically, to show that the slums are just as much the product of a market economy as the lush suburbs of south Liverpool. (Yarnit 1980, p. 182)

During this chapter and the preceeding one I have reviewed the kinds of adult learning in the community occurring in a group mode. The perspective adopted has been an historical one and most of the initiatives discussed began in the 1920s and 1930s. For the rest of the book two changes in substance and perspective are adopted. Firstly, the following three chapters concentrate on current activities; that is, those arising in the 1960s, 1970s and early 1980s. Secondly, the emphasis is placed firmly on practitioner roles and behaviours. Chapter 6 explores the ways in which educators can come to know the communities in which they are working — its structures, its power focuses, its educational resources — and to recognize the educational potential in particular situations.

Chapters 7 and 8 review the ways in which this potential can be realized through an examination of the efforts of adult educators to support that adult learning in the community occurring within both individual and group modes.

PART III

Supporting Adult Learners in the Community

SIX

Identifying and Researching Adult Learners in the Community

A precondition of adult educators being able to support the activities of adult learners in the community is the identification of such learners and the recognition of the educational component in community group activites. This chapter explores the different ways in which adult educators come to develop a knowledge of their communities and come to recognize the kinds of learning occurring therein. It examines a range of techniques from the use of informal observation and an anthropological style immersion in a community, to the more formal use of needs assessments and community surveys. The most appropriate methodological procedures for researching the activities of adult learners in the community are also discussed, and particular emphasis is placed on qualitative research strategies such as participant observation, open-ended interviews, and the application of grounded theory.

Assessing the Needs of a Community

The concept of need, like that of community, is a good example of a premature ultimate (Wiltshire 1973) in that once invoked it assumes a spurious finality preventing further analysis and discussion. Lawson (1979, p. 36) believes that a common stratagem of adult educators who are forced to explain why certain curricular elements are either present or absent from their programmes is to say that programmes are meeting the needs of adults in their locality. 'Need' is a term inspiring such reverence that its invocation is deemed justification enough for the educator's programming decisions. As Lawson argues:

> The concept of need in this context is used to extricate the organiser from his dilemma by apparently providing an objective basis on which to make

judgements. To say that one is meeting a need or that needs are being met is deemed to be a sufficient answer to the question 'why provide X?' in the programme. Like expressions of personal taste there is no possibility of a come back, no counter argument is appropriate, for the case is not argued, it is stated. (Lawson 1979, p. 36)

As with most premature ultimates, the introduction of the concept of need into a discussion tends to 'silence questions which need to be raised and block routes of inquiry which it would be possible to follow' (Wiltshire 1973, p. 26). The most crucial analytical route which is blocked or ignored is the one exploring the difference between needs and wants. Generally speaking, needs are referred to in the same breath as drives, wants, interests, preferences, wishes and demands. These expressions of desire or aspiration can, however, be considered equivalent only to *felt* needs. Felt needs are those which are perceived and expressed by the learners themselves — the need to learn to drive, to be more informed about the Middle Eastern political situation, or to develop culinary skills. As Chapter 4 argued, the expression of such felt needs by adult learners is the programmatic cornerstone of adult education for the community.

There is, however, another form of need which tends not to be distinguished from felt need or the expression of personal wishes and aspirations. This second form of need — what can be called prescribed need — is different in kind, not just in degree from felt need. It carries within it a sense of normative prescription so that declaring that a learner or a group of learners is in need suggests an imperative or command. To say 'you need this' means you should or you must have it. A prescriptive need is present whenever an educator, community developer or any external agency decides that adults are in a state of inadequacy, deficiency or inferiority when compared to states which the external educator decides are preferable. Monette (1977) calls such a need a normative need and, as he argues, it constitutes a value judgement entailing three propositions — 'that someone is in a given state, that this state is incompatible with the norms held by some group or by society, and that therefore the state of that someone should be changed' (Monette 1977, p. 118). It is this kind of needs assessment which characterizes adult education of the community as discussed in Chapter 4.

Felt needs are, therefore, of a different order from prescribed needs. On the one hand are simple expressions of desire by clients, on the other lie educators' prescriptions of the kinds of skills and competencies which they believe adults ought to acquire. These latter skills and competencies are diagnosed as essential irrespective of whether or not students see them as necessary. Of course, elements of the prescribed exist within any educational programme or, indeed, within wider programmes of socialization. To argue that all education should be self-education in that it is determined solely by learner desires is to deny the validity and importance of accumulated knowledge and experience contained within human (teachers) and material (libraries, data banks etc.) resources. The problem arises when the two kinds of need — felt and prescribed — are assumed to be synonymous.

Many writers in the field have recognized the difference between felt and prescribed needs. In North America, Griffith (1978) and Monette (1977) and in Britain, Wiltshire (1973) and Lawson (1979) have drawn our attention to this difference. Surprisingly, though, the recent handbook of practice on *Serving Personal and Community Needs Through Adult Education* (Boone *et al.* 1980) contains no reference to the considerable implications for adult education practice raised by whether the needs to be served are felt or prescribed. In a recent collection of papers on needs assessment Pennington (1980, p. 3) has opined that value judgements are unavoidable in such assessments. McMahon (1970) has also recognized that the following scenario is lamentably familiar to adult educators:

> Often there is the unfortunate pattern of the educator determining the need and offering the prescription (a course perhaps), and the client seeing the need differently and not responding to the proposed solution. (p. 11)

Newman (1979) has explored the difference between demand and need, and the ways in which an adult educator's prescription of individual or community needs can reflect condescension or a disguised authoritarianism. Just as writers on evaluation have noted the influence of stakeholders (those that have an investment in seeing a favourable evaluation produced), so Newman speculates that agencies sometimes identify needs which support their institutional *raison d'être*. He summarizes his experience in community needs assessment as follows...

> The adult educator must research his community as thoroughly as any community worker bent upon identifying needs, but he must set out to listen and learn. He must come to a community or situation with as few preconceived notions as possible. His aim should be to locate and respond as far as he is able to people's demands when they are clearly expressed; and to help people formulate and articulate their demands when the demands are not clearly expressed. (Newman 1979, p. 145)

It is the latter of these aims which poses particular problems for the educator trying to walk the notoriously slippery tightrope between providing sensitive assistance in the articulation of genuinely felt needs and falling prey to a benevolent authoritarianism. Interestingly enough, the practical injunction to listen and learn and to shed preconceived notions constitutes a practical parallel to the methodological assumptions underlying grounded theory (to be discussed later in this chapter).

The Community Survey

The conduct of a community survey is held by most adult educators to be a necessary prelude to the provision of an adult education programme. In practice, most programmers are so beset with a range of administrative and pedagogic duties that what was once seen as a necessary and intrinsic element of adult education provision becomes a discardable luxury. As a professor teaching programme planning and programme development courses I have often been aware that my students would never have the opportunity to put into practice the personal resolutions and professional injunctions to 'get to know the community'. Nonetheless, any adult educator who wishes to discover the range of informal adult learning occurring in the community must spend a considerable time exploring that locale. The point about the parallel educational universe, the invisible university, or the adult learning iceberg, is that the phenomenon represented by these metaphors — that of informal adult learning in the community — escapes questionnaires, surveys of premises or censuses, and tends not to be included in the records kept by City Hall.

The term survey research has come to be identified with particular data collection techniques, notably questionnaires or interviews. The term community survey as adopted by adult and continuing education programmers tends to be equated with check lists of possible courses or programme options delivered to, and completed by, a cross section of potential students. In the adult and community education literature as represented by Boyle (1981), Stark (1976), McMahon (1970), Knowles (1980a), Miller (1976) and Berridge (1973), the most common features of community surveys are:

1. Recruitment of a team of volunteers to administer the survey instrument.
2. Establishment of an advisory council or survey committee to advise on the purposes and design of the survey.
3. Collaboration with the mass media in alerting the local community to the prospect of a survey.
4. A training programme for volunteer workers in the survey.
5. Design of a sophisticated and exhaustive questionnaire to be personally administered by volunteers.
6. Holding of a town meeting to discuss the results of the survey.

In the 1975 Bay City community education survey, reprinted in Stark's (1976) *How To* handbook on *Conducting Community Surveys* the questionnaire to be administered was of census style proportions with approximately 200 multi-choice questions requiring a response. Such an undertaking, with the labour time that it involves on the part of the adult education programmer, is likely to be viewed as too ambitious for most practitioners. What may be just as fruitful as engaging in a long and complex piece of empirical research is to use secondary sources of information available in the community. Every community has a number of census reports, local government studies, surveys by organizations, businesses and other agencies which will yield basic information on the community structure. Local newspapers are a particularly useful source of information about those concerns seen by residents as particularly pressing. One technique I have found useful is to undertake a content analysis of 'readers' pages' or 'letters to the editor' in local papers. Although all adult and continuing education programmers will know of the individual who, singlehandedly, can conduct a one-person publicity campaign for a particular cause, it is a reasonable conclusion that a theme appearing in the letters page and explored by a number of different correspondents will reflect a wider community concern.

In an analysis of community observation techniques Brandt (1977) declared that "A community educator who does not take the time to study his community carefully and learn about the people in it is almost certain to fail" since "his own activities are bound to run into serious opposition before long and prove unproductive" (p. 143). He believed that the use of unobtrusive measures of examination — such as newspaper files, institutional publications and local government reports — would be most productive to the community educator with limited time and finance.

Perhaps the most important sources of community information, other than residents themselves, are the various community leaders in the political, business, social action, religious and educational spheres. As Knowles points out ...

> By the very nature of their work, their opportunities to take part in certain activities, or their personalities, some people in every community are especially well informed about the community as a whole or about certain segments or aspects of it. (Knowles 1980a, p. 113)

The problem with such sources is one of reliability. It is difficult to assess the extent to which one individual, no matter how insightful or experienced, can diagnose the problems or articulate the concerns of large numbers of community members. The chief prevention against receiving a distorted or filtered account of community concerns is, of course, to consult as many community leaders as possible.

To those seeking to implement a Freirean rationale in their work, seeking the opinions of local councillors and aldermen, labour leaders, priests and local volunteer workers may represent a regrettable paternalism in that the views and feelings of local residents never receive direct expression. Nonetheless. I would affirm that consulting a cross section of community leaders has considerable utility for any adult educator new to an area who is required to plan a programme almost immediately on arrival in the post. Indeed, I cannot conceive of a programmer doing otherwise if the programme is to stand any chance of success.

Informal Assessment Methods

Of greater relevance (than conducting formal community surveys) to the educator hoping to identify informal adult learning in the community is the process of community immersion. As earlier chapters have made plain one of the first principles of adult education work in community settings is for the worker to spend a considerable period of apparently 'unproductive' time with local community groups. This principle and practice was affirmed in Antigonish, at Highlander, in the Liverpool EPA and, indeed, is at the heart of Freirean philosophy. To a hard-headed School Board Director or Chief Education Officer such practice will probably be difficult for the practitioner to justify. It is no accident that those instances in which informal assessment and community immersion have been accepted as integral elements in an adult education programme have mostly been special projects or voluntary action efforts.

In an addendum to a piece on formal methods of community needs assessment Polsky (1976) has described his process of community 'infiltration' in seeking the 'tone' of a community. He argues that only if educators are aware of the hidden agendas of individuals and groups at different levels in the community, and only if such groups are convinced educators can be trusted, will information be offered that is accurate and revealing. Polsky regards such information as authentic and advocates talking to people on street corners and in stores as well as joining local action and interest groups as a participant rather than educational representative. Boyle (1981) has also recognised the importance of informal assessment methods, particularly when time and finance are unavailable for a lengthy formal survey. He advocates educators and other community workers locating themselves at 'listening posts' within communities such as taverns, churches and stores (p. 162).

Using listening posts as part of a community infiltration process to guage the tone of a community and gather authentic information — to any quantitatively oriented researcher schooled in the social survey tradition, such language will appear lamentably imprecise. However, it is only in using such informal community immersion and community infiltration techniques that the educator will be able to identify group settings and situations in which a teachable moment is enshrined.

An example from my own experience may illustrate the point. At one time I worked as a community education organizer in an adult education college in a rural area of scattered population. As part of my attempts to develop a knowledge of the informal community groups and learning networks in the area I agreed to be a guest speaker at a local women's group meeting. There was no institutional kudos involved in this act in that it resulted in no student recruitment or increased enrolment. After giving my talk I found that the group met every two weeks for informal discussion on matters of personal, social and political concern. Sessions in which guest speakers were present alternated with leaderless discussions. Knowing well the semantic and interpersonal traps which could ensnare discussion participants — even when a skilled leader was in charge — I suggested that I provide a package of background information to group members before each meeting. This package would contain statistical data on the matter in hand, abstracts of relevant studies and reports, proposed alternative explanations of the phenomenon under discussion, and suggestions for particular lines of inquiry. As I wrote in a recent paper:

> Since the group set the agenda of topics for discussion, and since I did not attend the meetings, I felt the group retained the responsibility for setting its own learning goals. This seems to me an example of an adult educator identifying, and then supporting, the educational component of community group activities. (Brookfield 1982a, p. 16)

A more detailed discussion of this initiative is contained in Chapter 8.

Qualitative and Quantitative Modes of Research

> 'Not everything that can be counted counts, and not everything that counts can be counted' (Cameron 1963, p. 13)

One of the most depressing aspects of methodological debates in the fields of social science and educational research is the ease with which writers can fall into the trap of adopting a vituperative, almost hysterical tone in their arguments serving only to obscure the validity of any propositions advanced. Anyone who advocates the adoption of qualitative modes of research as appropriate for a particular substantive area — such as adult learning in the community — can quickly be cast as a champion of qualitative research *per se* and, by inference, as an opponent of quantitative research. This combative, adversarial approach to intellectual debate is predicated on the establishing of a mutually exclusive (and wholly false) dichotomy between qualitative and quantitative methods. As professional reputations develop so proponents of differing views become entrenched in their commitment to one side or the other. Their time is then devoted to sniping at opponents' views rather than (a) actually doing research and (b) seriously considering the merits of alternative approaches. The following quotation illustrates this dichotomous adverserial mode of discourse most aptly:

> If one sociologist makes a personal observation about an event, we call it a hypothesis, an opinion or a guess. But if a thousand less intelligent and less interested people can be inveigled into filling out a return postcard, the tabulated total is regarded as research. Personally, I would rather trust the opinion of one bright trained observer than those of a thousand indifferent fools. (Cameron 1963, p. 28)

Superficially this is an appealing and seductive paragraph. However, the language, tone and content all serve only to create an apparent opposition between survey research (engaged in only by unintelligent, indifferent fools) and personal observation (the prerogative of bright sociologists). This creation and maintenance of a methodological dualism in the investigation of human behaviour can be traced back to the genesis of the discipline of sociology. The last century witnessed the rise of Comtean positivism (in which social behaviour was judged to be accessible to investigation using the methods of natural science) and its antonym in the Weberian notion of *verstehen* (the interpretative understanding of social action). Social scientists (including adult education researchers) have recast this schism in the form of quantitative versus qualitative methods.

The rationale underlying such polarities may be epistemological; that is, it may reflect a genuine and irreconcilable difference between contrasting views of the nature of reality and the most appropriate ways of understanding and expressing that reality. It is surely not too sceptical, however, to suspect that this kind of academic demarcation can also have a professional utility; researchers have a self-interest in perpetuating entrenched viewpoints regarding admissible methodologies and substantive concerns. A viewpoint is elaborated in a paper and prompts a number of refutations which, in turn, occasion replies to refutations. Individuals and departments become associated with particular perspectives and generate publications and posts out of this division.

This is not to argue for the imposition of an academic orthodoxy or a rejection of the advancement of knowledge through the exploration and possible synthesis of alternative viewpoints. It is rather to suggest that the advancement of knowledge is all too often conceived as occurring within methodological and conceptual tramlines. Methodologies, concepts, and classificatory schema are devised and refined without reference to their qualitative or quantitative counterparts and the two camps are deemed mutually exclusive. The vitriol generated in this battle is well illustrated in Stanislav Andreski's denunciation of social sciences as 'sorcery':

> It is a great pity that we do not have more works which, on the basis of careful and protracted observation, depict perceptibly the aspects of social reality which

escape the questionnaires and statistics. The reason for this scarcity is the wide acceptance of the dogma that nothing is worth knowing that cannot be counted, and that any information which is tabulated thereby becomes scientific — surely one of the grossest superstitions of our time, whose vogue can only stem from the fact that it enables a large number of people to make a living by indulging in easy pseudo-science. (Andreski 1972, p. 111)

It is to the credit of adult education as a field of research that many of its acknowledged leaders have rejected methodolatory and have advocated a methodological triangulation or pluralism. Although doctoral committees, tenure review boards, and journal editorial boards tend to look askance at qualitative methods, adult education luminaries have acknowledged that qualitative and intuitive modes are admissible and appropriate. Apps has proposed that adult educators should research evaluative and prescriptive questions (Apps 1973, p. 63) and Griffith believes that debate on the merits of inductive, qualitative and participatory research methodologies could breathe new vitality into adult education research world wide (Griffith 1979, p. 142).

The late Roby Kidd criticized the mutually exclusive nature of much debate on qualitative and quantitative modes of research and condemned the 'bland, homogenized, deodorized, anaesthetized prose with which we report most educational experiments, inventions, innovations' (Kidd 1981, p. 3). He argued that 'it is not possible, and may never be possible, to assign consistent numerical weights to all human attributes such as love, fear, rage, wonder, hope, responsibility' (Kidd 1981, p. 5). Finally, in the UK Ruddock has criticized the damaging and naive approach equating research with measurement. He advocates the use of non-metric qualitative research techniques, which are available in great variety, and a phenomenological scepticism regarding researchers' presentations of reality (Ruddock 1980, p. 81). The extent to which adult education research in North America and Britain has reflected this pluralism is documented in Brookfield (1982b, c).

Researching informal adult learning occurring in community settings is liable to be most accessible to qualitative modes of research. This implies no condemnation of quantitative approaches; indeed, the bulk of Tough's research into self-teaching, major learning efforts and intentional change is cast in a semi-quantitative mode. The present writer has also used quantitative survey techniques in his own research and undertook a study of the premier British social science statistician — Charles Booth — for his master's thesis (Brookfield 1974). However, qualitative research methods seem to be most appropriate for this particular field because:

1. Understanding such learning depends on the researcher appreciating the norms, values, codes and behaviours of the groups in which it occurs.

2. Recording such learning often relies upon direct observation of learning activities — sometimes with the researcher also functioning as co-learner.

3. Learners' activities are so idiosyncratic and diverse that they are often
unlikely to be amenable to incorporation in pre-coded questionnaire
categories.

4. An appreciation of the significance of learning acts can only come when the
researcher has gained the trust and confidence of the subject and such an
empathy is unlikely to emerge in the conduct of a survey questionnaire.

5. Adopting an emergent categorizations approach to the analysis of data allows
those themes and concerns most important to learners to emerge, rather than
those considered most important by researchers.

6. Recognizing that learning is occurring may only come after a period of
immersion in the culture and activities of learners, particularly since those
adults concerned may not consciously identify their activities as 'learning' or
'educational'.

In the rest of this chapter some of the chief features of qualitative research,
and their applicability to researching adult learning in the community, are
considered.

Interviewing Adult Learners in Community Settings

Interviews are a particularly appropriate tool of investigation for those
inquiries which have an idiographic rather than a nomothetic rationale;
that is, which are concerned with depicting the highly specific nature of
individual experience rather than advancing broad generalizations. Such
inquiries are located within the phenomenological tradition and rest on
the assumption that one person's formulation of a problem, or presentation of a dilemma, can encapsulate a wider reality. Hence, the
understanding of an individual caught up in a specific situation is seen by
Zweig as the key to the better understanding of the generic (Zweig 1965,
p. x) and 'qualitative researchers can study certain general social processes in any single setting or through any single subject' (Bogdan &
Taylor 1975, p. 12).

One of the chief difficulties with the interview as a research technique
is the expectation it arouses in potential interviewees that a certain pattern
of interaction will be followed. As I have argued elsewhere:

> The culture-specific associations surrounding the term 'interview' mean that in
> everyday discourse the word calls to mind television confrontations in which a
> detached questioner elicits information from a knowledgeable and articulate
> subject in a more or less hostile manner. Thus, the term is interchangeable with
> that of 'interrogation', since its only other common usage is in the context of
> the competitive and anxiety-provoking job 'interview'. (Brookfield 1981b,
> p. 13)

It will not be an unfamiliar occurrence for researchers into informal adult learning to realize that the individuals being studied may have experienced a number of 'interviews' in which they have been cast in the role of offender against institutional norms and conventions. As Holmes argued with regard to these occasions...

> To play the disinterested researcher may lead to being identified with that world. The result may be an apparently acceptable interview, with answers given to all questions, but that comes no nearer to an understanding of real feelings and perceptions than before one started. (Holmes 1976, p. 152)

One of the most readable and helpful essays on interviewing techniques, and in particular on how to overcome the mistrust and artificiality identified above by Holmes, is that of Ferdynand Zweig on 'The Art and Technique of Interviewing' (1965). Zweig had spent many years interviewing blue collar manual workers about their work, leisure interests, political behaviours and familial relationships. He regarded interviewing as 'a branch of a larger art, the art of conversation' (p. 245) and held that interviews should be a genuine exchange of experience, a true inter-view. Asking the same questions in the same order and with the same vocal inflections for each interview in a research project would only reduce the interviewer to being an appendage of methodology, a functionary whose task was rigidly to administer the interview schedule and record subsequent responses. Zweig believed that if the interviewer was to ask people to reveal their perceptions of activities which had great personal significance to them, then that interviewer must be prepared to voice his or her own enthusiasms, pleasures and anxieties. In my various research projects into informal adult learning over the years the following advice has served to determine my interviewing style:

> The act of interviewing does not need to sink to the level of mechanicalness. It can be a graceful and joyful act, enjoyed by the two sides and suffered by neither. What is more, my contention is that unless it becomes such an act it will only fail in its main function. One cannot conduct an interview by bombarding one's victims with a barrage of questions, which is only tiresome and tiring for both sides. The only way is to make an interview an enjoyable social act, both for the interviewer and the respondent, a two-way traffic, so that the respondent feels not a 'victim' but a true partner, a true conversationalist. (Zweig 1965, p. 245)

Grounded Theory

Qualitative research tends to be characterized by three features:

1. A substantive concern with the exploration of perceptions and attitudes, and with understanding the inner meaning and significance of behaviours.
2. A reliance on certain data collection techniques; open-ended interviews, participant and non-participant observation, and the use of unobtrusive measures
3. A prediliction for the application of grounded theory towards the analysis and coding of data, discernment of central themes, generation of hypotheses, and establishment of typologies and classifications.

The application of a grounded theory approach is particularly useful in investigating previously non-researched areas. To come to an area of research with no preconceptions concerning the most fruitful avenues of inquiry offered therein is hardly possible. In the very acts of assembling a research sample, deciding upon the study's investigative parameters, framing even a provisional interview schedule of appropriate questions, and devising an informal procedure for the recording of observed behaviours — all these require the researcher to express preferences regarding the themes to be investigated, thereby excluding the consideration of other possible features. However, in a grounded theory study the researcher does spend as much time as possible 'immersed' in and 'getting close to' the data. The collection and analysis of data occur concurrently and, as Darkenwald points out, verification is subordinated to discovery, while the reverse is true in experimental investigations (Darkenwald 1980, p. 68). Grounded theory has, therefore, a 'scene setting' function in studies of previously non-researched areas. It suggests categories, properties, typologies, classifications and hypotheses — a whole paradigm of investigation in fact — which can be refined in subsequent studies. In the field of research covered by this book — the learning of adults occurring in naturalistic community settings — the application of grounded theory is particularly appropriate.

The chief exponents of grounded theory are Glaser and Strauss and in their seminal *The Discovery of Grounded Theory* (1967) they advise that the study of a new field of research be undertaken 'without any preconceived theory that dictates, prior to the research, "relevancies" in concepts and hypotheses' (p. 33). In the adult education field grounded theory has been applied most notably in the study of adult literacy and adult basic education. In the national study of American adult basic education *Last Gamble in Education* (Mezirow *et al.* 1975) a team of field workers surveyed a sample of ABE classes to identify patterns of programme operation, classroom interaction and participant perspectives. In their introduction to the survey the authors describe their procedure of 'synchronic induction' thus:

Patterns that emerged were tested against the experiences in all other locations; and when mediating factors were reported in one place, they, too, were investigated by the entire network of field researchers to find out if they were occurring elsewhere... In this way conceptual categories were established and their attributes delineated. (p. x)

One of the authors of this report in an essay published some five years later described the way in which the category of 'failure reduction' — teachers' attempts to minimize students' public mistakes and thereby to reduce damage to students' self-esteem — was first recognized, then checked, then incorporated into the research through the formulation of theoretical propositions derived from this category. Darkenwald believed that a category such as failure reduction probably would never be discovered by observing the interaction of students and teachers in only one or two classrooms (Darkenwald 1980, p. 71).

In the major study of the impact of the British adult literacy campaign of the British Broadcasting Corporation (BBC) the grounded theory approach was applied and acknowledgement was made to the synchronic induction method of Mezirow *et al.* (1975). The researchers in the British study declared that 'what we were now seeking was the reality of the literacy experience as perceived by the participants' (Jones and Charnley 1978, p. 9). They began by consciously rejecting any hypotheses and simply talking to a group of literacy tutors and students. After team meetings to discuss the emerging common elements in these early tape recordings an *aide-mémoire* of interview prompts was devised. However, the authors of the study stressed that 'the method is reliable only if complete confidence can be established that the research is a genuinely open enquiry and that its boundaries are set by the interviewee' (Jones and Charnley 1978, p. 10). The overall approach was summarized thus:

The hypotheses emerge from the interpretation and analysis of the first research data. These are then tested against further primary data from further field work, and against information from other available sources and the hypotheses are refined or modified by discussion among the team. This process can be repeated as often as time and the nerves of the team will allow. (p. 10).

The stress is placed upon emergent themes, concepts and typologies in grounded theory since, in Glaser and Strauss's words, these 'usually prove to be the most relevant and the best fitted to the data. As they are emerging, their fullest possible generality and meaning are continually being developed and checked for relevance' (Glaser & Strauss 1967, p. 37). It is interesting to note, in passing, that one of the few classics in the field of adult education (already discussed in Chapter 3), Cyril Houle's *The Inquiring Mind* (1961), used a grounded theory approach before this procedure was granted that nomenclature. Houle announced that he had no conscious hypotheses at the outset of his investigation and that his chief purpose was to encourage his subjects to talk freely and frankly. His admisssion that themes (such as the significance of stimulators and of enclaves) emerged during the course of reading through the research (pp. 13 – 14) was a direct precursor of the notion of emergent categories and properties as developed by Glaser and Strauss.

The dangers of the grounded theory approach are obvious. Aside from the fact that it is extremely time consuming, there is the problem of researchers becoming so immersed in the data that they are unable to develop an overall perspective with regard to its main features. Typologies may be subject to such continual refinement that no clear framework for the management of material and coding of responses emerges. A research team may seize on what seem to be particularly fruitful avenues of inquiry early on in the study only to find that much time and effort has been invested in the exploration of thematic cul-de-sacs as these features remain unmentioned in subsequent interviews.

In a research field which is characterized by a history of developed and accepted hypotheses and experimental procedures, much of this exploratory effort is removed. However, in the investigation of adult learning in the community, where no generally acknowledged methodological paradigm exists to guide the researcher (though Tough's research design has been replicated by many), an inductive approach to the management of material is appropriate. Researching informal adult learning occurring within individual or group modes requires a flexible and developing methodology in which major themes and classificatory schema emerge only after a period of immersion in the data and reflection upon its internal logic. Too rigid an adherence to a preconceived theoretical framework in which the chief research concerns, the major concepts and preliminary hypotheses have all been previously formulated, may produce a neatly consistent and precise set of results. It can mean, however, that the finished research says more about the preoccupations of the researcher than the significance which learners ascribe to their actions.

Participatory Research

In recent years, thanks largely to the efforts of the participatory research group based on the International Council for Adult Education in Toronto, the principles and practice of participatory research have become familiar to adult education researchers. Those advocating the extension of participatory research emphasize the importance of community members in defining research problems, choosing appropriate methods for the gathering of data, and engaging in a collective analysis and interpretation of data. Such research is, therefore, planned for and applied by the community. The best formulations of the participatory research position are those of Hall (1975, 1978, 1979, 1981) and Conchelos and Kassam (1981). The chief critique of this approach has come from Griffith and Cristarella (1979).

Participatory researchers recognize that value judgements underlie the actions of researchers just as they affect those of adult education programmers and community workers. The most well-known exponent of the participatory research approach is Budd Hall, now Secretary General of the International Council for Adult Education (ICAE), who articulated the principles of participatory research after working in adult education research in Tanzania. During his time in Africa he became aware of fundamental shortcomings in the survey research methods he was using. In particular, he was involved in two research projects concerned with local elections and adult education programmes, both of which used carefully devised and pre-tested extended questionnaires as the data collection instruments. However, Hall found that 'my interpretation had to be based on my experience, my knowledge, my biases and my expectations' (Hall 1975, p. 25) and that 'the crucial task of interpretation depended on the insights that I managed to pull from tables and talks and books and hunches' (ibid.). This led him to formulate the following criticisms of survey research methods as used in adult education research:

1. The survey research approach oversimplifies social reality and is therefore inaccurate.
2. Survey research is often alienating, dominating or oppressive.
3. Survey research does not provide easy links to possible subsequent action.
4. Survey research methods are inconsistent with the principles of adult education.

In contrast to what are seen as oversimplified and alienating research methods is the participatory research approach. This approach has three important dimensions — 'a method of social investigation involving the full participation of the community, an educational process, and a means of taking action' (Hall 1979, pp. 53–54). The chief components of the approach are:

1. The definition of the research 'problem', the collection of data, and the analysis of results are activities in which the whole community or research population are integrally involved.
2. Research has a goal other than the 'pure' pursuit of knowledge or the building of academic careers. Hence, 'the ultimate goal of research is the radical transformation of social reality and the improvement of the lives of the people involved. The beneficiaries of the research are the members of the community itself' (Hall 1979, p. 54).
3. The substantive focus for participatory research tends to be the analysis of the current plight and future improvement of a range of powerless groups — minority groups, the poor and marginal sectors of society.
4. Participatory research is ultimately more accurate and therefore 'scientific'

than survey research since community participation and involvement at all stages in the research process ensures a truly authentic representation of social reality.

5. Participation in the research creates an awareness among community members of their own resources and results in a continued commitment to community development.

6. The participant researcher eschews the notion of an academic objectivity or detachment, instead becoming a committed participant, learner and advocate.

Participatory research tends to be identified with a Freirean emphasis on the liberation of peasant groups in Third World countries. However, elements of participatory research are present in the adult literacy project described earlier in this chapter and in the Antigonish, Highlander and Liverpool experiments analysed in Chapter 5. In Canada research projects with rural native communities, Latin American immigrant groups, and native people in Toronto have also been undertaken (Participatory Research Group 1980).

One of the most cogent critiques of the participatory research approach is that undertaken by Griffith and Cristarella (1979). The authors insist that participatory researchers are confusing community development with research, that they do not distinguish between the collection of knowledge and the application of results, that their commitment to improving the lot of their subjects distorts their perception, that they reject survey research methods *in toto* simply because they have occasionally been ineptly applied, and that the whole research process is altered because of the commitment of the researcher to a preconceived goal (that is, the improvement of the lot of community members or 'subjects'). They write: 'the term "participatory research" is a misnomer, applied idiosyncratically to activities not conducted primarily to advance knowledge, but rather to promote community development' (Griffith & Cristarella 1979, p. 18). There is no doubt that this comment is well made — participatory researchers are openly committed to a prescriptive improvement in the condition of the communities and groups with which they are working. However, participatory researchers do not see this as a criticism, but rather as a given, as a condition of their activity.

The tradition of participatory research is one which can be seen to have its methodological roots in the symbolic interactionist perspective of Mead (1934) and Blumer (1969) and the emphasis on understanding the inner meaning and significance of behaviours of Weber's *verstehende soziologie* (Weber 1949). It also calls to mind Collingwood's attempts to recreate the mental states of historical actors (Collingwood 1943). There is a connection with the anthropological research method of participant observation, which is characterized by 'a period of intense social interaction between the researcher and the subjects, in the milieu of the latter' (Bogdan &

Taylor 1975, p. 5). In the pursuit of needs assessment through community immersion identified earlier in this chapter participant observation is an essential technique. However, as Lofland declares 'It is precisely because it is the most penetrating of strategies, the most close and telling mode of gathering information, that it raises difficult social and moral questions' (Lofland 1971, p. 93). Chief amongst these is the declaration of the researcher's identity, the possibility of misinterpretation of the meaning and significance of behaviour, and the extent to which the participant observer's presence alters the phenomena under investigation (McCall and Simmons 1969). To participant researchers, however, the whole point of their involvement is to alter the phenomena under investigation. This is not a problem, but rather a necessary condition of their activity, since the purpose of research is to improve the lives of the community members with whom they are working.

Researching Adult Learning in the Community — An Example

As the authors of a riveting and revealing collection of sociological research odysseys have insisted, 'It is common knowledge that there has always been, perhaps necessarily, considerable divergence between how sociological research has actually been done and what is found in the textbooks' (Bell & Newby 1977, p. 9). The methodology chapters of theses or the prefaces to published books frequently present an account of the research process which is elegant, precise and logically consistent. As anyone who has undertaken research (particularly qualitative modes of research) knows, such impressive accounts tend to be *post facto* rationalizations of what is a haphazard and often frustrating activity. Above all, the importance of serendipity — of a lucky, chance occurrence — receives no mention. My first realization of the crucial importance of such fortuitous happenings came with my Masters thesis where my topic — the contribution of the Victorian social statistician and reformer, Charles Booth, to sociology — was 'suggested' upon my discovery that my landlord was Booth's grandson and had access to his complete writings and several unpublished pieces. Upon such fortunate accidents are academic careers launched.

As a conclusion to this chapter the following account of the inside story of a research effort is given. Since the chapter has up to this point consisted of generalized injunctions rather than specific examples of research, it seems a good idea to conclude with a brief exposition of one attempt to investigate adult learning in the community using qualitative methods and a grounded theory approach. Chapter 3 has already outlined the substantive findings of the study in the section on 'Successful Independent

Learning'. The study is the author's doctoral thesis and was conducted over four years (1976–80) in a rural area (Worcestershire) of the West Midlands of England. Its purpose was to be the investigation of the learning activities of a group of highly successful independent learners (Brookfield 1980a).

Serendipity as a Necessary Condition of Research

The story of the research project was characterized by a series of happy accidents, the first of which was the discovery (through a friend's recommendation) of Allen Tough's work on self-teaching, also discussed in Chapter 3. It was from reading *Learning Without a Teacher* (Tough 1967) that my ideas on the existence of a parallel educational universe of purposeful adult learning outside the formal adult education system received some early confirmation. The second happy accident was meeting someone who turned out to be an ideal research supervisor — Professor Henry Arthur Jones, then of the University of Leicester. This was accidental in that I had already been accepted as a doctoral candidate at another University but as a result of a meeting with Arthur Jones I decided to come to Leicester. Jones weaned me away from what I had assumed to be the expected mode of research for doctoral degrees (the use of survey questionnaires) and encouraged me to follow my suspicion that the comments and perceptions of interviewees (rather than my own preferences) should set the research agenda. I had originally assumed that the research would be a survey, using questionnaires and structured interviews, of a group of correspondence students and a smaller number of independent learners. In the event the proportions were reversed and it turned out to be an investigation of independent learners and a small subsample of correspondence students using open ended interviews. There were to be no preconceived hypotheses, nor any pretence that the twenty-five independent learners chosen were statistically representative of any larger population. Jones was quite willing to use artistic metaphors when talking of the study, while impressing upon me the importance of accuracy and precision in recording and interpreting data.

I was also lucky in my efforts to assemble what must be a fairly unusual sample; that is, adults who had attained public recognition as expert in their fields of interest without ever attending formal courses of instruction. Working as a community educator in the area had alerted me to the presence of seven or eight such individuals and all of these agreed to talk to me of their enthusiasms. It was during these conversations that the substantive themes for investigation in the subsequent interviews emerged.

Conducting Interviews

Earlier in the chapter I outlined the dangers of using structured interviews and the associations and expectations created in subjects upon hearing they were to be 'interviewed'. It was because of the dangers of alarming potential subjects that the initial letters of contact for the study deliberately avoided using the term 'interview'. Instead, the letters asked sample members to 'chat' or 'talk' about their interests and referred to these conversations being transcribed for research purposes. The hope was that the informal and non-threatening associations of these words would confirm that a reciprocal dialogue, not a staged question-and-answer session, was sought. Admittedly, the circumstances occasioning that dialogue could not be forgotten and it would be necessary to intervene if the interview was becoming repetitious or to probe an apparently casual, but revealing, aside. The intention was, however, to make the encounter as enjoyable for the subject as for the researcher.

Another way in which the interviews took on the character of conversations, of a dialogue between equals characterized by openness and a respect for the other's views, was seen in the frequency with which respondents declared that the encounter had been useful and revealing to them. Through being encouraged to reflect on their activities, to consider the broad features of their learning rather than specific substantive concerns, and to be forced to relay these reflections to an interested layman, the independent learners came away from their interviews with some insights into their own experiences. When learners said that they had 'just realized' something about their learning through talking about it, or that they had 'never thought about it like that before', it indicated that respondents as well as interviewer were finding the conversations to yield stimulating insights. There were also many times during the research when an expression of a genuine admiration for the independent learning activities of my 'subjects' came quite naturally to me. This was no calculating stratagem to put subjects off their guard in the hope of prompting an indiscreet revelation, but a spontaneous response to encountering repeated evidence of sustained commitment and considerable achievement.

Whenever possible the interviews were conducted in subjects' homes. The reasons for this were twofold; first, interviewees would regard themselves as being on familiar territory and less likely to feel intimidated than if they were expected to visit a researcher's office sited, perhaps, in a university or college building. Secondly, there was the opportunity for the researcher to see practical examples of the learning activity. The latter feature meant that the course of the interview could be altered, and interesting lines of inquiry pursued, through reference to particular artefacts. Asking about the other members in a photograph taken at an exhibition or society meeting, for example, would lead into a discussion on the use of enthusiasts' clubs and voluntary societies as informal learning networks.

If the subject agreed the interview was tape recorded and then transcribed. For some of the independent learners, however, the use of the tape recorder was considered intimidating and in this event I compiled an interview report (usually on the same day) based on notes made during the encounter and on my recollection of the conversation. In either case the subject was sent a copy of the interview report or transcript and invited to check its accuracy. This chance to see the researcher's record of the encounter was stressed as a condition of sample members agreeing to participate in the project. It was hoped that this would go some way towards removing the association between interview and interrogation and help to establish an open atmosphere characterized by reciprocity. Knowing that there would be no attempt by the researcher to tease out indiscreet revelations which would then be made public would help to build a trust between interviewer and interviewee. Also, by offering the subjects an opportunity to check the accuracy of interview summaries, and to suggest appropriate modifications and additions, the chance of a researcher paraphrasing a remark incorrectly, or misinterpreting an important point, would be considerably reduced.

Whenever possible questions were asked relating to specific events, to previous remarks, or to photographs, magazines and collectors' items at the subjects' homes. Grounding the exploration of a general theme within the context of a specific occurrence would, it was hoped, help the respondents to feel comfortable. Recounting the details of individual incidents instead of answering generalized, abstract questions would ease the subjects' anxieties resulting from expectations about interview protocol and the provision of 'correct' responses. It would be easier to discuss, say, the role of competitions in reinforcing motivation and directing the course of learning efforts, by commenting on a prominently displayed rosette or certificate and allowing the conversation to develop from that reference. For example, the following extract comes from an interview with a successful local fisherman who had earlier that day participated in a competition:

I've gone to the Avon today, really, geared up to fish the Severn because that's what I usually fish and that's what I'm geared up to fish. I've gone along with the wrong rod, which is too heavy, exerts too much power when I strike, and consequently I've lost fish through it. It's cost me a lot of money and I'm not very pleased about it! Because I didn't think enough about it before I went

Question: How could you have increased your chances of success then, before you arrived at the river?

By doing your homework. Firstly, you must know what sort of state the river is in, whether it's up, normal level, whether it's rising, falling — that's a must. Then you compare results, probably from the last three weeks on the venue. I always read the angling papers each week to find out what weights have been winning matches and what weights of fish have been getting in the prize money. It's the angler who catches the heaviest weight of fish that wins the money. I also get most of the results sent through to me anyway. We do a lot of talking in the local shop. We go in there and say what won the match at Huxley's on the Avon, what won the match at Stourport this week, how did friends get on, what did they do, how did they fish.

Rooting a question in the context of an incident occurring that same day here encouraged the respondent to talk about the general principles regarding the use of relevant knowledge to his best advantage and the function of peer groups (in this instance centred upon a fishing tackle shop) as information exchanges. A totally non-directive interview is impossible in that the researcher will bring to the encounter hunches, expectations of relevance, and an overall research concern which will inevitably influence the choice of those apparently casual, incidental comments selected for further exploration. As far as was possible, however, the interviews were self-generating in that new questions were asked in response to previous remarks. In the attempt to avoid a question and answer session the areas to which attention was directed were explored, wherever possible, though the clarification or elaboration of previous comments.

In any grounded theory research study it is inevitable that new categories and substantive themes emerge as the interview programme proceeds; indeed, this is the very *raison d'etre* of the method. One such category emerging in the study under discussion was that of 'attitude to learning'. The first mentions of distinctive attitudes towards their learning held by independent learners were subsumed under the general category of 'learning activity'. As the frequency and congruence of comment on this matter made it clear that independent learners shared a remarkably similar view of the fields of knowledge opening before them, so these attitudes were detached from the overall 'learning activity' category and awarded the status of a separate single category.

Similarly, the obvious significance attributed to competition participation by respondents in the early stages of the interview programme prompted the questioning of later subjects as to the extent of their competitive activities. The only hypothesis to receive formal testing was that proposed by Houle to the effect that no matter how intensely an individual may want to learn, he or she usually does not do so very actively if the marriage partner objects (Houle 1961, p. 43). Apart from this, all other generalizations, classifications and typologies used in the research, the selection of significant themes for further exploration, the organization of material into chapters, and the presentation of findings within these chapters, arose out of the researcher's continual re-reading and refinement of interview transcript comment over a period of three to four years.

SEVEN

Supporting Adult Learners in the Community: The Individual Mode

Principles of Adult Learning

Treatments of the psychology of adult learning vary in complexity and approach and this means that consensus on a set of first principles is hard to reach. Brundage and Mackreacher (1980), for example, offer thirty-six learning principles together with facilitating and planning implications resulting from these. A review of over 1,000 sources by Cross (1981) resulted in the development of a model of motivation to learning (the chain of response model) and a conceptual framework for understanding the characteristics of adult learners. This comprised two classes of variables — personal characteristics and situational characteristics. A representation of the much simpler, anecdotal approach to understanding adult learning is that of Jennifer Rogers who summarizes the main features of adult learning as follows:

> Adults learn best when they do not have to rely on memorizing, but can learn through activity at their own pace with material that seems relevant to their daily lives and uses their own experience. Finding 'right' answers at the first attempt seems important. Generous practice will reinforce new skills. Adults who have been out of touch with learning can often improve their educational performance dramatically if they are helped by 'learning to learn'.
>
> (Rogers 1979a, p. 59)

Simple formulations such as the above are known to most adult educators and are useful to new part-time teachers in the field. As Kidd acknowledged, however, the search for a generalized theory of adult learning 'may sound somewhat like a search for El Dorado, and no such magical or scientific theory is likely to arise or be formulated soon' (Kidd 1973, p. 188). In the most recent attempt to elaborate a set of first principles for adult education Darkenwald and Merriam (1982) proposed eight findings from learning process research to serve as a guide for educational practice. However, as they point out, most of the guidelines are as applicable to children as they are to adults and they need to be considered in conjunction with the unique qualities of adulthood — the adult's independent self-concept, ability to be a self-directed learner, and readiness and orientation to learning (Darkenwald and Merriam 1982, p. 112). All the aforementioned authors reveal a plurality of paradigms in their review of schools of adult learning theory. Darkenwald and Merriam (1982), for example, identify developmental themes, behaviourism, *gestalt* psychology, cognitive theorists and humanism as the chief theoretical approaches adopted in the investigation of adult learning theory. The theoretical paradigm underlying this writer's view of adult learning and teaching is the humanistic approach explored by writers such as Rogers, Maslow, Allport and Fromm.

The basic assumptions of humanistic philosophy and their relevance for adult education have been well summarized by Elias and Merriam (1980). Most readers will probably be aware of these assumptions so only a brief summation is necessary at this point. The chief twin tenets of humanist thought are:

1. Human beings are naturally beneficent, altruistic and good. It is the task of those determining the form of society to create environments which allow and encourage the expression of this innate goodness.
2. Human beings are truly free in the sense accepted by philosophers of free will. Humanists reject the thesis of determinism in which choices and individual acts are the inevitable and predictable result of antecedent causes (such as family upbringing or genetic inheritance). Human beings are faced with the moral necessity to make free choices in the conduct of their lives.

Adult educators who accept these propositions will not seek to impose their will on students in some kind of didactic, authoritarian manner; indeed, they may entirely reject the teacher – student division. The student is partially responsible for determining objectives and curricula whilst the educator becomes a facilitator of learning. The end result of such facilitation is the development of a fully realized person. Allport (1955) expresses this in terms of the individual's process of becoming and Maslow (1968) uses the term 'self-actualisation' to refer to this process of maturation. Carl Rogers (1969) has explored the connections between the humanistic practice of psycotherapy and the facilitation role of the educator. Rogers placed primary importance on the presence of independence in learning declaring that 'the only learning which significantly influences behaviour is self-discovered, self-appropriated learning' (Rogers 1969, p. 153). Such learning exhibits personal involvement, it is self-initiated, it pervades the behaviour and personality of the learner, and it is evaluated by the learner (p. 5).

The writer who has become most identified with the application of humanistic adult learning theory to the practice of adult education is Malcolm Knowles. The concept which is central to Knowles's thought is that of andragogy. Knowles borrowed the term in the 1960s from Yugoslavian adult educators and initially elaborated this in the first edition of *The Modern Practice of Adult Education* (1970) and *The Adult Learner: A Neglected Species* (1973). Andragogy is used by Knowles to refer to the mode of teaching and learning most appropriate to adults. This is contrasted to pedagogy, the mode most suitable to teaching and learning with children. Although Knowles initially formulated the distinction in dichotomous terms of andragogy *versus* pedagogy he now speaks of andragogy and pedagogy as points on a continuum of teaching and learning styles. In the years between the initial dichotomous formulation and his subsequent notion of a continuum the idea of andragogy has undergone critical analysis and conceptual refinement (McKenzie 1977, Elias 1979, Knudson 1980).

The concept of andragogy is premised on four assumptions regarding adult psychology which Knowles articulates as follows:

> 1) their self-concept moves from one of being a dependent personality toward being a self-directed human being; 2) they accumulate a growing reservoir of experience that becomes an increasingly rich resource for learning; 3) their readiness to learn becomes oriented increasingly to the developmental tasks of their social roles; and 4) their time perspective changes from one of postponed application of knowledge to immediacy of application, and accordingly, their orientation toward learning shifts from one of subject-centeredness to one of performance-centeredness. (Knowles 1980a, pp. 44–5)

Implications for practice arising from these assumptions as outlined by Knowles are legion. Of particular importance to our current concern — learning in the individual mode — are the following:

1. It is important to grant to the learner a degree of self-diagnosis with regard to learning needs.
2. The learner assumes partial responsibility for planning learning.
3. The teaching–learning transaction becomes the mutual responsbility of learners and teachers.
4. Evaluative procedures and criteria to judge successful performance become the partial responsibility of learners.
5. Experiential techniques of teaching are particularly suited to work with adult learners.

As we have seen in Chapters 5 and 6, and as the next chapter will also demonstrate, the implications identified above inform work with community groups as much as they do work with individuals. McCullough (1978) has explored the relevance of the concept of andragogy to work with community problem solving groups and we can see that these andragogical implications are applicable to groups as well as individuals. Knowles has neatly drawn together a number of practical injunctions and humanistic philosophical tenets which parallel the general principles inductively derived from the review of case studies in this book and from personal experience. Hence, we can say that there is a conceptual and practical link between working in a humanistic andragogical mode with self-directed learners and with community groups. In both instances the adult educator allows the learner(s) to set the agenda for learning, to prescribe needs, to define intermediate and terminal learning goals, and to evolve evaluative criteria. The educator assists where possible but does not attempt to remove from the adult(s) concerned the overall responsibility for the direction and execution of learning. The helping relationship is characterized by a respect for the integrity and independence of the adult(s) involved. Although the particular techniques appropriate to working with groups and with individuals may differ, the first principles involved are essentially the same.

Facilitating Learning — The Helping Relationship

It says much about the state of mind of some contemporary adult educators that the centrality of learner-centred education to the concept of andragogy is sometimes regarded as daringly innovative. As Srinivasan (1977) has pointed out, 'The basic philosophy and technique of counseling developed by psycotherapist Carl Rogers, for example, in the early 1940's show insights very similar to those which today are labelled revolutionary or at least highly innovative as if they were freshly discovered' (p. 7). In fact it is with Rogers that the notion of a 'helping relationship' in which learning or personal growth is 'facilitated' is most associated. Rogers defines a helping relationship as:

> A relationship in which at least one of the parties has the intent of promoting the growth, development, maturity, improved functioning, improving coping with life of the other. The other, in this sense, may be one individual or a group.
>
> (Rogers 1961, pp. 39–40)

This last point is important for, as Rogers acknowledges, the relationship of a community consultant to a community group exhibits these helping relationship aspects. The result of participation in such a relationship for the other (whether individual or group) will be an increased capacity for self-direction, self-initiated learning and creative adaptability. The help-ing relationship implements a general hypothesis which, to Rogers, 'offers exciting possibilities for the development of creative, adaptive, autonomous persons' (Rogers 1961, p. 38).

According to Brill (1973) a helping relationship is characterized by honesty and by acceptance so that the helper recognizes 'the uniqueness of the individual as a person who possesses the need and right to par-ticipate in making decisions about matters relating to his own welfare' (p. 48). It is also dynamic since all participate in, and change, the relation-ship. It is *not* a friendship, which is a relationship in which the needs of both participants are met more or less equally. Although elements of friendship may be involved Brill believes that friendship is separate from the 'purposeful, goal-directed, working interaction' (p. 51) which con-stitutes the helping relationship. Eisenberg and Delaney (1977) also specify characteristics of effective helping which include the ability to inspire trust, to recognize and eliminate self-defeating behaviour and to think systematically.

With regard to the relevance of the helping relationship to adult learn-ing in the community conducted in the individual mode, it is interesting to note that all Tough's major research into self-teaching, learning efforts, learning projects, and intentional change (reported in Chapter 3) has con-stantly recorded a desire on the part of independent adult learners for fur-ther assistance in conducting their learning. As Tough has maintained, however, there is a danger that 'educators will try to get their hands on the total range of adult learning and guide it, manage it, and stamp it with their seal of approval at the end' (Tough 1976, p. 71). I share this concern which I feel shares some similarities with the fears of those voluntaryists who are wary of the growth of mandatory continuing education discussed in Chapter 2. It is equally true, though, that professional adult educators dismiss the adult learning iceberg of informal, self-planned learning at their peril. After years of reflection on this matter Tough offers the follow-ing thoughts:

> I am often asked why we should become involved at all trying to facilitate a natural process that is already reasonably successful. 'We might mess things up and make them worse for people'. It is true that we could blunder in and insensitively do more harm than good. I would rather do nothing at all than harm a reasonably successful activity. If we thoroughly and accurately unders-tand the natural phenomenon before we try to be helpful, however, and if we try to fit into the person's natural process instead of making the person fit into ours, I believe we can be of great benefit. (Tough 1982, p. 76)

In an appendix to *The Adult's Learning Projects* (1979a) Tough discussed the relationship between helper and learner, distinguishing between help and control. He identified three variables the examination of which would help us understand the degrees of help and control in a relationship. These were (1) the actual influence of the helper; (2) the extent to which this influence is congruent with the amount desired by the helper; and (3) the extent to which the learner perceives a dysjunction between the amount of help received and the amount that the helper wanted to provide (p. 178). He believed that these variables could be used tentatively to prescribe certain characteristics of helpers and himself identified four clusters of characteristics of ideal helpers as follows. . .

(1) They are warm, loving, caring and accepting of the learners.
(2) They have high regard for learners' self-planning competencies and do not wish to trespass on these.
(3) They view themselves as participating in a dialogue between equals with learners.
(4) They are open to change and new experience and seek to learn from their helping activities. (Tough 1979, p. 183)

Tough also believed that it would be revealing and useful to study the motivations of those helpers most successful in assisting and encouraging learners. Other attempts to implement the helping relationship in the facilitation of independent learning are the *Guidelines for the Facilitation of Self-Directed Education* outlined by Knox (1974), the *Self-Directed Learning Readiness Scale* devised by Guglielmino (1978) and the *Policy Recommendations Related to Self-Directed Adult Learning* offered by Hiemstra (1980a). Penland (1981) has also discussed implications for the practitioner of research into self-directed adult learning.

The rest of this chapter discusses the kinds of support and assistance which can be given to the independent adult learner. Three broad types of help are identified: (1) the inculcation of the skills of mathetics, of learning how to learn; (2) the provision of assistance to learners in obtaining relevant resources, both human and material; and (3) the demonstration to the learner that experiential learning can be considered as significant, meaningful learning which can be as valid as that learning sponsored by formal higher and adult education institutions. These three forms of assistance are considered within a variety of settings (counselling services, learning exchanges, public libraries etc.) all of which deal with individual learners on a one-to-one basis.

Learning How to Learn — Mathetics and Learning Contracts

As Kasworm has noted, the current literature of lifelong learning emphasizes the significance of mathetics; that is, of 'learning how to learn' (Kasworm 1982). In both North America and Britain a number of writers have given considerable attention to the development of learning to learn skills among adult learners. Typical of such attention is the work of Smith (1982) and Gibbs (1981) and examples of courses designed to inculcate such skills have been given by Brookfield (1978a) Hutchinson (1979) and MacDonald (1982). Self-instruction manuals in the development of such skills are legion, some of the most respected being those of Knowles (1975), Rowntree (1976), Apps (1978) and Tough (1980).

Attempts to outline the development of learning to learn skills in informal settings have been made, in particular, by Tough, who has consistently identified the need to develop competencies in planning and executing learning among independent learners. In his essay on *Fostering Self-Planned Learning* (1979b) he declared that 'a large proportion of individuals are capable of dramatic improvement in their competence at self-planned learning' (p. 98). The competencies he identified as necessary to self-planned learning were those of choosing and performing appropriate preparatory steps, diagnosing what help is needed, and choosing and using helpful resources, until eventually the learner will be able to analyse the whole learning project. Tough also noted the importance of study skills in improving techniques of notetaking, fast reading, and memorizing. As he acknowledged, however, those books available on developing study skills tend to be for full-time students or adults returning to the higher education classroom.

At present, the models available within formal adult and higher education which have the greatest relevance for those working with adults in informal settings, are the experiments in non-traditional education which emphasize various learning contract arrangements. Berte (1975) defines learning contracts as 'written agreements or commitments between a student and a faculty member or faculty committee regarding a particular amount of student work and the institutional reward or credit for this work' (p. vii). These contracts specify learning goals, learning methods, evaluative measures and subsequent credit to be awarded and are usually deemed appropriate to higher education where the faculty wish to acknowledge the importance of developing self-education skills, to recognize a greater measure of equality between student and teacher, and to make each student's personal curriculum as grounded as possible in the student's immediate circumstances. The role of faculty becomes to 'assist the student with the development and clarification of learning goals, self-understanding, and self-direction' (p. 5). As MacKenzie *et al.* note, the learning contract 'is student-oriented and experience-based, in place of the traditional instruction-oriented and discipline-based system upon which higher education has traditionally depended' (Mackenzie *et al.* 1975, p. 365).

Three colleges which have documented their reliance on the learning contract method are the Empire State College (New York), the Minnesota Metropolitan State College and the Community College of Vermont

(*Mackenzie et al.* 1975). The masters degree programme in adult education at Saint Francis Xavier University in Nova Scotia has also based its operation on this approach. The Ed.D. in adult education through guided independent study (AEGIS) at Teachers College (Columbia University) places the negotiation of learning contracts at the centre of its activity. The verdict of one practitioner working within this mode at Empire State College is that learning contracts do nurture the development of learning to learn skills and that 'the student becomes more self-reliant, more disciplined, more independent. It seems highly plausible to assume that such a student remains a lifelong learner' (Worby 1979, p. 34). In the Sinclair Community 'College Without Walls' programme the use of learning contracts with adult students has led Cowperthwaite to conclude that such arrangements are highly individualized, related to the student's unique learning style, and serve to enhance the student's self-concept (Cowperthwaite 1980). Other documented examples of the use of learning contracts within adult and higher education are those of Percy & Ramsden (1980) in England and Neufeld and Barrows (1981) in Canada.

Learning contracts, like any other contractual form of arrangement, are framed on the assumption that the parties will behave in the manner specified in the contract. The problems of using learning contracts with adults who are learning in natural settings and who wish to maintain a sense of flexibility and personal control in their learning is that the contract can assume a fixed, reified status. Any learning behaviours other than those specified in the contract may come to be seen as 'irrelevant' or 'unproductive'. Tough has voiced this fear most cogently:

> My only concern with learning contracts is the possibility that they sometimes produce a feeling of being locked in. Even when the student is told that the contract can be renegotiated anytime, I worry that having the objectives and learning activities spelled out on paper will produce a reluctance to reconsider and modify them. (Tough 1982, p. 135)

Obviously, any attempt to use learning contracts with independent learners in order that their learning be purposeful and effective should include a waiver clause encouraging branching and divergence when appropriate. It is more than likely that anyone using this model — teacher – student arrangements within learning exchanges are probably the most common examples — will negotiate a contract in an atmosphere of relaxed flexibility.

Information, Counselling and Brokering Services

One of the most significant developments in the field of adult education over the last decade must be the growth of a host of information, advisory and counselling services for adults. Many of these do, of course, focus on career change and therefore have little directly to do with adults' pursuance of self-planned learning projects. As a past director of such a service (Brookfield 1977a), however, I know that a significant number of clients come seeking assistance with study problems, or with a desire to undertake self-planned learning projects but little experience or knowledge of this process. Those readers seeking information regarding the structures and principles of counselling for job change or entry to higher education are referred to the works of Di Silvestro (1981), Ironside and Jacobs (1977), Osborn, Charnley and Withnall (1981) and Goldberg (1980), all of which discuss the relevance of educational counselling to the development of self-directed learning capacities. Such a link is noted by Knox and Farmer (1977):

> The function of counseling and information services for adult learners consists of a wide variety of ways in which organizations that sponsor educational programs for adults provide information, advisement, guidance, and counseling to assist adults in selecting and planning their educative activities. (Knox and Farmer 1977, p. 392)

As articulated here, however, the rationale behind counselling and information giving appears to be to increase the institutional well-being of sponsoring agencies. This is particularly evident in Knox and Farmer's summary of information service functions where the authors declare that 'The purpose of such efforts is to increase the visibility and acceptance of the educational program and to encourage adults to participate' (Knox and Farmer 1977, p. 412). Such an orientation is not hard to understand given that most counsellors will be employees of providing agencies which will determine the success of counselling and information services by the criterion of increased enrolment. However, a number of services have developed in informal, community settings and while some of these are still oriented towards serving institutional ends (being established to reach disadvantaged groups) they are likely to exhibit a greater proportion of assistance to independent learners. Examples of community based (rather than institution based) counselling initiatives are the downtown 'drop-in' centres, education 'shops' or resource centres seen in a number of American, Canadian and British cities.

Of perhaps greater relevance to our discussion of supporting individual learning is the phenomenon of the educational brokering movement. Ironside (1981) identifies the brokerage model as one of four for community-based counselling. The strengths of the model are its independence, its voluntary nature, and the perception of clients and providers as being involved in a collaborative venture. However, educational brokerages generally suffer from funding problems, which, as Ironside points out, means that time and energy has to be spent looking for special project grants. This deflects staff from their main purpose and living with uncertain funding affects staff morale and discourages potential supporters.

Brokering agencies are often conceptualized as 'middlemen' or 'match-makers' between the range of educational institutions and resources, and the population of intending adult learners. Hefferman *et al.* (1976) define the missions of agencies as being to enable individuals to accomplish four objectives: (1) to define goals in their personal and working lives; (2) to set objectives for further education and training; (3) to select learning experiences to attain competencies and certification; and (4) to gain access to appropriate learning opportunities. These functions are performed through a range of procedures — information giving, counselling, referral, assessment, advocacy, and outreach. Unlike some other educational counselling and information services they are not seeking to maintain a particular educational empire by producing a regular stream of new recruits. Their perceived neutrality is their most valuable asset but also, as has already been acknowledged, their financial Achilles heel. Where an agency is seen as not serving the interests of a particular sector or institution then it has no special patronage upon which it can call in time of financial need. Most brokerage agencies established in the 1970s initially gained their funding from the Fund for the Improvement of Post-Secondary Education (FIPSE) project at the National Institute of Education. As Knowles points out, however, support for brokerage agencies was built into legislation in California, Massachussetts, New Jersey and Pennsylvania between 1974 and 1976 (Knowles 1980b, p. 39). Knowles also identifies perhaps the earliest example of this activity in the Educational Exchange of Greater Boston which has been providing educational information and counselling to adults since 1923.

In Massachussetts in 1974 a Regional Educational Opportunity Center (REOC) program was established in which five REOCs were charged with identifying disadvantaged adults who could benefit from education, with developing an inventory of educational opportunities in the regions, with assessing clients' needs and potential, and with matching clients with appropriate groups. In California attempts to introduce a bill establishing post secondary educational service centres foundered; however, the US Department of Labor has funded computer-based educational systems in Oregon, Alabama, Colorado, Massachussetts, Michigan, Minnesota, Ohio, Washington and Wisconsin. Finally, the Educational Information Centers (EIC) provisions of the federal Education Amendments of 1976 permit the EIC programme to make grants to states for the establishment of such centres. Powell noted that in 1979 forty four states and territories had submitted grant requests (Powell 1979).

The need for brokering agencies results from the diversity of educational opportunities in modern industrial society. Hefferman *et al.*

describe this as follows:

> At the one hand of the broker are several million Americans whose education has been interrupted by the responsibilities of early parenthood, economic pressures, social and cultural deprivation, frustration and low achievement in the classroom of their youth or by other impediments. At the broker's other hand is a vast and complex array of educational programs: private and public colleges and universities, community colleges, proprietary schools, correspondence schools, public schools' adult programs, employer sponsored training programs,and local state and federal agencies involved in education. (Hefferman *et al.* 1976, p. v)

The brokering agency serves as intermediary between educational opportunities and individual learners and uses information giving and counselling to achieve the matching of learners to opportunities. Recently, the goal of client empowerment — 'the promotion of clients' self-directedness, their sense of individual empowerment to make decisions and plans regarding their own lives and career goals' (NCEB 1981) — has become an important dimension of brokerage activities. Those clients who are empowered will become adept at using self-evaluation and planning techniques at critical stages in their lives. As the NCEB has acknowleged, however, the notion of teaching empowerment is almost a contradiction in terms. In words which recall the stream of humanistic psychology discussed earlier they assert that:

> Conditions can be set for individuals to recognise and to develop their own sense of personal agency, to become self-sustaining decision-makers and increasingly independent of institutional supports. (NCEB 1981, p. 4)

They do recognize, though, that personal and organizational factors can result in a supplicant relationship developing between client and broker. Staff who have developed pre-packaged exercises for career planning, and who are under pressure of large workloads, will be tempted to impose (in however beneficent a way) a preconceived solution onto a client's situation.

Public Libraries and Independent Learners

The community resource which is perhaps the most obvious target for adaptation as a medium through which to assist independent learners is the public library. As a survey of research into the functions of libraries points out, 'The public library is known to be more frequently visited by a wider range of people than adult education centres (and) it is viewed as a neutral area in society and therefore essential in any plan of lifelong learning' (Dadswell 1978, p. 7). In particular, 'Several writers agree that the public library is the type of institution which attracts and is more accessible to those people who would feel disadvantaged in relation to formal higher education or adult education institutions' (p. 7). The American Commission on Non-Traditional Study chose the public library for particular scrutiny and one of its chief recommendations was that the public library should be strengthened to become a far more powerful instrument for non-traditional education than is now the case (Gould 1973, p. 44). The same year the Russell report in Britain urged a greater co-operation between adult education centres and local libraries and stated that as well as being stock holders central libraries should be performing advisory functions (HMSO 1973; para 351) but it did not explore the role of individual library personnel in supporting independent learning.

It is in America that experiments in the facilitation of independent learning by public libraries have received the most serious implementation. In 1972 the Fund for Humanities organized a project to support ten public libraries in which the aim was to promote and offer a service of individualized information, advice, guidance and programming for would-be adult learners. This was the basis of the Adult Independent Learning Project in which eleven large public libraries established, as a pilot project, a Learners' Advisory Service 'for self-directed adults who wished to study independently, outside the traditional educational system' (Dale 1979, p. 85). Those participating were in Atlanta, Cleveland, Denver, Baltimore, Portland (Maine), Salt Lake City, St Louis, Tulsa, Woodbridge (New Jersey), and Worcester (Massachussetts). The learners' adviser/librarian was charged with two functions: firstly, to find out precisely what the learner wished to learn and secondly, to develop a plan to help the learner achieve that goal. During the period July 1975 to July 1976, 934 learners consulted the various services embarking on 969 learning projects. Thousands more contacted the service but did not fall into the category of individuals using the learners' adviser to determine needs and plan learning.

Dale (1980) interviewed sixteen of the learners' advisers on the differences between normal reference and readers' advisory work and learners' advisory work. Learners' advisory work was seen as entailing greater commitment and personal involvement and a systematic approach. It was felt important to be a good listener and to have a subject expertise in the learner's area of interest. The advisers were trained in the arts and techniques of programme planning and evaluation and in guiding learners in the use of study materials. The most useful training sessions were said to be those on adult psychology and interviewing techniques.

The lesson of this project is that there is a clear role within public libraries for one member of the library staff to be concerned with assisting novices in a particular area of interest (or, indeed, newcomers to library usage) to learn how to judge the level at which a book is written, how to choose the text best suited to their requirements, how to read books selectively so that information relevant to the task in hand is extracted, and how to find out what other, more suitable, texts are available. Depending on the staff available the adviser could be permanently on hand to deal immediately with referrals from the general 'Inquiries' desk. Alternatively, 'New Interests' surgeries could be advertised to be held at particular times or the inquirer could make an appointment to see the adviser at a later time. Were only one member of staff available to service several libraries, this person could become a peripatetic adviser (rather in the manner of local mobile libraries) agreeing to be at different libraries at the same time each week.

The aforementioned scheme would be expensive to implement since only a marginal increase in library usage would result from the efforts of the adviser. Other ways in which independent learners could be assisted are through the opening of academic libraries to the general public and through the library providing a home for brokering services. As Thresher (1979) points out, in terms of accessibility, neutrality, resources, mission, and financing, libraries are uniquely suited to serve as sites for brokering services. However, she does detect some resistance on the part of certain library staff to becoming involved in brokerage if such work entails any kind of counselling component. They feel uncomfortable with the amount of client self-revelation endemic to such work and all their formal training prepares them to deal with the organization, management and retrieval of materials and resources (books, microfiches, computers) rather than with uncertain and questing individuals. She does cite two examples of libraries in Cuyahoga (Ohio) and Forsyth County (N. Carolina) which use librarians as brokers, but acknowledges these instances are the exception.

A Chapter 4 affirmed, the term 'community' has become a fashionable catch-all term applied to a number of institutions and activities in the attempt to imbue these with an air of egalitarian, humanistic concern. The 'community library' is a concept which has lately received a considerable amount of attention in North America and Britain. To Passow (1973) the community library is one which exhibits an explicit pedagogic dimension in its orientations. Hence, these institutions are 'centers in which considerable teaching and learning takes place, of both a formal and informal nature' (p. 12) and they 'contribute to facilitating the means by which various individuals would become involved in the education and development of others' (p. 14). In Britain the role of libraries in amassing and disseminating community information has been explored by the library association in a consultative document. Community information services are defined as:

> services which assist individuals and groups with daily problem-solving and with participation in the democratic process. The service concentrates on the needs of those who do not have ready access to other sources of assistance and on the most important problems that people have to face, problems to do with their homes, their jobs and their rights. (Library Association 1980, p. 12)

Provision of such services can be accomplished in two ways, both of which are politically contentious. Libraries can accommodate an advisory centre staffed by librarians and others within their walls which would deal directly with community members and their problems. Alternatively, they can develop, as a second line resource, a specialized data bank for community workers and social workers who deal with such problems. Because of the advocacy role implicit in the former of these options, and the reticence noted by Thresher on the part of some librarians to undertake this, it is most likely that moves in this direction will concentrate on the assembling of community information resource banks for use by community workers and the helping professions.

Penland and Shirk (1981) have offered three indicators which can be applied to determine the degree of involvement in the community exhibited by library staff: (1) the number of outreach programmes they sponsor; (2) the degree of access which exists to information and referral services; (3) the existence of brokering and advisory services in libraries. In a survey conducted by Erteschik of projects funded under the US Library Services and Construction Act, worthwhile initiatives in the facilitation of independent learning by libraries were identified in Nassau County (New York) Philadelphia, St Clair Shores (Michigan) and Nashville (Erteschik 1977). Recently, in a major report on the future of adult and continuing education in the UK, libraries were seen as the natural sites for a proposed network of centres of independent learning. Such centres would be open to the general public as well as to registered full-time or part-time students and would prepare independent learning materials as well as performing a counselling role (Advisory Council for Adult & Continuing Education 1982, p. 121).

Learning Exchanges

A less expensive way in which libraries could assist independent learners would be for them to take responsibility for developing local skill exchanges. In these exchanges novices who wished to learn a particular skill would be able to contact people who had developed that skill and who would be prepared to instruct others in its acquisition. It may even be the case that the library need offer only accommodation for such a venture and that the compilation of a directory of skill models and the matching of clients and teachers would be undertaken by a volunteer. Libraries already serve something of this function through their provision of a well-placed bulletin board on which local societies can advertise forthcoming events and the address of their society secretary. Hence, one way for a newcomer to a field of interest to come to terms with that field is to contact the local enthusiasts' society.

There will, however, be individuals who feel unsure about approaching a local society and who simply prefer to consult a single person who is an acknowledged expert in the field, and who is prepared to assist interested beginners. There would be less danger of the novice losing interest because of the difficulty of understanding the 'grammar' of the new activity. The directory of skill models — persons prepared to instruct others in the acquisition of certain skills — could be sited in the library and take the form of a card index or loose leaf folder containing the names and addresses of persons willing to assist beginners in their particular specialisms. Users of the exchange would simply be handed the directory or, if the staff were available, could discuss their request with the librarian. This arrangement would then satisfy Illich's requirement that 'the operation of a skill exchange would depend on the existence of agencies which would facilitate the development of directory information and assure its free and inexpensive use' (Illich 1971, p. 92–3).

There is, however, a cautionary note to be expressed with regard to learners' use of learning exchanges. If an enthusiast were to place himself or herself entirely in the hands of an expert and to attribute to the expert the total responsibility for developing the learner's skills, this would contradict the basic requirement of independent learning, that the overall planning and execution of learning be the responsibility of the learner. To use a skill exchange in the context of an independent learning project the learner would have to enter the contract with the expert with a clear idea of the limited capabilities the learner wished to develop and a sense of their place within the overall project. To such an independent learner the danger of using a skill exchange would be that of developing a relationship of total dependence on the expert who would then be charged with setting the learner's goals and evaluating progress.

Concurrent with Illich's advocacy of skill exchanges is his notion of peer matching which lets 'each person specify the activity for which he sought a peer' (Illich 1971, p. 93). This idea is closer to the spirit of independent learning than that of skill exchanges in that the participants are, by definition, of equal status. In fact, as my own research (Brookfield 1980a) recorded, independent learners often need no formally-established peer-matching service, they merely contact their local enthusiasts' society. Illich himself acknowledges that 'a good chess player is always glad to find a

close match and one novice to find another. Clubs serve their purpose'
(Illich 1971, p. 94). Any peer-matching service established under the aegis
of a body such as the local public library, therefore, would be directed at
those individuals for whom no appropriate society existed. The librarian
would record the details of enthusiasts who wished to meet others engaged
in their field of activity and would make this information available to interested enquirers. These enthusiasts could, of course, use the 'small-ad'
columns of local papers or national enthusiasts' magazines to advertise for
like-minded partners. The peer-matching service of a local library would,
however, be permanently on offer and therefore more likely to result in
a successful contact than a 'one off' advertisement in the local or national
press, particularly if a beginner was trying to contact other novices.

As is the case with the skill exchange, the peer-matching service would
involve minimal expense, merely occasional publicity designed to attract
participants into the service and to advertise its existence locally, and
someone to update the directory and hand it over to interested inquirers.
In both skill exchanges and peer-matching services the spirit of independent learning is respected in that the responsibility for the initiation and
execution of the learning activity rests with the individual learner. There
is no attempt to absorb the learner into the formal education system and
no establishment of a scheme of institutional accreditation. Assistance is
available but, when requested, offered without entailing obligations on
the part of the learner who remains free to reject any skill model offered
and to withdraw from a peer-matching relationship.

In the last decade a number of skill exchanges have been established
and some of these have documented their development. The 1981 *National
Directory of Free Universities and Learning Networks* lists 251 organizations
which in 1980 offered 20,000 classes and referrals to over 300,000 participants (Free University Network 1981). Knox (1974) believes that the
learning exchange model has considerable utility for the development of
professional expertise and that it 'provides an example of a way in which
a professional can develop and utilize an informal interpersonal network
of peers as a vehicle for continuing his education' (p. 104). In his discussion of the relevance of learning exchanges for continuing professional
education he has identified twelve features of such exchanges which can
be used to facilitate self-directed education for health professionals.

The most famous learning exchange, and the one which has served as
a model to guide the efforts of others in this field, is The Learning
Exchange (TLE) founded in Evanston, Illinois in May 1971. Its co-
founder, Denis Detzel, had spent some time during the previous winter
at the Center for Intercultural Documentation (CIDOC) in Cuernavaca,
Mexico. The centre was founded by Illich and regular visitors included
Paul Goodman and Everett Reimer. In an early report on TLE Squires
(1974) recorded that 13,000 people had used the exchange in a period of

thirty-two months to explore over 1,800 different subject areas. By 1977 some 30,000 participants had registered to learn in over 3,100 topics (Lewis & Kinishi 1977). The *modus operandi* of TLE can be summarized as follows:

> If, for example, someone wants to learn Spanish, he or she can call or write The Learning Exchange and register that interest. The Learning Exchange then provides this person with the names and phone numbers of previous callers who have indicated an interest in teaching Spanish. That person then calls those potential Spanish teachers and works out whatever arrangements are mutually convenient and satisfactory... if a person is interested in finding a tennis partner, discussing a book, or in sharing any particular interest, that person can register as an 'interest-match'. The Learning Exchange will provide names and phone numbers of others who have similar interests and want to share them. (Squires 1974, p. 98)

Arrangements regarding costs and teaching/learning styles are the responsibility of teacher and learner, not the exchange co-ordinators. The rationale behind The Learning Exchange is that any community contains both potential skilled teachers and learners who wish to acquire the skills possessed by these teachers, and that an intermediary mechanism is needed to bring these parties together. In this respect it is similar to the brokerage model, although it exists independently of formal higher education and adult education opportunities.

The major report on the Evanston Exchange states the mission of the organization to be:

1. To develop a mechanism to assemble, order and disseminate information on educational/recreational resources and needs in Chicago.
2. To nurture the spirit of self-directed teaching and learning and to encourage interest sharing.
3. To assist private and public institutions to develop their educational/recreational programmes.
4. To become a self-financing organization.
5. To offer a model for the community utilization of educational/recreational resources which can be replicated in other settings. (Lewis & Kinishi 1977, p. 2)

Lewis & Kinishi claim that over 90 per cent of learners have been pleased with the instruction they have received and, interestingly, they record that almost one-third of teaching-learning arrangements are either free or undertaken according to barter principles. An example of the latter would be someone being taught to play the piano and, in turn, teaching the piano instructor to speak Spanish. From 1979 a membership fee was charged for registration in the exchange. Recent developments at TLE have included a Library Project to explore co-operation between the exchange and Chicago area public libraries and a Fund for the Improvement of Post-Secondary Education (FIPSE) supported project in the dissemination of information on the TLE model to other networks around the country. In interviews with personnel in three library affiliated networks in Corona (New York), Uniondale (New York), and Tallahassee, McElroy (1980) has recorded how a connection with the Evanston TLE has served to provide ongoing support to these developing initiatives. The names of these three services — 'Each One – Teach One', 'The Learning Connection', and 'The People Index' — give an idea of the principles of mutuality and sharing of expertise underlying their operation. McElroy offers her conclusions on the viability of libraries as sponsoring agencies for learning exchanges as follows:

> Public libraries, those respected institutions symbolizing intellectual freedom and free access to tools for living, have much to offer to and much to gain from this spirit of cooperation. An arrangement between two organizations — a public library and a free university or learning network — can be the beginning of a total community effort in support of self-directed learning. (McElroy 1980, p. 34)

Canadian and British examples of learning exchanges are harder to find. The 1981 *Directory* lists only the Toronto Skills Exchange under Canadian entries. In Britain the Centerprise project in East London has developed a skills exchange as part of its voluntary educational work. Rogers summarizes their efforts thus:

> In February 1973, two young Centerprise workers announced a learning exchange through local newsletters, churches and voluntary organizations, drawing, in a few months, over a thousand responses. Some were tutors, most were would-be learners wanting to know how to lay bricks, play the guitar, read and write, join a pensioners' sewing circle, clip poodles and much else. Except for musicians, tutors did not want to be paid. (Rogers 1979b, p. 136)

In their attempt to explore new ways of involving working class adults in adult education the workers in the Southampton New Communities Project encouraged the development of a skill and interest matching service (Fordham *et al.* 1979). They provided a board entitled 'What Would You Like To Do?' inviting people to record their interests. The purpose of the board was, in the words of workers in the project:

> simply to put people with similar interests and skills in touch with each other so that they might encourage each other, take responsibility for their own learning, and in the long term enable the team to determine the resources and approaches necessary to make this possible. (Fordham *et al.* 1979, p. 42)

About 100 participants were involved in the scheme but, as the authors of the report on its operation point out, the formal adult education sector experienced difficulty in responding to such informal initiatives. Groups were unable to arrange accommodation for their meetings in adult education premises and the workers in the project declared that structural changes in the provision of accommodation and services by formal adult education were necessary if the sum total of informal adult learning in the community were to be increased and its quality enhanced.

Experiential Learning

In Chapter 1 of this book I outlined the varieties and constituent features of that learning often termed 'experiential'. It is now appropriate to look at some of the ways in which the formal adult education and higher education system has attempted to grant credibility (and sometimes credit) to life experience. Tough (1982) sees the recognition of experiential learning as one of the forces leading to a reduction of professional control in education and there is no doubt that the major assumption underlying recognition of experiential learning — that purposeful learning of a high level can occur in the absence of accredited teachers or formal education institutions — has radical implications for the notion of professionalism. As the discussion in Chapter 1 indicated, there has developed a considerable debate over the merits of such learning and the extent to which it can be considered valid and comparable to learning occurring under the supervision of professional educators. Charges have been levelled against the recognition of experiential learning and its detractors have alleged that credentialling this learning constitutes a form of academic fraud. There is no doubt, however, that an awareness of the importance of experiential or 'prior' learning is now displayed by many institutions of higher education when considering the admission of adult students to degree courses. In Lipsett and Avakian's words 'Most colleges have already given a positive answer to the question "Should credit be granted for out-of-class learning?"' (Lipsett & Avakian 1981, p. 19). Their attention is now focused on ways of granting credit for such learning. These authors note, for example, that of Empire State College's 6,000 graduates, over 90 per cent have received some credit for experiential learning.

Gross (1977) has pointed out that it is the state of New York that has pioneered opportunities for adults to obtain credit towards college degrees through tests and other accreditation procedures. The Regents External Degree examinations in New York state test the level of preparation of candidates in various specialities and the College Level Examination Program (CLEP) awards scores for credit by examination which can be used to obtain varying amounts of credit remission at colleges and universities across the country. Under the CLEP programme in 1976–7, 385,000 tests were given with over 145,000 to servicemen and women through the Defense Activity For Nontraditional Support. The Regents Credit Bank will evaluate scores earned on various proficiency tests or courses taken in the military or business. This assessment can then be shown when applying for jobs or educational institutions. As I write this a recent Council for the Advancement of Experiential Learning (CAEL) newsletter records that the National League of Nursing has accredited the New York Regents External B.Sc. degree in Nursing (CAEL 1982). The degree can be awarded entirely by examination and since typical candidates are thirty-five years old and working full time this is probably the only way to obtain a degree while fulfilling domestic and occupational commitments. The rationale behind the performance examination mode is explained thus:

> These nursing examinations test different dimensions of nursing abilities and collectively they represent the repertoire of nursing competencies expected of new baccalaureate graduates in professional practice. The ability of candidates to meet the specified critical behaviours required by these documents that their learning is equivalent to that of campus-based students. (CAEL 1982, p. 6)

Jacobson (1976) has argued that the work of community action groups and neighbourhood study groups can involve research and writing which is at a level comparable to a graduate seminar. The major problem with such an operation is, of course, that in analysing outcomes of work undertaken in a group mode, the contribution of individual participants is obscured. An applicant for credit remission for work with neighbourhood community groups will have to know how to present evidence of his or her unique contribution and demonstrable achievements. In this discussion of experiential learning it might be interesting to look in more detail at some attempts to grapple with the administrative and educational problems caused by accrediting life experience.

The preparation of a portfolio of experiential learning is the technique used most frequently as a means of assessing the quality and extent of such learning. Rather like the preparation of dissertation proposals, or individual learning contracts, portfolio preparation is time consuming and an intellectually challenging exercise in itself. Students frequently fall into the trap of describing what they did — 'I worked on a voluntary community newspaper for six months' — rather than detailing what they have learned. A second problem is the inability of students to present a well-written articulate portfolio. To expect adults whose only writing for several years has been in the form of personal letters suddenly to be able to prepare an itemized, coherent testimony to their learning experiences framed in elegant prose is highly unrealistic. Thirdly, applicants for credit

have to relate their learning to syllabuses and degree objectives: adults unfamiliar with academic curricula will find it difficult to relate what may
appear to them to be mundane everyday experiences to the language of
formal academic disciplines.

An example from my own research (Brookfield 1980a) may illustrate
this last point. This was an apiarist who had kept bees for fifty years.
During my interview with him he revealed that he had devised and implemented a sophisticated experimental procedure whilst investigating effective techniques of beekeeping. He had access to a number of hives (some
his own, some of friends) and had applied the classic experimental technique of recording the performance of control and experimental groups.
In experimental investigations each lasting a five-year cycle he observed
how those hives in which he had introduced some variant compared to
those hives run on traditional lines. The amount of honey produced constituted an easily identifiable and verifiable index of evidence regarding
the success of different methods. The experience of this individual, as
relayed orally to a local professor of horticulture, subsequently formed the
basis of a book on bee swarm management which drew orders from
around the world. This was an individual, then, who had engaged in
intellectual inquiry of a high order and, moreover, who had devised the
format of such inquiry himself. He had exemplified the principles of
disciplined, self-directed inquiry of the type often said to epitomize, or to
be the end result of, higher education. Because of this individual's
problems in expressing himself in writing he would have found it very
difficult to prepare a portfolio specifying his accomplishments in the
required academic terminology. As it happened, this individual expressed
no desire to enter higher education or to gain recognition from the
academic world for his achievements. Had he wished so to do he would
have had to spend some considerable time acquiring basic literacy skills
prior to preparing and submitting a portfolio.

Techniques for assessing the educational value of experiential learning
have been discussed by Meyer (1975) and the CAEL have published two
guidebooks for faculty working in this field by Sharon (1977) and
Willingham (1977). It might be useful to conclude this discussion of experiential learning by examining in more detail one institution which has
attempted to provide adults with the opportunity to translate their relevant life-long educational experiences into college credits and degrees.
This institution, first visited by the author in Spring 1982, is Edison State
College, Trenton, New Jersey. The college is one of the nine state colleges
and was founded in 1972 by the New Jersey State Board of Higher Education. It was named after Thomas Edison whose knowledge of sciences and
engineering was obtained largely through study independent of formal
education institutions. The college has no teaching faculty and offers no
instruction and its students meet degree requirements through college

equivalency examinations devised and approved by the college, through individual assessment of college level learning by consultants engaged for that purpose, or through the transfer of credits earned at other educational institutions. Students can also use the college as a 'Credit Bank' so that all credits earned by the three aforementioned methods are entered on an Edison College transcript. These can then be transferred to another institution to complete degree objectives.

The mission of the college is 'to verify and to credential college-level learning, without regard to where or how that learning was acquired. It will grant credits, leading toward a degree, for any learning of college calibre and scope that can be verified through examinations or assessment or documented by official transcripts from other accredited colleges or universities' (Thomas A. Edison State College 1981a, p. 13). To accomplish this mission the college performs four functions:

1. It provides free academic counselling for any adults interested in pursuing a college education.
2. It awards its own baccalaureate and associate degrees.
3. It grants college credits to be used at Edison or transferred to another college.
4. It acts as a catalyst for adult education by awarding credits for in-service training courses sponsored by employers, labour organizations and government agencies.

Of particular interest to our discussion of experiential learning is the individual assessment option adopted by Edison College to award credit for previously non-certificated learning. The student who chooses this option prepares, with the assistance of an academic counsellor or programme adviser, a portfolio outlining the learning experiences and translating these into college level outcomes. This portfolio is then submitted to faculty assesors selected by the college. Credit may be awarded by these assessors on the portfolio itself or they may ask for more direct evidence of learning. In this case an oral examination, written examination, student performance or inspection of student products may be used. The college issues a guide to students entitled *Portfolio Assessment: the Student Handbook* (Thomas A. Edison State College 1981b) which is written to assist students in relating prior learning to college courses, in determining assessment objectives and in portfolio compilation. There is no limit to the amount of credit which can be earned through individual assessment, other than that of the student's own life experience.

An example of the use of individual assessment is given in the 1980–81 college catalogue. This is of a woman who had helped to found a theatre group and had been involved as an actress, stage manager, director and producer. In addition, she had been a Sunday school teacher. By presenting in her portfolio evidence of her theatre achievements and in an oral examination of her religious education she obtained twenty-five credits towards an Associate Arts degree.

A second example of an initiative in the field of experiential learning is the Community College of Vermont. This has no paid full-time faculty nor any permanent premises. Experts from the community are hired by the college to teach adults in churches, village halls, libraries, schools and other settings. The college specifies three areas of competencies — social, physical and intellectual — containing twenty goals. Students contract to achieve fifteen of these goals and local review committees award credit as appropriate. The contract comprises five elements; (1) a written account of the student's history and aspirations; (2) an outline of goals achieved;(3) a list of learning experiences; (4) evidence confirming these experiences; and (5) a portfolio containing examples of work (Daloz 1975). In an excellent review of innovatory local programmes in the US, Valley (1979) documents a number of external degree programmes which integrate procedures for the assessment of experiential learning. In the Twin Cities area a Metropolitan Assessment Service estimates learners' skills prior to enrolment in six local community colleges. A Life Experience Center at Edinboro State College awards college credit for naturalistic learning. The East Central College Consortium of seven liberal arts colleges in Ohio, West Virginia and Pennsylvania includes an assessment of experiential learning in its external degree programme.

As a postscript to this discussion of experiential learning it is perhaps worth noting that emphasizing a well-meaning recognition of the academic worth of such learning does carry within it certain dangers. The one which most worries this writer is that of coming to view experiential learning solely in terms of the credits such learning could be awarded were it to be transferred to an academic setting. It is not that great a step from acknowledging the academic credibility of some experiential learning to seeking always to conceptualize it in terms of its college course equivalency. This, of course, denies the innate validity and uniqueness of the learning. There is also the problem that college assessment of experiential learning tends not to be done experientially. The onus is on the student to use academic terminology in transferring experience into demonstrable learning outcomes that would be achieved in a college course. It could be argued that a true appreciation of experiential learning can only come when assessors themselves have experienced the inner tensions, conflicting pressures and contextual nuances of the student's learning situation. Translating an experience into formal academic terminology for the purposes of a portfolio submission does not convey the richness and subtleties of that experience. The whole tradition discussed in the previous chapter of qualitative research, of anthropological style participant observation, is one which recognizes the need to experience situations from a perspective inside those events. Only if assessors experience something of the boredom, frustration, complexity, and physical and intellectual challenge of, say, taking a group of urban teenagers on probation for an adventure weekend in the mountains, can the achievements of the student be fully appreciated. If we admit the validity of the affective dimension of learning and the importance of developing interpersonal skills, then we must be wary of assessing the educational worth of experience wholly by college course based cognitive criteria.

EIGHT

Supporting Adult Learners in the Community: The Group Mode

An axiomatic proposition of this book is that adult learning does not occur in a state of splendid isolation. Even those initiatives discussed under the individual mode in the previous chapter cannot be viewed as atomistic enterprises in which the learner acquires knowledge or skill in a social and intellectual vacuum. To recap my comments in Chapter 2, independent learning is characterized by two dimensions of independence: independence of institutional recognition and independence of externally imposed instructional control over the content and conduct of learning. Such independence does not imply an absence of peer support or expert assistance and the research documented in Chapter 3 illustrates the reliance of independent learners on various human resources.

In the present chapter I intend to review the attemps of some adult educators to support the learning occurring in group settings. There is an important difference between these initiatives and the three community development enterprises in the United States, Canada and Britain discussed in Chapter 5. In the Highlander, Antigonish and EPA projects educational activity was orientated towards, and grounded in, the advancement of various disadvantaged groups. Education was consciously applied as the handmaiden of community development and the success of the three initiatives discussed was estimated in terms of social improvement. Such improvement was viewed in terms of economic change and political reform as well as in an extension of educational opportunity. The case studies presented in the present chapter do not have such an overtly strong developmental component to them. They fall more within what might be called a liberal educational mode (as against a liberating mode, to continue the distinction made in Chapter 4) in which the pursuit of knowledge for purposes of enhanced aesthetic appreciation, increased intellectual awareness or heightened analytical power, is the avowed rationale of the enterpise. As we shall see, however, such activities tend to exhibit a redoubtable (and to some annoying) doggedness in generating wider social and political implications.

Social Change as an Educational Aim

Before reviewing some of these initiatives it is important that we examine some of the most frequently discussed issues concerning community roles for educators *qua* educators. There is a real debate concerning methods and content on this theme, particularly the extent to which educators can or should become agents of social change. Paterson (1973), for example, rejects what he calls the 'Dr Finlay' syndrome in which professional practice is widened to include the eradication of social ills. He feels the reasoning behind such practice is erroneous and that:

> It is up to society (and not the members of any professional group) to determine whether its institutions and practices are just or unjust: it is also up to society to determine whether the responsbilities of a particular professional group are being discharged adequately or inadequately. (Paterson 1973, p. 358)

Paterson declares that adult educators 'must work within existing society, and must accept its social (and educational) priorities' (ibid.). He feels that 'if adult education were to become harnessed to the promotion of a set of social causes, then it would become servile to those causes' (ibid.). Finally, in this challenging analysis, Paterson concludes that social change is a discussion topic for 'unbiased education' and not a political aim for the adult educator.

The orientation underlying Paterson's views is one of an holistic consensus in which 'society' is reified into an entity which hovers above, and exists separately from, the agglomeration of individuals it is ordering. There is an assumption that 'society' exerts a paternal benevolence in determining standards of conduct above and beyond the personal standards applied by individuals. The perspective is one which is very much that of the liberal community education model identified in Chapter 4 in which society is viewed as an harmonious whole. This neglects the fact that societies are generally composed of individuals and groups, many of which hold values, interests and aspirations which are contradictory. Stein (1964) has documented the eclipse of the *gemeinschaft*, consensus community and western societies might now be better described in pluralistic terms; that is, as comprised of an amalgam of diverse pressure groups, ethnic sub-cultures, social classes and interest groups of every conceivable function. Wherever serious dissension surrounds the criteria which are to be applied concerning the measure of social justice in a society, or the degree to which professional responsibilities are being adequately discharged, then the holistic consensus perspective must be considered seriously flawed.

The argument that educators must accept the social and educational priorities of society and that this entails the rejection of promoting a set of social causes appears to contain a logical fallacy. For, if educators do accept the social and educational priorities of a society (or to be more accurate of a particular ascendant group within that society) then they are supporting the set of social causes enshrined in those social and educational priorities. Just because priorities are held by a dominant group, or by a majority of individuals, does not defuse these priorities of any prescriptive elements. In working within existing society (to use Paterson's phrase) one is implicitly accepting the rightness of the ruling priorities and predominant values. The value choice signified by such an act of acceptance may not be as immediately apparent or publicly visible as that signified by adhering to a less popular or more radical set of priorities and values. Nonetheless, it represents just as much of a moral and ethical preference. Adherence to existing norms does not remove from such adherence the value choice contained therein.

In his article (Paterson 1973) and book (Paterson 1979), Paterson outlines the central tenets of his thesis and defends his ideas with commendable vigour. He advances arguments which are contentious and which, in the Freirean era, are unfashionable in the eyes of many younger practitioners and theorists. British adult educators are particularly fortunate to have two analytic philosphers (Lawson and Paterson) who have devoted their considerable intellectual talents to challenging the activist oriented model of adult education as represented by Freire and Lovett. Given that most writers in the adult education field simply refuse to acknowledge the value choices underlying professional preference Lawson and Paterson have done a service to the field by bringing the discussion of values to the forefront of intellectual inquiry. Indeed, the *ADULT EDUCATION* journal of the United Kingdom seems to confront contentious value and political questions with greater regularity than its American counterpart. Hence, we have critiques of social change as an educational aim (Paterson 1973), critiques of the concept of community education (Lawson 1977), exhortations to 'put politics back on the agenda' (Simey 1976) and 'calls to attack' against morally neutral practice (Ruddock 1974). In her piece Margaret Simey laments that 'The life blood of many a community movement is cut off at source by the embargo on the very moral and political purpose which could activate it' (Simey 1976, p. 226). Ruddock, too, calls for 'a sustained attack on educational provision (including much of adult education) which shows itself to be indifferent to social values' (Ruddock 1974, p. 375). He declares that 'The failure to debate this issue in concrete terms has long been a scandal' (p. 375) and advocates a scale of ethical principles for teachers and a code of good practice for educational managers.

Community Roles for Adult Educators

Role analyses of the activities of community adult educators have been undertaken by Jackson (1970, 1971), Davie (1980) and by those who have advanced the concept of the adult educator as animateur (Kidd 1971, Blondin 1971). Jackson is chiefly concerned with the contrasts in roles as adult educators work with professional groups and with informal volunteer groups. Like Lovett (a one-time colleague of Jackson) the 'most substantial challenge' facing adult education is seen as that of 'helping community groups whose members have received little formal education and have restricted opportunities to develop social, organisational and intellectual skills in their working lives' (Jackson 1970, p. 167). However, Jackson is also aware that more formal community groups concerned with social and welfare objectives are a clientele for the educator who works within a developmental framework. Because such groups tend to be led by professionals — teachers, youth workers, social workers and clergy — a different approach is needed from that adopted with informal, working class groups.

Jackson describes two approaches he has used in working with these more formal groups framed within a 'training the trainers' mode. The first is to hold seminars and lectures for groups composed of professional community workers, professionals in related fields (clergy, youth workers etc.) and volunteers. These seminars would develop a theory of practice in community development work and demonstrate the relevance of community development concepts through illustration with actual situations. A second approach is to arrange day conferences at which local government officers and political leaders would meet tenants' associations, community organizations and less formal 'street groups' to explore ways in which public participation in planning could be increased.

In the United States, Davie (1980) has recently identified four roles occupied by adult educators working in a developmental context. These four roles are those of analyst, investigator, organizer and agent. The analyst is concerned with studying community structures and problems in an impartial, unbiased manner. Such individuals would typically be university professors or consultants. The investigator also studies communities but undertakes this in collaboration with community members. The organizer works with disadvantaged and minority groups in furthering their interests through a process of consciousness raising and the inculcation of political skills. Finally, the agent is one who works for an organization such as the Cooperative Extension Service who is concerned to transmit information to community members on behalf of that organization.

This usage of the term 'agent' — as one who supports the interests and functioning of a corporate welfare agency — is in marked contrast to that attached to the term 'change agent'. The change agent is usually conceived of as more concerned with challenging institutional procedures and rationales than with serving their interests. Fessler (1976), however, also uses the more conservative definition of agent in his guidebook to facilitating community change. He sees social change as resulting primarily from institutional resolve declaring that most of the change efforts in our society are initiated by the paid employees of state and federal agencies and of some voluntary associations (p. 31).

A more radical role for community adult educators is that enshrined in the notion of the animateur. Jackson describes this as a professional role, midway between that of administrator and teacher (Jackson 1970, p. 174) and acknowledges its origins in French and French Canadian adult education. In France the notion of socio-cultural animation is at the heart of, and has now become a synonym for, the *éducation populaire* movement. *Education populaire* is a voluntary educational movement oriented towards individual fulfilment, community cooperation and a sense of civic responsibility. Titmus summarizes the process of animation as follows...

> Animation is not the transfer of knowledge from the animateur to the animated. It is essentially a process of learning by mutual interaction in which the animateur acts as a catalyst, a non-directive stimulant, a resource person in a democratic process. Indeed, socio-cultural animation, it is widely agreed, is self and group development by democratic means to a democratic end, although there is wide disagreement about the sense of democracy and democratic. (Titmus 1981, p. 141)

With regard to its educational dimensions, Titmus contrasts the animateur model of educational processes in which 'the emphasis is laid on the educational value of the experience itself, on the acquistion of learning skills, on personality development, rather than mastery of a body of information' (p. 143) with the acquisition of a predetermined body of knowledge characteristic of most adult education classes. Titmus records that socio-cultural animation has not realized the high hopes placed upon it by French educators, particularly with regard to its failure to transform society or result in a marked increase in the participation in formal education of the socially and educationally underprivileged.

Four aspects of the role of the animateur are identified by Kidd (1971, p. 148)...

1. To encourage a sense of self-control in individual development and community improvement.

2. To assist in developing skills of community action and education.
3. To nurture leadership abilities.
4. To clarify and evolve value judgements regarding personal growth and community change.

The element of community intervention apparent in Kidd's classification is also emphasized by Blondin (1971) who views the overall task of the animateur as one of social intervention to assist community groups to achieve commonly defined goals. Out of this activity 'the process of animation gives rise to a process of self-education, the essence of which is a heightening of the capacity for self-determination' (p. 160). A cherished ambition of every animateur is 'to achieve self-determination in a group of people, so that it becomes autonomous, that is, freed from its besetting automatisms and determinisms. Autonomy means that ability to make decisions and choices freely and to take the consequences' (ibid.). The workers in the New Communities Project on a public housing estate in England articulate precisely the sense of autonomy expressed by Blondin when describing the overall aim of their work. Their commitment was 'to increasing the independence, freedom and autonomy of people with regard to both the objective and subjective features of their environment' (Fordham *et al.* 1979, p. 193). This involved assisting individuals to realize that the most effective learning resources in a community were the human resources of individuals and networks of people.

The roles proposed for animateurs by Blondin are:

1. The animateur as an agent of rationalization: this is the process of developing skills of logical analysis, goal setting and evaluation as an aid to community development.
2. The animateur as an agent of socialization: to promote a sense of emotional and rational cohesion among group members.
3. The animateur as a channel of information: to assist in identifying relevant information of use to the group.
4. The animateur as an instigator of participation among group members.

(Blondin 1971, pp. 161–3)

Blondin's rationale underlying the animation process is a somewhat unusual one in that he sees the process as part of what he calls the 'war on poverty'. The poverty referred to is not material, however, but more a state of personal and collective powerlessness. Hence, the poor person is someone who cannot influence decisions and whose world view is not reflected in dominant social norms. This state of poverty exhibits strong elements of political apathy redolent of Oscar Lewis's 'culture of poverty' (Lewis 1961) in which those inhabiting such a culture transmit a stoical resignation regarding the impossibility of change to succeeding generations. The notion of constructive social action is alien to those in the culture of poverty and for Blondin the creation of an awareness that such a possibility exists is the *raison d'etre* of *animation sociale*. Hence, '*Animation sociale* thus becomes a basic weapon in the war on poverty, by placing in the hands of the poor some instruments for securing their advancement as a community' (Blondin 1971, p. 116). This idea can be seen to have direct conceptual and practical links with the liberating model of community adult education discussed in Chapter 4 in which adult education is seen as contributing to the collective advancement of working class, minority groups. It is also closely related to Alinsky's notion of the 'revolutionary organizer':

> A revolutionary organizer must shake up the prevailing patterns of their lives
> — agitate, create disenchantment and discontent with the current values, to pro-
> duce, if not a passion for change, at least a passive, affirmative, non-challenging
> climate. (Alinsky 1971, p. xxi–xxii)

In this analysis of community roles for adult educators we have covered the stylistic continuum of possible models of community work. At one end of the continuum stands the Cooperative Extension Service's transmission of organizational information to community members and at the other are the animation functions discussed in the preceeding paragraphs. The rest of this chapter considers some case studies of work with community groups which fall somewhere at a middle point on this continuum. The Free Universities, study circles, and the documentation of some of my own practice are initiatives which all exhibit a desire on the part of the educator to mix liberal and liberating aspects of community adult education. They are primarily concerned with educational processes rather than the overt promotion of collective political aciton. However, one outcome of participation in these educational processes is seen to be the inculcation, in individuals and groups, of the spirit of autonomous self-direction in the manner described earlier by Blondin. One obvious consequence of an increased sense of confident autonomy is a greater readiness to work for desired social changes.

Free Universities

The Free University movement constitutes one of the most remarkable and fascinating adult education innovations of the 1970s. In the decade which saw the research of Allen Tough receive widespread discussion and acclaim, in which the discussion of deschooling philosophies became common, and in which the notion of adult education as andragogy became an element central to the adult educator's vocabulary, the Free University movement represented a mass initiative in non-formal adult teaching and

learning. In its extra-institutional character, its emphasis on the inter-
changeability of teaching and learning roles, and its emphasis on student
control of curriculum and evaluation, the movement implemented some
of the andragogical injunctions arising out of the stream of research and
theory on self-directed learning. As the National Coordinator of the
movement writes, 'Free universities are helping to take learning away
from its institutionalized "providing" mode back to a time when learning
was a sharing process that both teachers and learners undertook together'
(Draves 1980, p. 19).

The origins of this movement which has so much significance for adult
education can be traced to a higher education context, specifically the Free
Speech movement at the Berkeley campus of the University of California
in 1964. The initial purpose of the movement was to organize and teach
courses in alternative political science to student activists on campuses
throughout the USA. This overtly political dimension declined as the
decade progressed and in the 1970s Free Universities came to function as
an important and viable alternative to traditional continuing education
programmes. As Draves writes:

> Free U's now serve housewives, the elderly, youth, farmers, city folk, and rural
> people. They are located in all types of communities from small rural towns in
> the midwest to large urban centers on the coasts. (Draves 1979, pp. 4–5)

The unifying principle of the movement is the recognition and implementation of the proposition that 'Anybody can teach, Anybody can
learn'. This demystification of the accreditation and curriculum approval
process means that Free Universities are in some ways a form of educational enterprise which resembles a pure, free market economy. If an
individual comes up with a good idea for a course there is no need to seek
the approval of academic committees, or to ground the course in existing
curricular paradigms. Hence, Free Universities can offer courses which
would be regarded as too esoteric by conventional continuing education
university departments. Such apparently esoteric courses may, however,
come eventually to be included within the curriculum of more conventional universities (as occurred with courses on holistic health and alternative technology, according to Draves).

In his book on *The Free University: a Model for Lifelong Learning* Draves
(1980) identified three core concepts behind the movement; that is, three
ideas professed by the most Free Universities with the least disagreement
and which give the movement its unique identity. These concepts are: (1)
responsibility for learning rests with participants as much as teachers; (2)
anybody can learn; (3) anybody can teach. To Draves the first of these
statements has both philosophical and structural ramifications. The Free
University becomes a linking mechanism, sharing many similarities with

the brokering agencies discussed in the previous chapter, which exercises a minimum of responsibility over content. It is 'a neutral passageway like a telephone line with no control or claim over the quality of content transmitted' (p. 122). Questions concerning the validity of knowledge, the appropriate behaviour for teacher and taught, and the criteria by which quality is to be assessed, become the responsibility of learners and teachers who are parties to the educational transactions.

The view of adult learning processes underlying the second tenet ('Anybody can learn') is one which regards knowledge as horizontal and which asserts that 'the entrance point to knowledge can be anywhere and that anyone should be able to learn anything at any point' (p. 126). Finally, the third 'Anybody can teach' principle is held by Free University advocates to be enshrined in the First Amendment's guarantee of freedom of speech. This grants the right to any individual to share knowledge, skills and ideas with any number of others, no matter how unorthodox such activities might appear to a majority. While many professional adult educators would applaud the notions that responsibility for learning is shared by learners and teachers, and that learning is possible for everyone, they are more critical and sceptical of this third idea. For, if it is really true that 'Anybody can teach', does not this imply that the professionally trained teacher is an individual possessing no special skills and differing in no noticeable manner from 'ordinary' citizens in terms of pedagogical competencies? It is not surprising that deschooling philosophies and Free University enterprises should both be regarded as threats to the teaching profession.

In fact, neither the deschooling philosophy nor the Free University movement denies the validity of a professionally trained teacher's expertise. Highly skilled teachers who possess a knowledge of the psychology of learning and have long practised the arts of diagnosing educational needs, group process management, and enhancing individual learning will be valued precisely for such abilities. The point is that such individuals do not and should not claim some kind of divine and exclusive right to be the sole transmitters of knowledge and skill. I said in Chapter 2 that the principles underlying voluntary learning and of those embodied in the democratic process were inseparable; so too the notion that ánybody can teach is at the heart of democratic theory. Professional teachers with wide experience of their craft will be particularly prized for their expertise. They have no need to fear the 'Anybody can teach' principle. However, they should also recognize that a great deal of purposeful teaching and learning occurs outside of their supervision, much of it complementary to formal educational provision. At certain times, in certain settings, for certain purposes, individuals will learn a variety of skills for which the 'teachers' will be friends, colleagues, or the learners themselves. The research discussed in Chapter 3 shows such an observation to be empirically accurate and not merely a philosophically desirable proposition.

The absence of 'quality control' over the content of courses and staff is at the heart of most critics' misgivings regarding the Free University movement. According to Draves (1980) the chief defences against teacher ineptitude are accurate, honest course descriptions and a continuous monitoring of classroom procedures. In those cases where several students complain about the quality of instruction, or the misleading nature of a course description, the instructor and curriculum are investigated by Free University personnel. If such a complaint is accurate the teacher is not allowed to operate under the aegis of the Free University again.

Draves also makes the point beloved of democratic libertarians that once an institution begins to exercise control over the ideas and knowledge deemed acceptable such an institution and its host society are likely to foster a repressive stagnation:

> Whole categories of classes branded as unorthodox or just plain wrong by traditional institutions have been allowed in free university catalogs. Free universities sense that, while out of ten crazy ideas, nine may be no good, that tenth idea may turn out to be something important to society. If we quash all ten ideas, which we would have to do because we don't know beforehand which idea will prove accurate, we quash creativity, imagination, and in the end, all social progress. (Draves 1980, p. 130)

Arguing for the freest exchange of ideas and knowledge possible does not, of course, absolve the Free University coordinator or any other adult educator from the necessity of making value judgements on those ideas he or she deems repugnant. Were an individual to propose teaching a course dealing with subject matter I felt to be immoral or socially harmful I would be compelled to refuse to allow such a course. To argue for a democratization of responsibility for teaching and learning and a healthy scepticism regarding 'appropriate' curricula does not mean the educator loses a sense of ethical correctness.

As well as the three core concepts outlined above as underlying Free University practice, eight other ideas are proposed as being of no little importance to the movement:

1. Informal structure: in particular, 'as little interference as possible with the experience of people interacting with people'.
2. Credentials as meaningless: Free Universities reject the notion of credentials as indicators of innate abilities and regard them as divisive. Hence, 'They serve to separate people, weed out, and provide gaps in society, but these distinctions are not very helpful to society as a whole'.
3. The community as a learning environment: the community is regarded as a total learning resource and Free Universities are seen as contributing to a more stimulating community environment.
4. Linking knowledge and action: neither knowledge nor institutions are neutral and by separating knowledge from action citizen participation is

discouraged. Free Universities are seen as providing 'forums in which positive constructive action can evolve' and as encouraging classes to engage in action projects and developmental activities.

5. Process over content: the most important educational purpose of Free Universities is not that of transmitting a certain body of knowledge. It is that of developing independent, self-directed learning skills.

6. Low cost and/or free education: an essential component in any truly lifelong education system.

7. Responsiveness to the community's characteristics: this means that there has been little or no standardization of educational practice or curriculum in Free Universities across the country.

8. Education for social change: Draves is open about this commitment of Free Universities to social change and the creation of a better society. In this case 'better' is defined in the following terms — 'one more responsive to human needs, to the poor, to the ideals of a democracy, to the development of the poorer nations on Earth and international understanding'. (Draves 1980, pp. 132–4)

Finally, how can the diverse amalgam of localized, autonomous institutions represented by the Free University network be viewed as a socially purposeful organism? To Draves the larger social function of the university is that of providing a sense of community (p. 279). Because American society in the post war era has become increasingly individualistic, personal and isolated, there is a need for institutions which affirm individuality within a sense of group wholeness. Free Universities are seen as institutions which 'have been able to create a sense of community, a structure in which education leads to community' (p. 282).

Study Circles

According to Titmus (1981) the annual enrolment in Swedish study circles represents over 60 per cent of the total Swedish adult population. Even for a society which is distinguished by the unusually high level of political credibility afforded to adult education, this is a remarkable statistic. In 1977–8 there were 339,924 circles with 3,178,687 participants. Study circles are defined by Titmus in terms of spirit rather than form. He writes that 'Friendship and community of effort towards a predetermined learning goal are the essential principles which unite them' (Titmus 1981, p. 76) and that this spirit is manifest in four features common to all circles — 'the element of comradeship, the principle that all, even the leader, shall participate in the work on equal terms, the prior choice of a limited field of study and the planned and systematic pursuit of it' (p. 69). As he very pertinently observes, however, the further education regulations which require a group to have a specialist teacher as leader in order to qualify for financial subsidy means that a mass network of such assisted circles is impossible in the United Kingdom.

Such a constraint does not exist in North America, however, and the *Great Books* programme, *Farm Forum*, and other mass living room learning experiments in receipt of grant aid did constitute forms of study circles. More recently, both Kurland (1979) and Osborne (1981) have called for a direct transference of the study circle model to the United States. Kurland advocates the extension of the study circle idea as a means of heightening political literacy. Study circles would allow citizens to discuss major political issues, to develop a personal position, and to engender a spirit of increased commitment to political participation. In a recent update of this 1979 proposal Kurland notes that the New York State Study Circle Consortium is running over 400 study circle programmes in community agencies, hospitals, businesses, health centres, churches, libraries, and homes (Kurland 1982, p. 30).

The director of the Consortium has noted how the andragogical, self-directed, participatory nature of the study circle process can induce frustration and confusion among students. She believes such feelings are the chief reasons for the dropout from circles and cites interviews with facilitators and participants in support of this assertion (Osborne 1981, p. 78). In her outline of two case studies Osborne recounts how study circle participation has resulted in community-problem solving. In one case a group's investigation of the history of a local church resulted in an application to the federal government for the designation of that church as an historic site. In the second case, an Albany neighbourhood health centre trained fourteen adolescents to run peer study circles on sex education themes, particularly birth control and venereal disease. She also mentions a nascent study circle initiative in which community groups can use a specially developed study guide (Willison 1980) to assess community needs and plan positive action.

In Britain the National Extension College (NEC), a non-profit distance education institution, has recently (July 1981) established a research project attempting to identify study circles run as self-help learning groups in the United Kingdom. In their first newsletter (NEC 1982) are identified the Attleborough Learning Exchange (a computer based exchange to match teachers and learners) and the 'Brain Train' (a railway commuter study clubs scheme). In the latter scheme twenty-eight train routes have offered commuter study clubs over a four year period. Ninety per cent of the study groups are led by commuters themselves, who act as unpaid volunteers. Curricula are determined by the results of questionnaires to passengers which ask travellers to suggest subjects they would like to study and invite tutors to volunteer to teach these subjects. Groups meet once or twice a week until they feel a change is appropriate and no payment is required of learners or expected by tutors.

Supporting Adult Learners in the Community — A Case Study

This section is avowedly personal and impressionistic in that it recounts my own experience of attempting to implement some of the ideas I have outlined regarding supporting adult learners in the community. The setting for this case study — an adult education college in the rural West Midlands of England — may seem so idiosyncratic and specific as to make comparisons or general injunctions appear invalid. The usefulness and applicability of any general observations made are judgements which must rest with the individual reader. I do feel, however, that outlining some of the principles, practices and problems I faced in my attempts to support non-institutional learning from within an institutional setting will be of interest to those who wish to know the experience which underlies this author's advice which has appeared throughout the book. There may also be features of this particular experiment which will be replicable in other settings.

The focus of this case study is Malvern Hills College, a specialist adult education and art centre opened in 1973 in the rural county of Hereford and Worcester in England. The college was to serve as the county centre for adult education and was established with the purpose of exemplifying many of the recommendations of the then recently published Russell Report (HMSO 1973) — a national report on the development of British adult education. In a paper published soon after the college's initiation its Principal cited the college as an example of '*Russell Recommendations Exemplified*' (Hayens 1974). He outlined the consultative meetings held with a range of academic, ancillary and administrative staff and the determination to work with voluntary societies. The intention was to emphasize student and society participation in the college so that notions of members and subscriptions (rather than students and fees) and groups and lists (rather than classes and registers) became predominant. The mission of the college was summarized as follows:

> The objective is not at some future time to have achieved a set and repetitive programme, but to have a flexible situation, responsible to the community and receptive to its demands, regularly having the invigoration of new and additional ideas and projects. (Hayens 1974, p. 183)

I joined the college staff in January 1974 as the newly-appointed Lecturer/Organizer in Community, Social and Environmental Development. My colleague and head of department, Bob Claiden, had been professionally trained in adult education at the University of Nottingham and was strongly committed to the notion of informal, community-based adult education. To him the criteria to be applied to the success of the department were not to be found in class sizes or numbers of courses. Rather, we were to place considerable emphasis on working with autonomous community groups in the surrounding area seeking to elicit their definitions of meaning and usefulness and to provide a supportive educational service within such a framework. Bob was particularly keen on developing training courses with leaders of children's playgroups. He was also interested in building a programme for the disabled. My own interest was in working with independent learners in an individual and group mode.

All, then, seemed set fair in that I occupied a professional position which many in my field would envy. I was in a new job and therefore had no burden of professional precedent upon me. I was working in a newly created college and new department which had, moreover, been established to implement the recommendations of a new, major government report on adult education. Finally, both my Principal and Head of Department were committed to a departure from class based notions of adult education provision in favour of a more informal, community-based mode.

A Community Survey

The first task to be undertaken by the Department of Community, Social and Environmental Development was that of a community survey. This had been called for by the working party which advised the Board of Governors on the conversion of the college to an adult education centre (it had previously been a college of further education with full and part time students aged between 16 and 18). The survey was charged 'with the particular objectives of identifying sections of the population and parts of the geographical area where more efforts should be made' (Hayens 1974, p. 182). The responsibility for conducting this survey fell to the Department of Community, Social and Environmental Development.

We decided to concentrate on three particular tasks. Firstly, we used the secondary data which were available to us in local libraries and voluntary organizations regarding the socio-economic profile of the region. Data derived from the decennial national census conducted by the British government relating to the area was easily located in the local library. The last census had been conducted in 1971 so a comprehensive source of recent socio-economic data was readily available. This enabled us to construct a profile of the social class and age composition of the area. Such an endeavour was personally very useful to me since I had moved to the area to take up the post, never before having even visited the region other than for my interview.

A second task of the survey was to document the amount and variety of premises which existed in the scattered rural villages served by the college and which might be used for some kind of outreach, satellite provision. To this end we visited social service, church and local authority offices as well as voluntary bodies in our attempt to compile a register of church halls, village halls and other buildings which might serve as a setting for some kind of adult education activity. Finally, we decided to visit a range of local education leaders; figures who, in their respective villages, were prominent members of different groups. We talked to clergy, voluntary society coordinators, local councillors, teachers, social workers, playgroup leaders and others whose experience we thought might prove relevant. That there are problems of possible distortion and paternalism in this method has already been acknowledged in Chapter 6. However, it did seem the quickest and cheapest way to collect an amount of reasonably reliable information on community characteristics and needs.

One last feature, which had considerable implications for subsequent programme development, is worth mentioning. Soon after my arrival I accompanied a local social worker on her daily round of local casework visits. The purpose of this was to give me an experiential sense of some of the problems of the community I had entered. I was also involved in organizing a training course for volunteer social workers and felt that only if I had an appreciation of the daily casework of professional social workers could I begin to devise a course for volunteers which would develop complementary social work skills. As a result of accompanying this worker on her rounds both Bob and I became volunteer social workers ourselves, each working with different cases. Hence, while we were organizing a training course for social workers (taught by an experienced professional) we were also undergoing the volunteering experience ourselves and attending as students the course we had helped to organize.

Educational Advisory Service
The first procedural change in my practice which resulted from the survey was the establishment of an Educational Advisory Service in the summer of 1974. This was established for two purposes, the first of which was to assist clients in negotiating the maze of formal educational opportunities existing in adult, further and higher education. This first function was an (unknowing) implementation of the brokerage model discussed in the previous chapter on supporting learning in the individual mode. The second function was to offer advice and assistance with study problems to adults who were experiencing difficulty in coming to terms with a new subject area. This second function was similar to that provided by the Learners' Advisory Services in American public libraries (discussed in Chapter 7) which were established under the Adult Independent Learning Project. In both instances adults were given help in planning and executing independent learning projects with regard to locating community resources and developing independent learning skills. The operation of the service was documented (Brookfield 1977a) and it was recognized as one of the new wave of advisory, counselling and informa-

tion services for adults which were established in the late 1970s in the United Kingdom (ACACE 1979).

The service was offered free to all members of the local community and no distinction was made between clients who were enrolled as college students and those outside the college who used the service with no thought of future enrolment in mind. The service was available on one or two evenings a week when no appointment to see the counsellor (myself) was necessary. Alternatively, clients could make an individual appointment during the week. The service did, of course, deal with many who decided to participate in the adult education activities of the college. Hence, adults wishing for sustained advice on the planning and execution of an independent learning project could enrol in the Home Study Service for a series of individual tutorials on their project. Alternatively, adults exploring possible higher education opportunities through the advisory service would on occasion be advised to undertake a 'Return to Study' course as a preparation for participation in the formal world of higher education. It is to these two services that attention is now turned.

Home Study Service

The development of the Home Study Service was the result of expressed student needs. A number of adults had contacted me to say that they were intending to become students in the Open University and that they wished for some form of preparatory study. However, since they were unable to attend introductory courses to Open University study such preparation would have to be home based. For a while I simply prepared essay questions together with suggested reading, sent these off to individual students and marked the results. As word of this arrangement began to spread, and more requests for supervision began to emerge, I decided to establish what I originally called a Correspondence Tuition Service. I quickly decided that this was a serious misnomer since students were engaged in negotiating individual learning contracts, not following pre-packaged correspondence courses, and changed the title to the Home Study Service. The operational procedures of the service were simple.

> Students at present register on a termly basis for a supervised course of study designed to meet their individual needs. On receipt of an enquiry I meet the student (if this is possible) for a short interview to find out exactly what he or she hopes to gain from the service. . . Whatever the enquiry, however, the initial contact and the mutual definition of a provisional scheme of work are of crucial importance. When there is a minimum of face to face contact between teacher and student, both must be as sure as possible of each other's expectations. (Brookfield 1977b, p. 41)

As I stressed in a paper on the service written for an American audience

(Brookfield 1978b) the diagnostic interview at which student objectives were clarified, and the means to attain these objectives discussed, was of crucial importance to the scheme. It was during these interviews that the chief features of each individual student programme were settled. The interviews were run on a negotiated learning contract basis and both tutor and student were free to veto elements of the projected work scheme as appropriate. Four categories of programme were typically requested and devised:

1. Vocationally oriented programmes — mostly students who wished to prepare for 'O' or 'A' level examination entry (the British equivalent to high school completion diplomas and grade 12 examinations) or to enrol as adult students in higher education.
2. Liberal/Non-Vocational programmes — where students explored an area of study for its innate fascination.
3. Study Skills programmes — in which the student wished to develop or improve particular skills such as notetaking or essay planning.
4. Assistance with learning projects — where I would assist in the execution of an already devised learning project. Learners in this category would frequently have been clients of the Educational Advisory Service.

Adminstrative and auditing purposes required Home Study Service participants to enrol as 'normal' college students but in practice the time, place and format of any tutorials were matters to be decided upon by tutor and student. I would meet students in their homes, sometimes at weekends, and we would be ready to alter our mutually agreed programme as seemed appropriate and desirable. The Home Study Service was an example of adult education in the community in that tuition took place in students' homes as well as within a college setting, and in that the responsibility for setting learning goals rested with the learners. It was cast in an individual mode in that students worked with the tutor on a one-to-one basis through individually negotiated learning contracts. The rationale behind the service was one based upon perceptions regarding the temperament of potential clients in the service. Hence, this form of individualized learning contract arrangement was seen 'as a method of teaching particularly well suited to certain temperaments, rather than a medium which is employed only for geographical reasons' (Brookfield 1978b, p. 20). The students for whom the service was intended comprised 'those individuals who temperamentally dislike a total concentration on group learning procedures and who feel uncertain as to how they would cope with the emotional pressures and the academic pace of group work' (Brookfield 1978b, p. 20). Such students would include many from working class backgrounds with an unhappy experience and negative memory of classroom activities.

'Return to Study' Programme

With the Educational Advisory Service and the Home Study Service a degree of informality had been maintained through three devices; the tutoring or counselling had been on occasion home based, the negotiation of learning activities (in the Home Study Service) had involved a substantial element of learner influence, and the service to Educational Advisory Service clients had been offered free of charge and with no implication or expectation of subsequent institutional enrolment. The third component in the evolving programme was to provide a more formal series of courses designed for adults who wished to return to systematic study of some kind but who felt themselves to be inadequate in terms of the academic skills necessary to success in formal educational settings. In a paper analysing the problems experienced by such students the rationale for organizing the courses was expressed as follows:

> I would suggest that the adult's domestic and occupational circumstances make for several characteristic problems which occur with greater frequency amongst this category of student than any other. These students' low self-evaluation with regard to those younger than themselves, their personal, colloquial style of presentation, their search for unequivocal answers — these are the kinds of problem with which tutors of adults lately returned to study will have to deal and the solution of which will require the adult to undergo perceptual alterations as well as presentational improvements. (Brookfield 1979b, p. 96)

In a survey of three years course membership on a range of 'Return to Study' courses (Brookfield 1978a) it was noticeable that there existed a majority for whom course membership represented these adults' first acquaintance with the world of adult education. To this extent the courses were fulfilling the remit I had imposed upon them which was to attract students with unhappy memories of formal schooling who nonetheless wished to confront again the challenge of an intellectual quest within a formal educational setting. However, students did not exhibit any noticeable educational or social deprivation and the same survey noted that 'the students attending "How to Study" courses seem to be typical of what is considered by many as the traditional adult education clientele ... a group of students who are approaching middle age, engaged predominantly in intermediate or skilled occupations (if not working as full-time housewives) and containing a preponderance of female members' (Brookfield 1978a, pp. 364–5).

The courses centred chiefly on the development of the survival skills deemed necessary to higher education students. Most of these were cognitive — the development of critical analysis, skimming, notetaking, essay planning, examination preparation. However, adult students also need to understand and manage the affective changes concomitant on higher education participation. They have to alter a poor self-image as learners and to develop sufficient confidence to participate in seminars. Hence, the courses contained seminars on the adult learner (intended to demonstrate the learning strengths endemic to adulthood) and discussion techniques. Previous 'Return to Study' students were invited to address new groups and, as I have written elsewhere, 'their accounts of the academic, familial and emotional demands of higher education participation exhibited an authenticity and relevance much appreciated by course members' (Brookfield 1981d, p. 5).

The three initiatives discussed so far can be conceptualized as occupying points along a continuum representing the relative formality of adult learning arrangements. At its least formalized point was the Educational Advisory Service. This was a community service, (not an in-house facility only for college students) which charged no fee to clients. Through informal and confidential counselling clients were able to clarify opportunities available and to discuss the consequences of various choices. They were also able to consider their plans for independent learning activities. The Home Study Service allowed for a greater degree of structure in that learners were able to negotiate individually oriented programmes of study. Some tutorials arranged within this service were located in learners' houses and responsibility for choices regarding curriculum development, criteria for evaluation and work to be completed rested primarily with learners. Finally, the 'Return to Study' courses resembled traditional modes of study in that they were sponsored by a formal adult education institution and entailed the usual practice of enrolment in a class which met regularly under the supervision of a tutor. The last initiative to be considered — the Supporting Autonomous Adult Learning Groups scheme — was community based in every way possible and falls clearly into the mode of adult education in the community as outlined in Chapter 4.

Supporting Autonomous Adult Learning Groups
The National Housewives Register (NHR) is a network of womens' study groups in the British Isles which meet regularly at two-weekly intervals in order to discuss non-domestic issues, primarily those of social concern. They meet in private homes and alternate visits by outside speakers with informal, leaderless discussion sessions. I became aware of the existence of this network when one of my students in a Sociology class declared herself to be the secretary of a local NHR group and asked me to come along and talk to the group one evening. I agreed and subsequently found myself in the living room of a farmhouse in the midst of the Herefordshire countryside talking to twenty or so NHR members about the role and effects of television in British society. The session was not part of any formal college course and my chief purpose in agreeing to meet the group (other than being intrigued by the idea of discovering a network of informal

study circles in my own professional back yard) was to increase the visibility of the college as an adult education resource.

Upon learning of the group's arranging to meet at least once a month for leaderless discussions I began to speculate on the possibility of offering some form of assistance which would enhance the educational experience which was occurring without seeking to bring the initiative under the aegis of the college. I knew about the living room learning, study circles and learning box schemes in America, Sweden and Australia and thought that some form of modest analogue might be introduced with the NHR groups. I suggested, therefore, that participants in the leaderless discussions might find the sessions more satisfying if all had access before the discussion to a package of relevant material. I offered to assemble the package and to loan these materials to the group in return for a single termly payment.

The rationale behind the experiment, therefore, was that a prior acquaintance by all participants with the subject matter under discussion would make for a more effective interchange. Several days before the group was due to meet the secretary collected a resource pack from me which was distributed to group members in her area. The resource pack received by each participant consisted of several pieces of material: (1) a sheet of relevant statistical data; (2) extracts from relevant studies and reports; (3) proposed alternative explanations of the phenomenon under discussion (where appropriate); and (4) key questions as suggested topics to be explored during the discussion.

The key features of this experiment were that the group set the agenda of topics for discussion and relayed these to me, and that I did not attend the meetings. The group therefore retained the responsibility for setting its learning goals and my function was to make the pursuit of these goals more enjoyable and productive. Because these discussions were held in group members' living rooms, because the context of such discussion was under the control of participants, and because in my contact with the group I did not seek to convert them into a formal adult education class, this seems to me an example of adult education in the community as already conceptualized in Chapter 4. In the brief paragraph which appeared in the college calendar describing the scheme I tried to place the onus for initiating contact as much as was possible with the groups themselves and to emphasize that I was not seeking an insidious conversion of such groups into formal college classes:

> For those groups and organizations which meet regularly for educative discussions in each other's homes or in settings other than educational institutions, the department offers support through the provision of back-up resource material. If any group of people is meeting for the discussion of issues of social and personal concern, they are invited to contact the department to see if a resource package of information relevant to the discussion can be provided beforehand.

The charge can easily be levelled against educators engaged in such experiments that in the act of assembling a resource package they are exercising a form of institutional hegemony. The selection of what are considered important or relevant materials for the package and the way in which explanations are presented or reports summarized invariably reflect the prejudices of the compiler. To those alarmed at the prospect of insidious influence, however, I would only say that the alternative prospect of meandering, competitive and intolerant discussions is doubly disturbing. The dangers of diversion and status competition within the discussion group were heightened in this case by the lack of access to library materials endured by these rural NHR members. It is also important to record that the group members were most appreciative of the opportunity to receive a package of materials relevant to their meeting and that they did, indeed, made good use of these.

Let me end this discussion of the Supporting Autonomous Adult Learning Groups scheme by summarizing once again its underlying rationale:

> Even under the control of skilled and informed tutors, discussion seminars can become unmanageable emotional battlegrounds with student efforts directed more to the furtherance of self-esteem than the productive exchange of ideas and experience. It is essential then, that leaderless groups are composed of members with some knowledge of the topic under scrutiny and the provision of a preparatory resource package can help to secure this necessary condition (Brookfield 1979a, p. 368)

I left the college in September 1980 to spend a year as a Visiting Professor in Adult Education at the University of British Columbia, Vancouver, Canada and subsequently to work for the United Kingdom Advisory Council on Adult and Continuing Education (ACACE) and at Columbia University in New York. Although the years I spent as a community adult educator in rural England seem to be light years removed from my subsequent professional adventures, those years formed the practitioner bedrock upon which my subsequent theoretical speculations and research activities have been built. In the summer of 1982 I learned that the college which had been created as a county adult education centre in the post-Russell euphoria had ceased to enjoy funding from the public purse (that is, the local education authority). The college fell under the aegis of a charitable trust and the full time adult education staff were transferred to other public education institutions in the area.

Training Community Adult Educators

Programmes of professional training for adult educators in both North America and the United Kingdom vary with regard to the community education component included therein. In my time as a professor and student of adult education in British, Canadian and American universities I have been struck by the institution-based nature of much adult education training. Courses which are the staple of postgraduate adult education programmes (particularly in North America) are those of Programme Planning and Evaluation, Adult Psychology, Organization and Management of Adult Education, Instructional Methods, and Foundations. Programme planning courses can be cast in a community adult education mode but the tendency is to concentrate more upon recruitment and marketing procedures, instructional design, or curriculum development, than upon working with community groups. The adult educator is viewed as an institution bound planner working in a classroom based mode to construct and administer a self-financing program.

Qualities and Competencies
In a three-year study by the British Community Work Group the qualities required by the community worker were identified as follows:

1. An ability to build relationships characterized by trust and confidence.
2. An ability to adapt to different circumstances.
3. A sensitivity to a group's pace and an ability to adjust to this.
4. A capacity to work towards long-term objectives.

(Community Work Group 1973)

As the authors of the report acknowledged, 'The workers' own views of their roles and functions, when presented in this shorthand form, suggest a bewildering multiplicity of tasks, often conflicting and thus demanding a considerable range of skill and knowledge, as well as personal qualities of objectivity and integrity' (p. 25). It can be argued that such affective abilities as identified in 1 and 3 above cannot be taught in a training course, only learned experientially in real-life settings. One answer to this is to stress simulation and gaming exercises using case studies to recreate as closely as possible situations educators would encounter in the course of their work.

A major community education training text using this approach is that of Berridge, Stark and West (1977) who present twenty-four cases covering eight areas in which community educators have to develop skills: creating community awareness, planning and implementing, staffing, coordinating community efforts, developing policies and procedures, financing, exercising leadership, and evaluation. Their belief is that 'case studies re-create a reality which may be vicariously experienced by trainees in classroom settings' and that 'the case study is one of the most effective ways to share insights and sharpen skills' (p. ix). One adult education professor who has attempted to train community adult educators in graduate courses and non-credit workshops is **Roger**

Hiemstra. In his course on 'Community and the Adult Educator' he identifies nine performance objectives or competency expectations for community educators:

1. To identify vertical and horizontal pulls, strengths and weaknesses in a community.
2. To undertake a community power analysis and recognize the primary power actors.
3. To identify potential and actual educational resources in a community.
4. To recognize indices for studying a community.
5. To construct a community change/social action model.
6. To analyse potential community problem-solving programmes.
7. To recognize strengths and weaknesses of the applicability of community education procedures to local situations.
8. To discuss the ramifications of economic, political and social changes for local community adult education programmes.
9. To appreciate the difference between community planning needs in rural and urban settings.   (Hiemstra 1980b, p. 27)
                                                            1982, p. 2)

These competency expectations are developed through gaming and simulations and the use of case study material. Thompson (1980) has also developed an experientially based training course for community educators. His in-service, in-house model of 'Training for Bridge Building' presents an in-service training course for staff which introduces issues surrounding developments in the district in which the community education centre is located.

Leading Informal Study-Discussion Groups
One of the most frequently replicable skills required of educators working with informal community groups is that of leading group discussions. In American, Canadian and British adult education the discussion group has come to be regarded as the mode of teaching and learning most suited to adult education. Rogers and Groombridge argue, for example, that 'Adult education probably uses the discussion method of learning more widely and more successfully than any other sector of education in Britain' (Rogers and Groombridge 1976, p. 55). Discussion has also been invested with a social and political significance wider than the educational. In the 1940s Essert advised American adult educators to look on membership in a discussion group as a substitute for the neighbourly *gemeinschaft* lost in urban development during the twentieth century (Essert 1948, p. 275). Such an association between the use of discussion and rejuvenation of community (and sometimes the creation of democracy) means that the literature of discussion method occasionally betrays an evangelical fervour which makes it imperative that practitioners distinguish between prescriptive rhetoric and objective analysis.

The role of the discussion leader is one which affords numerous opportunities for deliberate or inadvertent manipulation, in particular the temptation to distort group processes to ensure that a 'tidy' or 'productive' discussion occurs. One common danger is for tutors committed to democratic discussion procedures to open their first meeting with a new group with a declaration that no preconceived curriculum has been devised and that content is the responsibility of participants. Such a tutor is likely to ask 'What would you like to discuss?' at the opening of a session thereby confusing and unsettling participants in a subject area or skill domain. Participants will, by definition, sometimes be unable to specify the particular aspects of a new area of knowledge they would like to consider. When this happens and the tutor is faced with a lack of response the temptation is to reduce the embarrassment of both parties by reverting to a syllabus reflecting the tutor's own prejudices.

In actuality, it should not be a cause for concern that a group of individuals with diverse backgrounds, meeting for the first time in an unfamiliar setting, should not be able immediately to devise an agreed, intellectually sound scheme of work. Expectations of what group membership will entail (derived from schoolday recollections), anxieties both anticipated and experienced regarding the competitive dimensions informing many group activities, the lack of experience in expressing opinions in group settings — all these factors conspire against any shared intellectual endeavour.

A more insidious way in which tutors manipulate discussions can be seen in the attempt to 'guide' a discussion to a previously specified conclusion. A tutor will profess discussion to be a free exchange of ideas among equals with the tutorial role altered to that of resource person or facilitator. However, in the subsequent discussions only those comments which support tutor perceptions of progress toward a 'group' goal will be selected for emphasis.

To Paterson (1970), however, it is logically inadmissible to proclaim that a discussion is taking place if the tutor has already determined the progress and outcome of the encounter. This is because a distinguishing characteristic of discussion is the true equality of the participants, one dimension of which is their opportunity to alter the course of the discussion as seems appropriate. 'Guided' discussion thus becomes a contradiction in terms since discussion is a democratic, participatory exchange of opinion which has as a necessary condition the removal of the tutor from a privileged position of domination. For Paterson, 'True discussion cannot be directed, or even guided, for to attempt to do so is in effect to opt out of the discussions, to close one's consciousness to alternative interpretations' (Paterson 1970, p. 47). Watkins (1975) also observes that in such guided discussions 'the learning which takes place is that permitted and sanctioned by the tutor and not necessarily what the student most needs' (p. 7).

This process of manipulation is graphically summarized by Paterson and his words should strike a chord in many a reader of this book who has been a teacher or student in adult education. A manipulative tutor, then, will 'unobtrusively and skilfully synthesize the various discussion contributions of his students, by judicious selection and emphasis, into a neatly structured and rounded proposition or body of propositions, which are then represented as the ''conclusions'' of the ''class discussion'' ' (Paterson 1970, p. 47). When this occurs the unanswered questions, the points of genuine dissension and the inconvenient facts are all ignored in the desire to present a 'conclusion' in the discussion. However, the value of using discussion method lies in its process features as much as the ability to produce lucid conclusions. It is more important that participants clarify points of dissension, propose and assess alternative explanations and attempt to understand each other's perceptions, than that a coherent 'conclusion' be advanced as the sum total of the group's efforts.

A final temptation to which discussion leaders are liable to fall is that of constantly 'rephrasing' participants' contributions, supposedly on behalf of the group. Where group members are relatively inarticulate or unused to public articulation of their thoughts the leader will be tempted to 'help' the student present an idea to the group. This form of benevolent misrepresentation results in the tutor declaring 'What I think you're really getting at is. . .' or asking 'Isn't what you're saying. . .' and it takes courage and confidence to reply 'No, you've misrepresented my meaning'. This is particularly the case when the adult does not wish to be labelled as an uncooperative member.

The use of discussion must be considered a calculated risk since the course of the subsequent encounter cannot be charted at the outset. It is this very uncertainty, however, which is the essence of the attraction of the discussion method to leader and participants. When members feel they are involved in shaping the form and content of an educational transaction then their interest and commitment will be enhanced and a truly participatory, democratic encounter is taking place.

NINE

Conclusion: A Personal Postscript

Value Choices and Contextual Variables

In the overview chapter introducing this volume, three broad purposes were ascribed to the work. Firstly, it was to assess the empirical validity of the frequent assertions made by educators regarding the extent and quality of informal, independent adult learning. Secondly, it was to illuminate the educational component of much developmental and activist work occurring in communities. Finally, the book was to review the ways in which adult educators could work with independent adult learners to support and enhance their learning. Such a review would explore the connections which could be made between formal educational institutions and informal learning occurring within individual and group modes.

In this postscript I do not wish to restate a case made earlier or to review ground which has already been covered. However, there are some final personal observations I wish to make on the nature of work with adult learners in community settings.

The first of these observations refers to the value judgement element in much of this work. Anyone who chooses to work with independent learners in individual or group modes will realize early in their operations that choices have to be made regarding the groups and individuals which are felt to be deserving of educators' attentions. If adult learning is truly ubiquitous and (as Tough's research suggests) many more adults would like assistance with their learning than currently manage to use the range of professional services on offer, then those who make themselves publicly available to provide such help will be deluged under a flood of demand.

The choice of which individuals and groups to assist out of all those expressing a desire for help will, of course, depend partly on the nature of the assistance required and the subject or skill expertise possessed by the educator. However, if we accept that there are transferable andragogical skills which can be applied in a number of different individual and group settings, then considerations other than those purely of technique will come into play. Institutional preferences and biases may well compel the individual educator to seek to work with certain kinds of clients. Indeed, where an institution and employee are matched in terms of their professional outlook there will be no sense of institutional compulsion experienced by the practitioner. An adult basic education specialist working for a social welfare agency will naturally seek to work with disadvantaged groups and such a preference will reflect and coincide perfectly with institutional concerns. There will, however, be occasions when educators will have to choose between groups competing for their attention and assistance. In such cases the decision as to which to assist (Womens' Rights lobbyists, Consumer Advocacy Groups, Chamber of Commerce or Conservationist Societies) will be strongly affected by the personal value system of the individual educator. The decision as to which of several potential individuals or groups to assist cannot be taken solely on mechanistic, techniques-orientated grounds. It is a second order decision which will depend on the values, ethics and moral stance of the educator.

It is regrettable that the programme development and programme planning literature in adult education does not address this fact. The assumption seems to be that programme planning or development is an applied skill which exists somehow independently of political and moral considerations. It is as if the programmer is a morally denuded automaton inhabiting an ethical vacuum. The programmer's task becomes simply one of applying 'how to' principles to working with clients almost irrespective of the nature of any educational situation. The literature of programme planning and development is full of prescriptive, exemplary advice regarding the conducting of needs assessments and clientele surveys, the setting of programme objectives, and the correct form of instructional design. Rarely are there any descriptions of the institutional pressures faced by programmers or allusions to the importance of the programmer's personal sense of priorities and values. Yet the professional reality familiar to readers of this book is that limited resources in terms of finance, accommodation and manpower mean that programmers have to make choices regarding the programmes they will sponsor and support.

These considerations — the nature of institutional biases, the programmer's personal concerns, the kinds of requests for assistance made to educators and the range of resources available — are all contextual variables. To assume that programme planning principles or evaluative procedures are easily replicable in a number of different settings is to ignore the professional workaday reality of most adult educators. The existence of the kinds of contextual variables identified above means that educators have to develop idiosyncratic, situationally-specific styles of professional performance in working with different client groups, hired instructors and administrators. However much writers of textbooks and those engaged in teaching on professional development courses of any kind (and I include myself in this category) may offer exemplary guidelines and first principles of good practice, they should not forget that such advice will inevitably be altered by the contextual variables outlined above.

Gibbs (1981) is one of the few writers with the courage to admit to breaking what many people regard as the accepted practice in his field, in this case the teaching of study skills. Realizing that the general exhortations of *How To Study* skills cookbooks bore little relation to his own and his students' study habits, he designed a manual which acknowledged the idiosyncratic nature of study behaviours and then used this as an esential component in developing required skills. Such initiatives are rare in the adult education programme planning literature.

Accepting Ambiguity – The Limbo of the Informal Educator

Adult educators exploring the links which can be made between formal adult education and the world of informal, independent learning soon come to a realization that a state of ambiguity is almost a given condition of their work. There will be ambiguity, first and foremost, with regard to clients' wishes in terms of learning goals and objectives. A scenario familiar to educators working with would-be independent learners and community groups is that of encountering a strongly felt and stated desire to learn or to act, but an absence of any specific focus for such learning or action. In this situation the educator has to apply a self-denying ordinance with regard to the temptation of offering benevolent advice at too early a stage in the relationship with the client(s). On the other hand, nothing is guaranteed to produce more annoyance in initially enthusiastic client groups than an educator ostentatiously displaying a commitment to Rogerian, non-directive principles and refusing to answer direct requests for advice and guidance with equivalent directness. Continually to turn queries on their head and ask questioners 'Well, what do you think'?, can engender suspicion and annoyance at helpers' apparent unwillingness to declare personal opinions. It turns educators, in clients' eyes, into people who fastidiously and consciously are distancing themselves from the rest of the group by virtue of some supposed superiority of perception or judgement. Such a perception is hardly likely to inspire the atmosphere of reciprocity necessary to such work.

Ambiguity will also probably be manifest in the institutional attitude adopted towards those who choose to work in an informal mode with groups and individuals. The *raison d'etre* of most adult education programming tends to be the increase of student numbers through ever more plentiful courses and classes. Anyone who challenges this rationale runs a professional risk of being denied the opportunity to climb the ladder of institutional reward bestowed in the form of job promotion or increased funding. On the other hand, it may sometimes serve an institution's needs very conveniently to be able to wheel out a token informal or outreach worker whose clients will be from groups proportionately under-represented in the general student clientele. Most adult education pro-grammers will know of individuals who work with community groups in an informal mode and who occupy the lowest position on the institutional ladder of job prestige and institutional resources. However, when those same institutions are attacked for the élitist nature of their provision, then the outreach worker suddenly becomes the object of institutional ap-proval. This shift in the focus of institutional attention often lasts no longer than the period of political concentration or external criticism of the rigidity or élitism of the institution's programme. Once this threat is removed the educator then becomes assigned to that peculiar professional limbo so familiar to (though not beloved of) community workers, outreach workers and informal educators of all kinds.

The characteristics of this state of limbo are dichotomous, if not con-tradictory. On the one hand there often exists an institutional indifference to the effort of educators. The battles which educators and community workers have to fight to maintain resources and secure institutional recognition leave scars which take the form of a sense of professional marginality and isolation. In opposition to this, however, lies the intense satisfaction of receiving genuine testimony to the effects such work can have on individuals' lives. Those who have no commitment to profes-sional advancement and who are not dependent upon institutional patron-age have no need to flatter or dissemble. When they express their appreciation, therefore, they are making an authentic, intensely personal statement. I well remember during one period of my professional life when the sense of marginality surrounding my activities was so profound as to induce what almost became a sense of professional paranoia, the emotional sustenance provided by students' expressions of appreciation.

Aside from the deep satisfactions derived from expressions of genuine appreciation there are two other self-protective stratagems which informal educators can adopt to ensure their professional survival and personal sanity. The first of these is the generation of a network of professional con-tacts. In Chapters 3, 7 and 8, I made reference to the use of peer groups as learning networks and the importance of such networks in the maintenance of motivation as well as sources of information. The same principles hold true for educators working with such learners. Con-ferences and other gatherings of educational brokers, Free University workers and community educators will have a reference group function as well as occasioning an exchange of information regarding techniques. Attendance at conferences and regional meetings, subscription to and readership of relevant journals, the development of contacts through personal correspondence — all these serve to reinforce the informal educator's sense of professional identity or camaraderie. Without the contact with such a reference group the life of the educator would be lonely indeed.

A second stratagem which serves to protect informal community educators from a morale sapping sense of institutional exclusion is the acquisition of a degree of political astuteness. The educator who can identify the local focuses of educational power in terms of key decision makers, and who then can arouse public opinion to the pitch where such decision makers are fully aware of the importance of a programme to large numbers of potential voters and taxpayers, is fortunate indeed. Such a person is well equipped to combat the periodic attempts to withdraw grant support or to divert the educator's energies into more conventional channels. I well remember a period in my professional life when I spent a significant amount of time cultivating contacts with journalists, writing to newspapers, organizing public meetings and collecting petition signatures — all because the programme in which I was working was faced with a series of threats concerning the withdrawal of funds which seemed to emerge almost as regularly as (and to coincide with) the autumn leaves turning brown. As an educator I resented having to devote so much time to developing skills more appropriate to political lobbyists or pressure group advocates. A healthy sense of *realpolitik* made me aware, however, that unless I conducted a quick self-teaching project in the development of such skills my programme was under threat of extinction. A degree of shrewdness regarding techniques which can be used to influence educational decision makers is, therefore, an attribute which is essential to informal educators.

The absence of attention to this political dimension in role analyses of adult educator competencies is a striking feature of the professional literature. Monette has identified the technological and service-orientated preoccupation apparent in the literature of adult education and the lack of acknowledgement given to the existence of value judgements underlying practice. He writes 'There seems to exist in adult education a fear of unmasking the value choices underlying adult educational practice, as if once identified they might prove embarrassing to this "service oriented" profession' (Monette 1979; p. 87). Yet, as has repeatedly been emphasized in this book, all practice is based on some value framework, covert or overt. At certain times the values underlying the activities of practitioners will be opposed to those supporting the institutional rationale. When this occurs practitioners will need all the political astuteness they possess in order to argue for their programme. Yet there exist no chapters in programme planning and programme development textbooks regarding the political skills needed by practitioners if their activities are to reach their full potential. The political constraints upon adult education programmers and the skills such practitioners will need to maintain their activities are contextual variables (to use my earlier phrase) totally ignored in the literature of applied programme development skills.

Finally, in closing this book it is as well once again to elucidate the perennial dilemma of educators working in the mode of humanistic facilitation of independent learning with individuals or groups. There is a fine line to be drawn between the sensitive provision of assistance to the dimly felt needs of a beginning learner and the benevolent, but nonetheless authoritarian, manipulation of learner behaviours. Boyle expresses this dilemma thus:

> One recognizes a real dilemma in that as programmers and through the manipulation of human behaviour within an educational experience, we impose our values on the clientele. The dilemma violates a fundamental value of the freedom and opportunity to choose. However, there exists no formula for structuring an effective change situation where such manipulation is totally absent. (Boyle 1981; p. 147)

Boyle suggests that the most that can be hoped for is that educators and learners be aware of the values each hold. This is certainly a first step and it underscores one of the chief themes of this book; namely, that practice is value based and that choices which educators make reflect institutional preferences and personal biases. In any situation where a teaching–learning transaction occurs a temporary imbalance, in terms of expertise, is present. However, such an imbalance need not imply any necessary assumption of innate superiority nor enshrine any permanent dysjunction of esteem. The parties to the transaction are by turns learners, by turns teachers. Within the world of formal adult education the tendency is for such temporary imbalances to become ossified in institutional structures or conventions. The independent learners whose stories are recounted in this book experienced no such consciousness of inferiority. In their readiness to share knowledge with other inquiring minds and in their view of intellectual exploration as a journey of unending challenge and discovery, they exemplify all that is best in the humanistic process of adult teaching and learning.

Bibliography of References
Cited in the Text

Adams, Frank 'Highlander Folk School: Getting Information, Going Back and Teaching It' *Harvard Educational Review* 42 (1972): 497–520

Adams, Frank *Unearthing Seeds of Fire: The Idea of Highlander* Winston-Salem, N. Carolina: John F. Blair Publishers, 1975

Addams, Jane *Twenty Years At Hull House* New York: New American Library, Signet Classics, 1910

Advisory Council for Adult and Continuing Education (ACACE), *Links to Learning* Leicester, England: Advisory Council for Adult and Continuing Education, 1979

Advisory Council for Adult and Continuing Education (ACACE) *Continuing Education: From Policies to Practice* Leicester, England: Advisory Council for Adult and Continuing Education, 1982

Agnew, John A. 'The Danger of a Neighbourhood Definition of Community' *Community Education Journal* 7 (1980): 30–31

Alinsky, Saul D. *Rules for Radicals: A Practical Primer for Realistic Radicals* New York: Random House, 1971

Allport, Gordon W. *Becoming: Basic Considerations for a Psychology of Personality* New Haven: Yale University Press, 1955

Andreski, Stanlislav *Social Sciences as Sorcery* London: Andre Deutsch, 1972

Apps, Jerold W. 'Toward a Broader Definition of Research' *Adult Education (USA)* 23 (1973): 59–64

Apps, Jerold W. *Study Skills: For Those Adults Returning to School* New York: McGraw Hill, 1978

Apps, Jerold W. *Problems in Continuing Education* New York: McGraw Hill, 1979

Arensberg, C.A. and Kimball, S.T. *Family and Community in Ireland* Cambridge, Massachussetts: Harvard University Press, 1968, 2nd ed.

Armstrong, Kathleen Anne *Masters of Their Own Destiny: A Comparison of the Thought of Coady and Freire* Vancouver: Center for Continuing Education, University of British Columbia, Occasional Paper n. 13, 1977

Baillie, Susan 'Limits of the Process Perspective' in Warden, John (ed.) *Process Perspectives: Community Education as Process* Charlottesville, Virginia: Mid-Atlantic Community Education Consortium, 1979

Barnard, Henry *Connecticut Common School Journal* 1 (1838) Quoted in Knowles,

Malcolm S. *A History of the Adult Education Movement in the United States* Huntington, New York: Robert E. Krieger, 1977

Beard, Ruth *Teaching and Learning in Higher Education* Harmondsworth: Penguin Books, 1972

Bell, Colin and Newby, Howard *Community Studies: An Introduction to the Sociology of the Local Community* London: Allen & Unwin, 1971

Bell, Colin and Newby, Howard (eds) *The Sociology of Community: A Selection of Readings* Portland, Oregon: Frank Cass & Co. Ltd, 1974

Bell, Colin and Newby, Howard (eds) *Doing Sociological Research* London: Allen & Unwin, 1977

Bensman, A.J. and Vidich, J. *Small Town in Mass Society: Class, Power and Religion in a Rural Society* Princeton: Princeton University Press, 1958

Berridge, Robert A. 'A Process Oriented Community – Tipp City, Ohio' *Community Education Journal* 1/3 (1971): 13–16, 22

Berridge, Robert A. *Community Education Handbook* Midland, Michigan: Pendell Publishing Co., 1973

Berridge, Robert A. and Stark, Stephen 'The Process Model in Action' *Community Education Journal* 5/6 (1975): 43–7

Berridge, Robert A., Stark, Stephen and West, Phillip T. *Training the Community Educator: A Case-Study Approach* Midland, Michigan: Pendell Publishing Co., 1977

Berte, Neal A. *Individualizing Education by Learning Contracts* San Fransisco; Jossey Bass, New Directions in Higher Education no. 10, 1975

Biddle, William W. and Biddle, Loureide J. *The Community Development Process* New York: Holt, Rinehart & Winston, 1965

Birch, A.H. *Small Town Politics* Oxford: Oxford University Press, 1959

Blondin, Michael *'Animation Sociale'* in Draper, James A. (ed.) *Citizen Participation: Canada* Toronto: New Press, 1971

Blumer, Herbert *Symbolic Interactionism: Perspective and Method* Englewood Cliffs, New Jersey: Prentice Hall, 1969

Bode, C. *The American Lyceum: Meeting of the Mind* New York: Oxford University Press, 1956

Bode, R.L. 'Living Room Learning' in Burch Glen *Accent on Learning: An Analytical History of the Fund for Adult Education's Experimental Discussion Project 1951–1959* Washington D.C.: Fund for Adult Education, 1960

Bogdan, Robert and Taylor, Steven J. *Introduction to Qualitative Research Methods: A Phenomenological Approach to the Social Sciences* New York: John Wiley & Sons, 1975

Boone, Edgar J., Shearon, Ronald W., White, Estelle and Associates *Serving Personal and Community Needs Through Adult Education* San Fransisco: Jossey Bass, AEA/USA, 1980

Booth, Charles *Charles Booth's London* Fried, A. and Elman, R. (eds) Harmondsworth: Penguin Books, 1971

Borzak Leonore (ed.) *Field Study: A Source Book for Experiential Learning* Beverly Hills: Sage Publications, 1981

Boshier, Roger 'Motivational Orientations of Adult Education Participants: A Factor Analytic Exploration of Houle's Typology' *Adult Education* (USA) 21/2 (1971): 3–26.

Boucouvalas Marcie *Interface: Lifelong Learning and Community Education* Charlotesville: Mid-Atlantic Center for Community Education, Research Report 79–104, 1979

Boyd, Robert D. and Apps, Jerold W. *Redefining the Discipline of Adult Education* San Fransisco: Jossey Bass, AEA/USA, 1980

Boydell Tom *Experiential Learning* Manchester: Manchester Monographs in Adult Education, University of Manchester, 1976

Boyle, Patrick G. *Planning Better Programs* New York: McGraw Hill, 1981

Brandt, Richard M. 'Community Observation' in Brabach, Harold J. and Decker, Larry E. (eds) *Planning and Assessment in Community Education* Midland, Michigan: Pendell Publishing Co., 1977

Brill, Naomi I. *Working With People: The Helping Process* Philadelphia: J.B. Lippincott Co., 1973

Brookfield, Stephen D. 'Charles Booth and Sociology' Reading: University of Reading, Dept. of Sociology, M.A. Thesis (Unpublished) 1974

Brookfield, Stephen D. 'Educational Advice for Adults' *Education and Training* 19 (1977a): 137–9

Brookfield, Stephen D. 'A Local Correspondence Tuition Service' *Adult Education* (UK) 50 (1977b): 39–43

Brookfield, Stephen D. 'Learning How to Learn: the Characteristics, Motivations and Destinations of Adult Study Skills Students' *Adult Education* (UK) 50 (1978a): 363–8

Brookfield, Stephen D. 'Individualizing Adult Learning: An English Experiment' *Lifelong Learning/The Adult Years* 1 (1978b): 18–20

Brookfield, Stephen D. 'Supporting Autonomous Adult Learning Groups' *Adult Education* (UK) 51 (1979a): 366–9

Brookfield, Stephen D. 'Adult Study Problems' *Journal of Further & Higher Education* 3 (1979b): 91–6

Brookfield, Stephen D. 'Independent Adult Learning' Leicester: University of Leicester, Ph.D Thesis (Unpublished) 1980a

Brookfield, Stephen D. 'The Nature of Independent Adult Learning' *Continuing Education* 1 (1980b): 2–3

Brookfield, Stephen D. 'Independent Adult Learning' *Studies in Adult Education* 13 (1981a): 15–27

Brookfield, Stephen D. 'Overcoming Culture-Specific Limitations on Interviewing' *Adult Education Research Conference* (AERC) *Proceedings* De Kalb, Illinois, 1981b

Brookfield, Stephen D. 'The Adult Learning Iceberg: A Critical Review of the Work of Allen Tough' *Adult Education* (UK) 54 (1981c): 110–18

Brookfield, Stephen D. 'Preparing Adult Students for Entry to Higher Education: Continuing Education Initiatives in the U.K.' *Canadian Journal of University Continuing Education* (1981d): 4–9

Brookfield, Stephen D. 'Community Adult Education' *Community Education Journal* 9 (1982a): 14–16

Brookfield, Stephen D. 'Adult Education Research: A Comparison of North American and British Theory and Practice' *International Journal of Lifelong Education* 1 (1982b): 157–67

Brookfield, Stephen D. 'Adult Education Research in North America and Britain: A Comparative Analysis of Perceptions and Practice' *Adult Education Research Conference (AERC) Proceedings* Lincoln, Nebraska, 1982c

Brown, Frank B. *Education By Appointment: New Approaches to Independent Study* New York: Parker Publishing Co., 1968

Brundage, Donald H. and Mackreacher, Dorothy *Adult Learning Principles and Their Application to Program Planning* Toronto: Ministry of Education, Ontario, 1980

Bryson, Lyman *Adult Education* New York: American Book Co., 1936

Buttedahl, K. 'Living Room Learning' in Kidd J.R. and Selman Gordon (eds) *Coming of Age: Canadian Adult Education in the 1960's* Toronto: Canadian Association for Adult Education, 1978

Cameron, William Bruce *Informal Sociology: A Casual Introduction to Sociological Thinking* New York: Random House, 1963

Campbell , M. Donald 'Community Education for Group Growth' in Boyd, Robert D. and Apps, Jerold W. *op. cit.*, 1980

Chamberlain, Martin N. 'The Professional Adult Educator: An Examination of His Competencies and of the Programs of Graduate Study which Prepare him for Work in the Field' Chicago: University of Chicago, Ph.D. dissertation (unpublished), 1960

Clark, Kathleen 'Independent Learning: A Concept Analysis' *Proceedings of a Conference on Independent Learning* Vancouver: Center for Continuing Education, University of British Columbia, W.K. Kellog Report 7, 1973

Clark, Michael 'Meeting the Needs of the Adult Learner: Using Nonformal Education for Social Action' *Convergence* 11 (1978): 44–53

Coady, Moses M. *Masters of Their Own Destiny* New York: Harper & Brothers, 1939 (Reprinted in 1980 by Formac Publishing Co., Antigonish, Nova Scotia)

Coady, Moses M. 'Adult Education in Action' A reprint of part of a broadcast given in 1938 *Learning* 2 (1979): 6

Coggins, Chere C. 'Individual Growth through Community Problem-Solving' in Boyd, Robert D. and Apps, Jerold W. *op. cit.*, 1980

Coleman, James S. 'Differences Between Experiential and Classroom Learning' in Keeton, Morris T. and Associates *Experiential Learning: Rationale, Characteristics and Assessment* San Fransisco: Jossey Bass, 1976

Colllingwood, R.G. *The Idea of History* Oxford: Oxford University Press, 1943

Community Education Development Centre (CEDC) *Community Education Developments: U.K. 1982* Coventry: Community Education Development Centre, 1982

Community Work Group *Current Issues in Community Work* London: Routledge & Kegan Paul, 1973

Compton Freeman H. 'Community Development Theory and Practice' in Draper, James A. (ed.) *Citizen Participation: Canada* Toronto; New Press, 1971

Compton J. Lin and McClusky, Howard M. 'Community Education for Community Improvement' in Boone, Edgar J., Shearon, Ronald W., White, Estelle E. and Associates *Serving Personal and Community Needs Through Adult Education* San Francisco: Jossey Bass, 1980

Conchelos, Greg and Kassam, Yussuf 'A Brief Review of Critical Opinions and Responses on Issues facing Participatory research' *Convergence* 14 (1981): 52–64

Conger, D. Stuart *Canadian Open Learning Systems* Prince Albert, Canada: Saskatchewan Training Research and Development Station, Dept of Manpower and Immigration, 1974

Conger, D. Stuart 'Canadian Open Learning Systems' in Kidd, J.R. and Selman, G. (eds) *Coming of Age: Canadian Adult Education in the 1960's* Toronto: Canadian Association for Adult Education, 1978

Conti, Gari J. 'Rebels with a Cause: Myles Horton and Paulo Freire' *Community College Review* 5 (1977): 36–43

Convergence 'Independent Study: Three Reports from Asia' *Convergence* 5 (1972): 70–79

Copeland, Harlan G. and Grabowski, Stanley M. 'Research and Investigation in the United States' *Convergence* 4 (1971): 23–30

Council for the Assessment of Experiential Learning (CAEL) *CAEL News* 5 (1982)

Cowperthwaite, G. 'Options for Lifelong Learners: The External Degree' in Heerman, B., Coppeck, Enders Cheryl and Wise, Elizabeth (eds) *Serving Lifelong Learners* San Francisco: Jossey Bass, New Directions for Community Colleges no. 8, 1980

Cremin, Lawrence A. *American Education: The Colonial Experience 1607–1783* New York: Harper & Row, 1970

Cross, K. Patricia *Adults as Learners: Increasing Participation and Facilitating Learning* San Fransisco: Jossey Bass, 1981

Cunningham, Phyllis M. and Hawking, James 'Literature Review of Research on MCE for Professionals' in Heaney, Tom (ed.) *Task Force on Voluntary Learning Report* Chicago, AEA/USA, 1980

Dadswell, G. 'The Adult Independent Learner and Public Libraries: A New Perspective for the Library Service' *Adult Education* (UK) 51 (1978): 5–11

Dale, Sheila 'The Adult Independent Learning Project: Work with Adult Self-Directed Learners in Public Libraries' *Journal of Librarianship* 11 (1979): 83–106

Dale, Sheila 'Another Way Forward for Adult Learners: The Public Library and Independent Study' *Studies in Adult Education* 12 (1980): 29–38

Daloz, L.A. 'Giving Education Back to the Learner' *International Journal of Career and Continuing Education* 1 (1975): 97–102

Danielson, Michael *The Politics of Exclusion* New York: Columbia University Press, 1976

Darkenwald, Gordon G. 'Field Research and Grounded Theory' in Long, Huey B. & Hiemstra, Roger and Associates *Changing Approaches to Studying Adult Education* San Fransisco: Jossey Bass, AEA/USA, 1980

Darkenwald, Gordon G. and Merriam, Sharan B. *Adult Education: Foundations of Practice* New York: Harper & Row, 1982

Davie, Lynn E. 'Group Transactions in Communities' in Boyd, Robert D. and Apps, Jerold W. *op. cit.*, 1980

Davis, Allison, Gardner B.B. and Gardner M.R. *Deep South* Chicago: University of Chicago Press, 1944

Davis, James A. *Great Books and Small Groups* New York: Free Press, 1961

Day, Michael 'On Behalf of Voluntary Adult Education' in Heaney, Tom (ed.) *Task Force on Voluntary Learning Report* Chicago: AEA/USA, 1980

Decker, Larry *People Helping People: An Overview of Community Education* Midland, Michigan: Pendell Publishing Co., 1978 (rev. ed.)

Dennis, N. 'Popularity of the Neighbourhood Community Idea' in Pahl, R.A. (ed.) *Readings in Urban Sociology* Oxford: Pergamon Press, 1968

Dickinson, Gary *Teaching Adults: A Handbook for Instructors* Don Mills, Ontario: General Publishing Co., 1979

Dickson, David 'Is the Community School an Effective Model for Neighbourhood-Based Community Development?' *Community Education Journal* 2 (1981): 18–21

Di Silvestro, Frank R. (ed.) *Advising and Counseling Adult Learners* San Fransisco: Jossey Bass, New Directions in Continuing Education 10, 1981

Draves, William A. 'The Free University Network' *Lifelong Learning/The Adult Years* 3/4 (1979): 4–5, 30

Draves, William A. *The Free University: A Model for Lifelong Learning* Chicago: Follett Publishing Co., 1980

Dressel, Paul L. and Thompson, Mary M. *Independent Study: A New Interpretation of Concepts, Practices and Networks* San Fransisco: Jossey Bass, 1973

Driscoll, W.J. 'New Developments and Changes in Independent Study' *Convergence* 5/2 (1972): 26–36

Effrat, Maria *The Community: Approaches and Implications* New York: Free Press, 1974

Eisenberg, Sheldon and Delaney, Daniel M. *The Counseling Process* Chicago: Rand McNally Publishing Co., 1977 (2nd ed)

Elias, John 'Andragogy Revisited' *Adult Education* (USA) 29 (1979): 252–5

Elias, John and Merriam, Sharan B. *Philosophical Foundations of Adult Education* New York: Robert E. Krieger, 1980

Elsey, Barry 'Voluntary Organisations and Adult Education' *Adult Education* (UK) 46 (1974): 391–6

Erteschik, Ann (ed.) *Library Programs Worth Knowing About* Washington D.C.: Office of Libraries & Learning Resources, U.S. Office of Education, 1977

Essert, Paul L. 'The Discussion Group in Adult Education in America' in Ely, Mary L. (ed.) *Handbook of Adult Education in the United States* New York: Teachers College, Columbia University, 1948

Faris, Ron *The Passionate Educators: Voluntary Associations and the Struggle for Control of Adult Educational Broadcasting 1919–1952* Toronto: Peter Martin Associates, 1975

Farquharson, Andrew 'Peers as Helpers: Personal Change in Members of Self-Help Groups in Metropolitan Toronto' Toronto: University of Toronto, Doctoral Dissertation, (Unpublished), 1975

Fellenz, Robert A. and Coker, Larry W. 'Toward a Definition of Adult Education, Community Education and Community Development' in *Yearbook of Adult and Continuing Education 1979–1980* Chicago: Marquis Academic Media, 1980

Fessler Donald R. *Facilitating Community Change: A Basic Guide* La Jolla, California: University Associates, 1976

Filkin, Elizabeth and Yarnit, Martin 'When a Second Chance is a Good Thing' *Times Higher Education Supplement* 22 February, 1980

Fletcher, Colin 'Community Studies as Practical Adult Education' *Adult Education* (UK) 53 (1980a): 73–8

Fletcher, Colin 'The Theory of Community Education and its Relation to Adult Education' in Thompson, Jane L. (ed.) *Adult Education for a Change* London: Hutchinson, 1980b

Fletcher, Colin 'The Forseeable Future' in Fletcher, Colin and Thompson, Neil (eds) *Issues in Community Education* Lewes, Sussex: Falmer Press, 1980c

Fletcher, Colin and Thompson, Neil (eds) *Issues in Community Education* Lewes, Sussex: Falmer Press, 1980

Fordham, Paul, Poulton, Geoff and Randle, Lawrence *Learning Networks in Adult Education: Non-Formal Education on a New Housing Estate* London: Routledge & Kegan Paul, 1979

Frankenburg, Ronald *Communities in Britain: Social Life in Town and Country* Harmondsworth: Penguin Books, 1966

Free University Network *1981 National Directory of Free Universities and Learning Networks* Manhattan, Kansas: Free University Network, 1981

Freire, Paulo *Cultural Action for Freedom* Cambridge, Massachussetts; Harvard Educational Review, 1970

Freire, Paulo *Pedagogy of the Oppressed* Harmondsworth: Penguin Books, 1972

Gagné, Robert M. 'Learning Research and its Implications for Independent Learning' in Weisgerberger, R.A, (ed.) *Perspectives in Individualized Learning* New York: F.E. Peacock Publishers, 1971

Gagné, Robert M. *Essentials of Learning for Instruction* Hinsdale, Illinois: Dryden Press, 1975

Gagné, Robert M. *The Conditions of Learning* New York: Holt, Rinehart & Winston, 1977 (3rd ed.)

Gans, H.J. *The Levittowners* London: Allen Lane, 1967

Gardner, John W. *Self Renewal* New York: Harper & Row, 1963

Garfinkel, Harold J. *Studies in Ethnomethodology* Englewood Cliffs, New Jersey: Prentice Hall, 1967

Gartner, Alan P. 'Credentialing the Disenfranchized' in Keeton, Morris T. and Associates *Experiential Learning: Rationale, Characteristics and Assessment* San Fransisco: Jossey Bass, 1976

Gaventa, John and Horton, Billy D. 'A Citizen's Research Project in Appalachia, U.S.A.' *Convergence* 14 (1981): 30–42

Gibbs, Graham *Teaching Students to Learn: A Student-Centred Approach* Milton Keynes: Open University Press, 1981

Glaser, Barney G. and Strauss, Anselm L. *The Discovery of Grounded Theory: Strategies for Qualitative Research* Chicago; Aldine Publishing Co., 1967

Goldberg, Joan C. 'Counseling the Adult Learner: A Selective Review of the Literature' *Adult Education* (USA) 30 (1980); 67–81

Gould, Samuel B. (ed.) *Diversity by Design* San Fransisco: Jossey Bass, 1973

Grantham, Marilyn and Dyer, D.A. 'Community Development as an Educational Process' in Stubblefield, Harold W. (ed.) *Continuing Education for Community Leadership* San Fransisco: Jossey Bass, New Directions for Continuing Education 11, 1981

Griffin, Virginia 'Self-Directed Adult Learners and Learning' *Learning* 2 (1978): 6–8

Griffith, William S. 'Paulo Freire:: Utopian Perspectives on Literacy Education for Revolution' in Grabowski, Stanley M. (ed.) *Paulo Freire: A Revolutionary Dilemma for the Adult Educator* Syracuse, Syracuse University Publications in Continuing Education, 1972

Griffith, William S. 'Educational Needs: Definition, Assessment and Utilization' *School Review*, May 1978: 382–94

Griffith, William S. 'Adult Education Research – Emerging Developments' *Studies in Adult Education* 11 (1979): 125–44

Griffith, William S. and Cristarella, Mary C. 'Participatory Research: Should it be a New Methodology for Adult Educators?' in Niemi, John A. (ed.) *Viewpoints on Adult Education Research*: Columbus, Ohio: ERIC Clearinghouse on Adult, Career & Vocational Education, Information Series No. 171, 1979

Gross, Ronald *The Lifelong Learner* New York: Simon & Schuster, 1977

Gross, Ronald 'Independent Scholarship: Passion and Pitfalls' *Chronicle of Higher Education* 22(16) 1981: 56

Gross, Ronald *The Independent Scholar's Handbook* Reading, Mass.: Addison-Wesley, 1982

Guglielmino, Lucy *Self-Directed Learning Readiness Scale: A Measurement of One's Current Readiness for Self-Directed Learning* Boca Baton, Florida: Guglielmino Associates, 1978

Hall, Budd L. ''Participatory Research: An Approach for Change' *Convergence* 8/2 (1975): 24–31

Hall, Budd L. 'Breaking the Monopoly of Knowledge: Research Methods, Participation and Development' in Hall, Budd L. and Kidd, J.R. (eds) *Adult Learning: A Design For Action* Oxford: Pergamon Press, 1978

Hall, Budd L. 'Participatory Research: Breaking the Academic Monopoly' in Niemi, John A. (ed.) *Viewpoints on Adult Education Research* Columbus, Ohio: ERIC Clearinghouse on Adult, Career & Vocational Education, Information Series No. 171, 1979

Hall, Budd L. 'Participatory Research, Popular Knowledge and Power: A Personal Reflection' *Convergence* 14 (1981): 6–19

Hall, Budd L. and Kidd J.R. (eds) *Adult Learning: A Design for Action* Oxford: Pergamon Press, 1978

Hallenbeck, Wilbur C., Verner Coolie, London, Jack and Bergevin, Paul *Community and Adult Education* Washington D.C.: Adult Education Association of the U.S.A., 1962

Hallenbeck, Wilbur C. 'Community in the Theory and Practice of Adult Education' in Hallenbeck, Wilbur C. *et al. op. cit.* 1962

Harrison, Bernard 'The Teaching–Learning Relationship in Correspondence Tuition' *Teaching at a Distance* 1 (1974): 2–8

Harrison, John 'Community Work and Adult Education' *Studies in Adult Education* 6 (1974): 50–67

Hart, J.K. *Adult Education* New York: Thomas Y. Cromwell, 1927

Hayens, Arthur 'Russell Recommendations Exemplified' *Adult Education* (UK) 47 (1974): 179–83

Heaney, Tom (ed.) *Task Force on Voluntary Learning Report* Chicago: AEA/USA, 1980

Hefferman, J.M., Macy, Francis U. and Vickers, D.F. *Educational Brokering: A New Service for Adult Learners* Syracuse: National Center for Educational Brokering (NCEB), 1976

Her Majesty's Stationery Office *Adult Education: A Plan For Development* London: Her Majesty's Stationery Office (HMSO), 1973

Heywood C.L. 'Broadcasting Adult Education Half a Century Ago' *Adult Education* (UK) 54 (1981): 242–5

Hiemstra, Roger *The Educative Community: Linking the Community, School and Family* Lincoln, Nebraska: Professional Educators Publications, 1972

Hiemstra, Roger 'The Educative Community in Action' *Adult Leadership* 24 (1975): 82–5

Hiemstra, Roger *Lifelong Learning* Lincoln, Nebraska: Professional Publications, 1976a

Hiemstra, Roger 'The Older Adult's Learning Projects' *Educational Gerontology* 1 (1976b): 331–41

Hiemstra, Roger (ed.) *Policy Recommendations Related to Self-Directed Adult Learning*

Syracuse: Syracuse University, Division of Educational Development & Adminstrative Studies, Occasional Paper 1 1980a

Hiemstra, Roger 'Adult and Community Education: Mobilizing the Resources of the City' in Franklin, Spikes W. (ed.) *The University and the Inner City: A Redefinition of Relationships* Lexington, Massachussets: Lexington Books, D. C. Heath & Co., 1980b

Hiemstra, Roger 'Teaching Community Adult Education Skills and Knowledge' Paper distributed as a portion of the symposium on *Community Adult Education: A Review of Principles, Practice and Philosophy* Lincoln, Nebraska: *Adult Community Research Conference Proceedings* 1982

Highlander Research and Education Center *Highlander Reports: October 1980* New Market: Tennessee, 1980

Hill, F. E. and Williams, W. E. *Radio's Listening Groups* New York: Columbia University Press, 1941

Himmelstrup, Per. Robinson, John and Fielden, Derrick *Strategies for Lifelong Learning: A Symposium of Views from Europe and the U.S.A.* Esbjerg, Denmark: University Centre of South Jutland/Association for Recurrent Education, 1981

Holmberg, Borje *Distance Education: A Survey and Bibliography* London: Kogan Page, 1977

Holmes, John 'Thoughts on Research Methodology' *Studies in Adult Education* 8 (1976): 149–63

Houle, Cyril O. *The Inquiring Mind: A Study of the Adult Who Continues to Learn* Madison: University of Wisconsin Press, 1961

Houle, Cyril O. *The Design of Education* San Fransisco: Jossey Bass, 1972

Houle, Cyril O. 'Deep Traditions of Experiential Learning' in Keeton, Morris T. and Associates *Experiential Learning: Rationale, Characteristics and Assessment* San Fransisco; Jossey Bass, 1976

Houle, Cyril O. *Continuing Learning in the Professions* San Fransisco: Jossey Bass, 1980

Hutchins, Robert M. Preface to Adler, Mortimer J. and Wolff, P. (eds) *A General Introduction to the Great Books and to a Liberal Education* Chicago: Encyclopedia Britannica Inc., 1959

Hutchinson, Enid 'Return to Study Courses' *Adult Education* (UK) 52 (1979): 98–103

Illich, Ivan *Deschooling Society* Harmondsworth: Penguin Books, 1971

Ironside, Diana J. 'Community Counselling for Adults' in Di Silvestro, Frank R. (ed) *Advising and Counselling Adult Learners* San Francisco: Jossey Bass, New Directions in Continuing Education 10, 1981

Ironside, Diana J. and Jacobs, Dorene E. *Trends in Counselling and Information Services for the Adult Learner* Toronto: Ontario Institute for Studies in Education, 1977

Jackson, Keith 'Adult Education and Community Development' *Studies in Adult Education* 2 (1970): 165–72

Jackson, Keith 'Community Adult Education — the Role of the Professional Adult Educator' *Adult Education* (UK) 44 (1971): 165–72

Jacobson, Marilyn D. 'Academic Credit for Life Learning' *Adult Leadership* 25 (1976): 98–100, 125

Jennings, Bernard (ed.) *Community Colleges in England and Wales* Leicester: National Institute for Adult Education, 1980

Jensen G., Liveright A. A. and Hallenbeck W. C. (eds) *Adult Education: Outlines of an*

Emerging Field of University Study Washington D.C.: Adult Education Association of America, 1964

Johnstone, John W. C. and Rivera, Ramon J. *Volunteers for Learning: A Study of the Educational Pursuits of American Adults* Chicago: Aldine Publishing Co., 1965

Jones, Arfon 'Sidney Stringer School and Community College' in Fletcher, Colin & Thompson, Neil (eds) *op. cit.*, 1980

Jones, H. A. and Charnley, A. H. *Adult Literacy: A Study of its Impact* Leicester: National Institute for Adult Education, 1978

Jourard, Sidney M. 'Fascination: A Phenomenological Perspective on Independent Learning' in Gleason, G.T. (ed.) *The Theory and Nature of Independent Learning*, Scranton, Pennsylvania: International Textbook Co., 1967

Kaplan, Michael H. and Schwartz, Terry Ann 'Community Education: A Vehicle for Community Problem Solving' in Stubblefield, Harold W. (ed.) *Continuing Education for Community Problem Solving* San Fransisco: Jossey Bass, New Directions for Continuing Education 11, 1981

Kasworm, Carol 'An Explanatory Study of the Development of Self-Directed Learning as an Instructional/Curriculum Strategy' Maryland: *Lifelong Learning Research Conference Proceedings*, University of Maryland, 1982

Kelly, Thomas *A History of Adult Education in Great Britain* Liverpool: Liverpool University Press, 1970 (2nd ed)

Kennedy, William B. 'Highlander Praxis: Learning with Myles Horton' *Teachers College Record* 83 (1981): 105 – 19

Kerensky, Vasil M. 'Ten Educational Myths: A Community Educator's Perspective' *Community Education Journal* 8/2 (1981): 9 – 13

Kerensky, Vasil M. and Melby E. *Education II* Midland, Michigan: Pendell Publishing Co., 1972

Keuscher, Robert M. 'Why Individualize Instruction?' in Howes, Virgil M. (ed.) *Individualization of Instruction: A Teaching Strategy* New York: Macmillan Co., 1970

Kidd, J. R. (ed.) *Learning and Society* Toronto: Canadian Association for Adult Education, 1963

Kidd, J.R. 'Adult Education, the Community, and the Animateur', in Draper, James A. (ed.) *Citizen Participation: Canada* Toronto: New Press, 1971

Kidd, J. R. *How Adults Learn* New York: Association Press, 1973

Kidd, J. R. 'The Fiftieth Anniversary of the Antigonish Movement' *Learning* 2/4 (1979): 6

Kidd J. R. 'Research Needs in Adult Education' *Studies in Adult Education* 13 (1981): 1 – 14

Kirkwood, Colin 'Adult Education and the Concept of Community' *Adult Education* (UK) 51 (1978): 145 – 51

Kirkwood, Robert 'Importance of Assessing Experiential Learning' in Keeton, Morris T. and Associates *Experiential Learning: Rationale, Characteristics and Assessment* Jossey Bass, San Fransisco, 1976

Knowles, Malcolm S. *The Modern Practice of Adult Education: Andragogy versus Pedagogy* New York: Association Press 1970

Knowles, Malcolm S. 'The Relevance of Research for the Adult Education Teacher/Trainer' *Adult Leadership* 20 (1972): 270 – 72, 302

Knowles, Malcolm S. *The Adult Learner: A Neglected Species* Houston, Texas: Gulf Publishing Co., 1973 (2nd ed., 1978)

Knowles, Malcolm S. *Self-Directed Learning: A Guide for Learners and Teachers* Chicago: Association Press, 1975

Knowles, Malcolm S. *A History of the Adult Education Movement in the United States* Huntington, New York: Robert E. Krieger Publishing Co., 1977

Knowles, Malcolm S. *The Modern Practice of Adult Education: From Pedagogy to Andragogy* Chicago: Follett Publishing Co., 1980a (rev. ed.)

Knowles, Malcolm S. 'The Growth and Development of Adult Education' in Peters, John M. and Associates *Building an Effective Adult Education Enterprise* San Fransisco: Jossey Bass, AEA/USA, 1980b

Knox, Alan B. 'Lifelong Self-Directed Education' in *Fostering the Need to Learn — Part One: Monographs and Annotated Bibliography on Continuing Education and Health Manpower* Syracuse: Syracuse University, 1974

Knox, Alan B. and Associates *Developing, Administering and Evaluating Adult Education* San Fransisco: Jossey Bass, 1980

Knox, Alan B. and Farmer, Helen S. 'Counseling and Information for Adult Learners' *International Review of Education* 23 (1977): 387–414

Knudson, Russell S. 'An Alternative Approach to the Andragogy/Pedagogy Issue' *Lifelong Learning/The Adult Years* 3/8 (1980): 8–10

Kolb, David A., Winter, Sara K. and Berlew, David E. 'Self-Directed Change: Two Studies' *Journal of Applied Behavioural Science* 4 (1968): 453–71

Kreitlow, Burton R. and Associates *Examining Controversies in Adult Education* San Fransisco: Jossey Bass, AEA/USA, 1981

Kulich, Jindra 'The Adult Self-Learner: An Historical Perspective' in Kidd J. R. and Selman G. (eds) *Coming of Age: Canadian Adult Education in the 1960's* Toronto: Canadian Association for Adult Education, 1978

Kurland, Norman 'The Scandinavian Study Circles: An Idea for the United States?' *College Board Review* 114 (1979): 20–23

Kurland, Norman 'The Scandinavian Study Circle: An Idea for the U.S.' *Lifelong Learning/The Adult Years* 5/6 (1982): 24–7, 30

Laidlaw, A. F. *The Campus and the Community: The Global Impact of the Antigonish Movement* Montreal: Harvest House, 1961

Lawson, Kenneth 'Community Education: A Critical Assessment' *Adult Education* (UK) 50 (1977): 6–13

Lawson, Kenneth *Philosophical Concepts and Values in Adult Education* Milton Keynes: Open University Press, 1979 (rev. ed.)

Lengrand, Paul *An Introduction to Lifelong Education* London: Croom Helm, 1975

Lewis, Oscar *Children of Sanchez: Autobiography of a Mexican Family* New York: Random House, 1961

Lewis, G. R. and Kinishi, Diane R. *The Learning Exchange* Evanston, Illinois: The Learning Exchange, 1977

Library Association *Community Information: What Libraries Can Do* London: The LibraryAssociation, 1980

Lindeman, Eduard *The Meaning of Adult Education* New York: New Republic, 1926 (Reissued in 1961 by Harvest House Publishers, Montreal)

Lipsett, L. and Avakian, Nancy A. 'Assessing Experiential Learning' *Lifelong Learning/The Adult Years* 5/2 (1981): 19–22

Little, David 'Adult Learning and Education: A Concept Analysis' in *Yearbook of Adult and Continuing Education 1979–1980* Chicago: Marquis Academic Media, 1979

Lofland, John *Analyzing Social Settings: A Guide to Qualitative Observation and Analysis* Belmont, California: Wadsworth Publishing Co., 1971

Long, Huey B. *Continuing Education of Adults in Colonial America* Syracuse: Syracuse University Publications in Continuing Education, 1976

Long, Huey B. ' "How To" Literature in Colonial America' *Lifelong Learning/The Adult Years* 3/9 (1980): 12–14

Lotz, Jim 'Thoughts on Community Developers' *Adult Leadership* 21 (1972): 79–81

Lotz, Jim 'The Antigonish Movement: A Critical Analysis' *Studies in Adult Education* 5 (1973): 79–112

Lotz, Jim *Understanding Canada: Regional and Community Development in a New Nation* Toronto: N.C. Press, 1977

Lovell, Bernard R. *Adult Learning* London: Croom Helm, 1980

Lovett, Tom 'Community Adult Education' *Studies in Adult Education* 3 (1971): 2–14

Lovett, Tom *Adult Education, Community Development and the Working Class* London: Ward Lock Educational, 1975

Lovett, Tom 'The Challenge of Community Education in Social and Political Change' *Convergence* 11/2 (1978): 42–51

Lovett, Tom 'Adult Education and Community Action' in Thompson, Jane L. (ed.) *Adult Education for a Change* London: Hutchinson, 1980

Lowe, John *Adult Education in England and Wales: A Critical Introduction* London: Michael Joseph, 1970

Luikart, Clark *Social Networks and Self-Planned Adult Learning* Chapel Hill, North Carolina: University of North Carolina Extension Bulletin 61, 1977

Lynd, R. S. and Lynd, H. M. *Middletown: A Study in Contemporary American Culture* New York: Harcourt Brace, 1929

Lynd, R. S. and Lynd, H. M. *Middletown in Transition* New York; Harcourt Brace, 1937

Macdonald, Carolyn 'A University Introduction to Study' *Adult Education* (UK) 55 (1982): 7–11

MacIver, R. M. and Page, C. H. *Society: An Introductory Analysis* London: Macmillan Papermac, 1961

Mackenzie, N., Postgate, N. and Scupham, R. *Open Learning; Systems and Problems in Post Secondary Education* Paris, Unesco Press, 1975

Maslow, Abraham H. *Toward a Psychology of Being* New York: D. Van Nostrand Co., 1968

Massachussetts Department of Education *Community Education: An Action. Handbook* Boston; Center Research Incorporated, Massachussetts Department of Education, 1979

McCall, George J. and Simmons, J. L. *Issues in Participant Observation: A Text and Reader* Reading, Massachussetts: Addison-Wesley Publishing Co., 1969

McCatty, Cressy 'Patterns of Learning Projects Among Professional Men' Toronto: University of Toronto, Ph.D Doctoral Dissertation (unpublished), 1973

McCullough, K. Owen 'Andragogy and Community Problem Solving' *Lifelong Learning/The Adult Years* 2/2 (1978): 8–9, 31

McElroy, Meredith *The Nature of Cooperation between Public Libraries and Free Universities/Learning Networks* Manhattan, Kansas: Free University Network, 1980

McGee, Leo 'Crediting Life Experiences Can Lead to Fraud' in Kreitlow, Burton, R. and Associates *Examining Controversies in Adult Education* San Fransisco: Jossey Bass, AEA/USA, 1981

McKenzie, Leon 'The Issue of Andragogy' *Adult Education* (USA) 27 (1977): 225–9

Mclure, Larry, Cook, Sue Carol and Thompson, Virginia *Experience Based Learning: How to Make the Community Your Classroom* Portland, Oregon: NorthWest Regional Educational Laboratory, 1977

McMahon, Ernest E. *Needs — of People and their Communities — and the Adult Educator* Washington D.C.: Adult Education Association of the U.S.A., 1970

Mead, George Herbert *Mind, Self and Society* Chicago: University of Chicago Press, 1934

Merriam, Sharan B. 'Ben Franklin's Junto Revisited' *Lifelong Learning/The Adult Years* 2/10 (1979): 18–19

Meyer, P. *Awarding College Credit for Non-College Learning* San Fransisco: Jossey Bass, 1975

Mezirow, Jack, Darkenwald, Gordon G. and Knox, Alan B. *Last Gamble on Education* Washington D.C.: Adult Education Association of the U.S.A., 1975

Mezirow, Jack 'Perspective Transformation' *Studies in Adult Education* 9 (1977): 153–64

Midwinter, Eric *Priority Education: An Account of the Liverpool Project* Harmondsworth: Penguin Books, 1972

Midwinter, Eric *Patterns of Community Education* London: Ward Lock Educational, 1973

Miller, Harry L. *Teaching and Learning in Adult Education* New York: Macmillan, 1964

Miller, James W., 'Community Needs Assessment' in Klevens, Chester (ed.) *Materials and Methods in Continuing Education* Canoga Park, California: Klevens Publications Inc., 1976

Mills, C. Wright *The Sociological Imagination* Harmondsworth: Penguin Books, 1959

Minzey, Jack D. and Le Tarte, Clyde *Community Education: From Program to Process* Midland, Michigan: Pendell Publishing Co., 1972

Minzey, Jack D. and Le Tarte, Clyde *Community Education: From Program to Process to Practice* Midland, Michigan: Pendell Publishing Co. 1979

Monette, Maurice L. 'The Concept of Educational Need: An Analysis of Selected Literature' *Adult Education* (USA) 27 (1977): 116–127

Monette, Maurice L. 'Need Assessment: A Critique of Philosophical Assumptions' *Adult Education* (USA) 29 (1979): 83–95

Moon, Rexford G. and Hawes, Gene (eds) *Developing New Clienteles of Adult Students* San Fransisco: Jossey Bass, New Directions for Experiential Learning 7, 1980

Moore, Michael G. 'Towards a Theory of Independent Learning' *Journal of Higher Education* 44 (1973a): 661–79

Moore, Michael G. 'Speculations on a Definition of Independent Study' Vancouver: *Proceedings of a Conference on Independent Learning* Center for Continuing Education, University of British Columbia, W. K. Kellog Report 7, 1973b

Moore, Michael G. 'A Model of Independent Study' *Epistolodidaktika* 1 (1977): 6–40

Moore, Michael G. 'Independent Study' in Boyd, Robert D., Apps, Jerold W. and Associates *Redefining the Discipline of Adult Education* San Fransisco: Jossey Bass, AEA/USA, 1980

Morris, Henry *The Village College* Cambridge; Cambridge University Press, 1924

National Advisory Council for Adult Education (NACAE) *Terms, Definitions, Organizations and Councils Associated with Adult Learning* Washington D.C.: NACAE, 1980

National Council for Educational Brokering (NCEB) 'Three Key Issues: Evaluating Educational Providers, The Counseling Link, Empowerment' Syracuse: *Bulletin of National Council for Educational Brokering* 6/2 (1981)

National Extension College (NEC) *Study Circle Newsletter* 1 (1982)

Neufeld, V. and Barrows, H. 'A Problem-Solving Design: McMaster Medical School' in Herman, Reg (ed.) *The Design of Self-Directed Learning* Toronto: Dept of Adult Education, Ontario Institute for Studies in Education, 1981

Nevada State Department of Education *A Process Model for Community Development* Carson City, Nevada: Department of Education, 1977

Newby, Howard 'In the Field: Reflections on the Study of Suffolk Farm Workers' in Bell, Colin and Newby, Howard (eds) *Doing Sociological Research* London: Allen & Unwin, 1977

Newman, Michael *The Poor Cousin: A Study of Adult Education* London: Allen & Unwin, 1979

Ohliger, John 'What Happened to the Canadian *Farm Radio Forum?*' *Adult Education* (USA) 18 (1968): 176–87

Ohliger, John 'Is Lifelong Adult Education a Guarantee of Permanent Inadequacy?' *Convergence* 7/2 (1974)

Organisation for Economic Cooperation and Development (OECD) *Learning Opportunities for Adults Vol. 1* Paris: OECD, 1979

Osborn Marilyn, Charnley Alan and Withnall A. *Educational Information, Advice, Guidance and Counseling for Adults* Leicester: National Institute for Adult Education, Review of Existing Research in Adult and Continuing Education, Vol. 6, 1981

Osborne, Karen Quallo 'Informal Adult Learning and Public Policy Issues: The Study Circle Approach' in Stubblefield, Harold W. (ed.) *Continuing Education for Community Leadership* San Fransisco: Jossey Bass, New Directions for Continuing Education 11, 1981

Park, Robert E. *Human Communities: The City and Human Ecology* New York: Free Press, 1952

Participatory Research Group 'Participatory Research Group' Information leaflet Toronto: International Council for Adult Education, 1980

Passow, A. H. 'Trends in Learning and Education Affecting Community Library Services' in Garrison, G. (ed.) *Total Community Library Service* Chicago: American Library Association, 1973

Paterson, R. W. K. 'The Concept of Discussion: A Philosophical Approach' *Studies in Adult Education* 1 (1970): 28–50

Paterson, R. W. K. 'Social Change as an Educational Aim' *Adult Education* (UK) 45 (1973): 353–9

Paterson, R. W. K. *Values, Education and the Adult* London: Routledge & Kegan Paul, 1979

Pedler, Mike 'Teaching Students to Learn' *Adult Education* (UK) 45 (1972): 87–91

Penfield, Kathy 'Prospects for a Learning Society' *Adult Leadership* 24 (1975): 40–44

Penland, Patrick R. *Self-Planned Learning in America* Pittsburgh: Book Center, University of Pittsburgh, 1977

Penland, Patrick R. 'Self-Initiated Learning' *Adult Education* (USA) 29 (1979a): 170–79

Penland, Patrick R. 'Individual Self-Planned Learning in America: Summary Report' in *Yearbook of Adult and Continuing Education 1979–1980* Chicago: Marquis Academic Media, 1979b

Penland, Patrick R. 'Self-Directed Adult Learning: Implications for the Practitioner' Anaheim, California: Paper presented at the 1981 AEA Commission of Professors meeting on *Self-Directed Adult Learning*, 1981

Penland, Patrick R. and Shirk, J. C. 'The Public Library as a Community Resource' *Community Education Journal* 9 (1981): 14–17

Pennington, Floyd C. (ed.) *Assessing Educational Needs of Adults* San Francisco: Jossey Bass, New Directions for Continuing Education 7, 1980

Percy, Keith and Ramsden, Paul *Independent Study: Two Examples from English Higher Education* Guildford: University of Surrey, Society for Research into Higher Education, 1980

Perraton, Hilary 'I Sat in H. G. Wells's Chair' *Teaching at a Distance* 13 (1978): 1–4

Peters, John M. and Gordon, Susan *Adult Learning Projects: A Study of Adult Learning in Rural and Urban Tennessee* Knoxville: University of Tennessee, 1974

Peters, R. S. 'Education as Initiation' in Archambault, R. D. (ed.) *Philosophical Analysis and Education* London: Routledge & Kegan Paul, 1965

Polsky, Harlan L. 'Community Needs Assessement — Another Viewpoint' in Klevens, Chester (ed.) *Materials and Methods in Continuing Education* Canoga Park, California: Klevens Publications Inc., 1976

Poster, Cyril D. *The School and Community* London: Macmillan, 1971

Powell, Susan A. 'State Policies: Plans and Activities' in Peterson, Richard E. and Associates *Lifelong Learning in America: An Overview of Current Practices, Available Resources and Future Prospects* San Fransisco: Jossey Bass, 1979

Rée, Harry *Educator Extraordinary: The Life and Achievement of Henry Morris* London: Longman, 1973

Rees, A. *Life in a Welsh Countryside* Cardiff: University of Wales Press, 1950

Reimer, Everett *School is Dead* Harmondsworth: Penguin Books, 1971

Riesman, David *The Lonely Crowd: A Study of the Changing American Character* New Haven: Yale University Press, 1961

Roberts, Hayden *Community Development: Learning and Action* Toronto: University of Toronto Press, 1979

Rockhill, Kathleen 'Professional Education Should Not Be Mandatory' in Kreitlow, Burton W. and Associates *Examining Controversies in Adult Education* San Fransisco: Jossey Bass, AEA/USA, 1981

Rogers, Carl R. *On Becoming a Person: A Therapist's View of Psychotherapy* Boston: Houghton Mifflin Co, 1961

Rogers, Carl R. *Freedom to Learn* Columbus, Ohio: Charles E. Merrill, 1969

Rogers, Jennifer *Adults Learning* Milton Keynes: Open University Press, 1979a

Rogers, Jennifer 'Independent Learning in the Post-Compulsory Sector in the United Kingdom' in *Learning Opportunities for Adults Vol. 2: New Structures, Programmes and Methods* Paris: Organisation for Economic Cooperation and Development, 1979b

Rogers, Jennifer and Groombridge, Brian *Right to Learn: The Case for Adult Equality* London: Arrow Books, 1976

Rogers, Maria 'Autonomous Adult Learning Groups' in Ely, Mary L. (ed.) *Handbook of Adult Education in the United States* New York: Teachers College, Columbia University, 1948

Rowntree, Derek *Learn How to Study: A Programmed Introduction to Better Study Techniques* London: Macdonald & Jane's Publications, 1976 (2nd ed)

Ruddock, Ralph 'A Time to Attack' *Adult Education* (UK) 46 (1974): 372–6

Ruddock Ralph *Perspectives on Adult Education* Manchester: University of Manchester, Dept of Adult Education, Monograph No. 2 1980 (2nd ed)

Scottish Education Department *Adult Education: The Challenge of Change* London: Her Majesty's Stationery Office, 1975

Seay, Maurice F. and Associates *Community Education: A Developing Concept* Midland, Michigan: Pendell Publishing Co., 1977

Seeley, J. R., Sim, R. A., and Loosley, E. W. *Crestwood Heights* New York: Wiley, 1963

Seller, Maxine S. 'Success and Failure in Adult Education: The Immigrant Experience' *Adult Education* (USA) 28 (1978): 83–99

Sharon, A. *Assessing College Credit for Non-College Learning* San Fransisco: Jossey Bass, 1975

Shawen, Neil M. 'The American Lyceum and Adult Education' *Lifelong Learning/The Adult Years* 2/7 (1979): 8–11, 27

Sheats, Paul H., Jayne, Clarence D. and Spence, Ralph B. (eds) *Adult Education: The Community Approach* New York: The Dryden Press, 1953

Sim, Alex R. *Canada's Farm Radio Forum* Paris: UNESCO, 1954

Simey, Margaret 'Let's Put Politics Back on the Agenda' *Adult Education* (UK) 48 (1976): 223–7

Smith, Robert M. *Learning How to Learn: Applied Learning Theory for Adults* Chicago: Follett, 1982

Smith, Virginia B. Foreword to *Experiential Learning: Rationale, Characteristics and Assessment* Keeton, Morris T. & Associates San Fransisco: Jossey Bass, 1976

Squires, Gregory D. 'The Learning Exchange: An Innovation in Adult Education' *Adult Leadership* 23 (1974): 98, 109

Srinivasan, Lyra *Perspectives on Non-Formal Adult Learning: Functional Education for Individual, Community and National Development* New York: World Education, 1977

Stacey, Margaret *Tradition and Change: A Study of Banbury* Oxford: Oxford University Press, 1960

Stark, Stephen L. *Conducting Community Surveys* Midland, Michigan: Pendell Publishing Co. 1976

Stein, Maurice R. *The Eclipse of Community* New York: Harper & Row, 1964

Stewart, Brian 'A Community Adult Education Service' *Adult Education* (UK) 49 (1976): 69–74

Stock, Arthur 'Introduction' in Jennings, Bernard (ed.) *op. cit.*, 1980

Strong, Marie 'The Autonomous Adult Learner' Nottingham: University of Nottingham, M.Ed. dissertation (unpublished) 1977

Stubblefield, Harold W. 'The Aims of the American Adult Education Movement in the 1920's: A Historical Analysis' *Adult Education Research Conference Proceedings* Ann Arbor, Michigan: AERC 1979

Stubblefield, Harold W. (ed.) *Continuing Education for Community Problem Solving* San Francisco: Jossey Bass, New Directions for Continuing Education 11, 1981

Stubblefield, Harold W. and Hunt, Thomas 'The Case of Jane Addams and the Revisionist Historians: A Framework for Writing a History of Adult Education' *Adult Education Research Conference Proceedings* Lincoln, Nebraska: AERC, 1982

Thomas A. Edison State College *Thomas A. Edison State College 1980–1981 Catalog* Trenton, New Jersey: 1981a

Thomas A. Edison State College *Portfolio Assessment: The Student Handbook* Trenton, New Jersey: Thomas A. Edison State College, 1981b

Thompson, Neil 'Training for Bridge Building' in Fletcher, Colin and Thompson, Neil (eds) *op. cit.*, 1980

Thresher, Jacquelyn 'Public Libraries are Natural Homes for Brokering Services, But Are Librarians 'Natural' Brokers?' National Center for Educational Brokering (NCEB) *Bulletin* 4/5, 1979

Titmus, Colin *Strategies for Adult Education: Practices in Western Europe* Chicago: Follett, 1981

Tough, Allen M. 'The Assistance Obtained by Adult Self-Teachers' *Adult Education* (USA) 17 (1966): 30–37

Tough, Allen M. *Learning Without a Teacher: A Study of Tasks and Assistance during Adult Self-Teaching Projects* Toronto: Ontario Institute for Studies in Education, Educational Research Series 3, 1967

Tough, Allen M. *Why Adults Learn; A Study of the Major Reasons for Beginning and Continuing a Learning Project* Toronto: Ontario Institute for Studies in Education 1968

Tough, Allen M. 'Self-Planned Learning and Major Personal Change' in Smith, Robert M. (ed.) *Adult Learning: Issues and Innovations* DeKalb: Northern Illinois University, Dept of Secondary and Adult Education, 1976

Tough, Allen M. 'Major Learning Efforts: Recent Research and Future Directions' *Adult Education* (USA) 28 (1978): 250–63

Tough, Allen M. *The Adult's Learning Projects: A Fresh Approach to Theory and Practice in Adult Learning* Toronto: Ontario Institute for Studies in Education, 1979a (2nd ed)

Tough, Allen M. 'Fostering Self-Planned Learning' in *Learning Opportunities for Adults Vol. 2: New Structures, Programmes and Methods* Paris: Organisation for Economic Cooperation and Development, 1979b

Tough, Allen M. *Expand Your Life: A Pocket Book for Personal Change* New York: College Entrance Examinations Board, 1980

Tough, Allen M. *Intentional Changes: A Fresh Approach to Helping People Change* Chicago: Follett, 1982

Valley, John R. 'Local Programs: Innovations and Problems' in Peterson, Richard E. and Associates *Lifelong Learning in America: An Overview of Current Practices, Available Resources and Future Prospects* San Fransisco: Jossey Bass, 1979

Verner, Coolie 'Definition of Terms' in Jensen *et al., op. cit.* 1964

Verner, Coolie 'Community Action and Learning: A Concept Analysis' in Draper, James A. (ed.) *Citizen Participation: Canada* Toronto; New Press, 1971

Violas, P. C. 'Jane Addams and the New Liberalism' in Karier, C. J., Violas, P. and Spring, J. (eds) *Roots of Crisis: American Education in the Twentieth Century* Chicago: Rand McNally College Publishing Co., 1973

Warden, John W. *Process Perspectives: Community Education as Process* Charlotesville: Mid-Atlantic Community Education Consortium, 1979

Warden, John W. 'Community Education as a Political Act?' *Community Education Journal* 7/3 (1980): 5–10

Warner, L. W. and Lunt, P. S. *The Social Life of a Modern Community* New Haven: Yale University Press, 1941

Watkins, Roger 'Co-operative Learning in Discussion Groups' *Teaching at a Distance* 2 (1975): 7–9

Watts, Owen F. 'Adult Education at a Distance: The Box Scheme in Western Australia'' *Studies in Adult Education* 10 (1978): 14–27

Weaver, D. *The Emerging Community Education Model* Flint, Michigan: National Community Education Association, 1972

Weber, Max *The Methodology of the Social Sciences* New York: Free Press, 1949

Wedemeyer, Charles A. 'Independent Study' in Deighton, Lee C. (ed.) *The Encyclopedia of Education Vol. 4* New York: Macmillan Co., 1971

Whale, Brock W. 'The Community as a Place to Learn' in Baker, Harold B. (ed.) *The Teaching of Adults Series* Saskatoon: University of Saskatchewan, 1976

Williams, W. M. *The Sociology of an English Village* London: Routledge & Kegan Paul, 1956

Williams, Wyn and Robins, Wayne R. 'Observations on the Californian Case' in Fletcher, Colin and Thompson, Neil (eds.) *op. cit.*, 1980

Willingham, W. *Principles of Good Practice in Assessing Experiential Learning* Princeton: Council for Experiential Learning, Educational Testing Service, 1977

Willison, M. *The Rainbow Starts Here* Albany: Study Circle Consortium, University of the State of New York, 1980

Wiltshire, Harold C. 'The Concepts of Learning and Need in Adult Education' *Studies in Adult Education* 5 (1973): 26–30

Worby, Diana 'Independent Learning: The Uses of the Contract in an English Program' *Lifelong Learning/The Adult Years* 2/6 (1979): 32–4, 42

Wright, Joan 'Community Learning: A Frontier for Adult Education' in Boyd, Robert D., Apps, Jerold W. and Associates *op. cit.*, 1980

Wright, Joan 'Community Learning' in *Community Education: A Review of Principles, Practice and Philosophy* Lincoln, Nebraska: Adult Education Research Conference Proceedings, 1982

Yarnit, Martin 'Second Chance to Learn, Liverpool: Class and Adult Education' in Thompson, Jane L. (ed.) *Adult Education for a Change* London: Hutchinson, 1980

Young, Michael and Willmott, Peter *Family and Kinship in East London* Harmondsworth: Penguin Books, 1962

Zorbaugh, H. W. *The Gold Coast and the Slum* Chicago: University of Chicago Press, 1929

Zweig, Ferdynand *The Quest for Fellowship* London: Heinmann, 1965

Index

accreditation, 17,18, 26
  see also assessment, credit
activist orientated model of adult
  education, 175
activists, 8, 9
adult education, 1–4, 9–11, 29–30,
  60, 61
  and community development, 78
  for the community, 84–5
  in the community, 85–7
  of the community, 87–9, 94
  see also community education,
    education
Adult Education Association of
  America, 2
Adult Independent Learning Project
  (1973) USA, 160, 187
adult learners, 2, 137–8, 152–4
  see also independent learners
adult learning
  in the community, conceptual
    analysis, 11–15
  and community action, 104–6
  definitions of, 1–4, 11–12, 13–15
  groups, 4–6, 7–8; in the 18th &
    19th centuries, 90–4
  principles of, 149–52
  projects, 38–9
  ubiquity of, 1–4, 43–4, 198
The Adult Learning Iceberg, 34, 86
adult literacy, 74, 140
adult psychology, training sessions, 160
advisory work, libraries, 160
age, of independent learners, 42, 44–5
aims, of education, 28–9
amateur scholarship, 48

ambiguity, of role of informal educator,
  200–3
American Commission on Non-
  Traditional Study, 5–6
andragogy, 5, 27, 93, 103–4, 116,
  151–2, 199
animateurs, 7, 36, 89, 106, 176, 177–9
Antigonish Movement, 9, 71, 107–11
Appalachian Alliance, 116
assessment
  of experimental learning, 169
  of needs of community, 85, 128–30,
    133–4
  see also accreditation, credit,
    self-assessment
assistance, 37, 40, 46, 152–4, 198
  see also supporting adult learners in
    the community
Atlantic Canada Center for Community
  Education, Nova Scotia, 71
attitudes to learning, 52–3
autonomous learning, 27–8; groups, 5,
  90–4
autonomy, 178
avocational academics, 47–9
avocational liberal pursuits, 38

BBC
  study of adult literacy campaign, 140
  Wireless Discussion Groups, 97–8
Boston Community Schools
  Programme, 77
'Brain Train', commuter study groups,
  184
British Community Work Group, 194
brokerage, *see* educational brokering

California Community Schools, 77
Centerprise Project, London, 166
'change agent', 177
Chicago school of urban community studies, 63, 64
citizenship, 28, 88
Citizenship School, Johns Island, S. Carolina, 113
classroom learning, 39
clientele, of contemporary community education, 74
clubs, *see* societies
Coady, M., 110–11
cognitive skills, 190
community
    concept of, 8, 60, 61–3, 64–5
    creation of sense of, 65–6
    as educative influence, 82
    as learning resource, 8, 74, 85, 86, 87, 92, 182
    see also neighbourhood
community action, 104–6
community advisory councils, 75, 76
Community Association, 75
Community College, Vermont, 171
community development, 76, 78, 79, 106–7
community education, 7–9, 66–70, 73–8, 79, 81
Community Education Development Centre (CEDC), Coventry, 71, 73
community leaders, 132
community learning, 99–101
'community library', 161–2
community power, 63, 80–1
community problem-solving, 80–1, 101–4
community roles
    for adult education, 117
    for adult educators, 176–9
Community Schools, 70–3, 74, 77
community sentiment, 63
Community Survey, 131–3, 186–7
community transactions, and adult education, 9–11
Community Work Group, 105
community workers, 65–6, 194
competitions, 55, 57

conflict, needs of, 67–8, 81, 102
consultancy duties, 54
contemporary community education in the US and Britain, 73–8
contextual variables, 198–200
continuity learners, 36
continuing professional education, 29, 30
Cooperative Extension Service, 176–7, 179
co-operative movement, 9
Cooperative Program in Educational Administration, 72
correspondence study, 22, 23–4
costs, of tuition and transportation, 42
    see also financial costs
counselling, function of adult education, 119–20, 156–8
credentials, meaningless, 182
credit, for experiential learning, 29, 167–8, 169–71
    problems of, 171–2
    see also accreditation
credit courses, 39
credit unions
    Liverpool EPA, 119
    Nova Scotia, 9, 108–9
critical confidence, 56

Danish folk schools, 112, 117
democracy, 33, 103, 181
democratic procedures ignored, 75
'Design for Action', 89
development community, 8, 78, 89, 106–7
disabled, 186
disadvantaged groups, 9, 69, 74, 176
discussion groups, 97–8, 195–7
discussion group setting, 91–2
duration
    of learning, 39, 51
    of self-teaching projects, 37

economic impetus to community education, 109, 111
Edison State College, Trenton, New Jersey, 169–70

education, 8
  aim of, 28–9
  as initiation into body of knowledge,
    88
  as political act, 69–70
  see also adult education, community
    education
Educational Advisory Service, 187–8
educational brokering, 157–9, 161, 187
educational counselling, 119–20,
  156–8
Educational Exchange of Greater
  Boston, 158
educational needs, *see* needs
Educational Priority Area Project
  (EPA), Liverpool, 72, 117–25
educative community, 82–4, 85, 92
efficiency of learning, 2, 13
  see also quality of learning
enthusiasm, impetus for independent
  learning, 48
ethnic groups, 74, 75
ethical objections to MCE, 31–2
evaluation, of independent learning,
  55–6
evaluation techniques and procedures,
  151
experiential learning, 16–19, 167–72
experiential techniques of teaching, 151
experts, role in independent learning,
  33

facilitating learning, 152–4
  see also assistance
Farm Forum, 5, 95–6
felt needs, 129, 130
financial costs, for independent
  learners, 26
  see also costs
Flint, Michigan, 71, 108, 111
formal instructional setting, of adult
  learning in community, 13–14, 15
Free Universities, 5, 27, 30, 164,
  179–83
Freire, P., 110–11, 112, 114
Fund for the Improvement of Post-
  Secondary Education (FIPSE) 158,
  166

function, communities of, 61, 63

'*gemeinschaft*' type communities, 62, 66,
  67
geographical location, as concept of
  community, 62, 63, 64–5
goals, 15, 67, 79, 81, 86, 88
The Great Books Programme, 6, 30,
  92, 98–9
grounded theory, 7, 50, 51–2, 56,
  138–41
grounded research study, 148
group discussion, 121–2
group mode, independent learning,
  46–7
groups, adult learning in the
  community, 4–6, 7–8; in the 18th &
  19th centuries, 90–4
  see also discussion groups, ethnic
    groups, pressure groups, residents'
    groups, self-help groups
group transactions, and adult
  education, 9–10

help to independent learners, *see*
  assistance
Hiemstra, R., 82–3, 85
Highlander Folk School, 9, 71, 111–17
Highlander Research and Education
  Center, Knoxville, Tennessee, 115
history
  of adult education, 4–6, 10–11
  of self-learning, 2
Home Study Service, 188–9
Horton, M., 112, 114
Houle, C., 35, 36
Hull House, Chicago, 93
humanistic approach to adult
  education, 150, 151

immersion in community, 86, 117, 128,
  133
immigrant self-help group, 11
impetus
  to community education, 109, 111
  for independent scholarship, 48

independence in learning, 24–6, 41–2, 173
independent learners
  age of, 44–5
  assistance for, 152–4
  and public libraries, 159–62
  successful, 49–57
independent learning
  as aim of education, 28–9
  and correspondence study, 23–4
  definition, 2, 3–4, 22, 24–6, 32–3
  evaluation of success, 55–6
  in the group mode, 46–7
  synonyms, 26–9
  see also adult learning, learning
independent learning skills, 2
independent scholarship, 48
individual growth, potential for, 78, 104
  see also self-actualisation, self-fulfilment
individual mode, 34, 149
individual instructions, 22, 23
industrial training, 29
informal assessment methods, of needs, 133–4
informal community groups, 4–5
informal learning networks, 53–4
informal study discussion groups, 195–7
information services, 156–9
information sources, for self-learning, 42
  see also resources
inner city, educational component of regeneration, 118
'The Inquiring Mind', 35–6
in-service training programmes, 29
Institute of Community Studies, London, 64
institutional implementation of community education, 70–3
institutions, role of in adult education, 1–2, 3, 4, 67, 70
intentional changes, 39–40
interest, communities of, 61, 63
interviewing techniques, training sessions, 160

interviews
  in community settings, 137–8, 145–8
  open-ended, 35, 51
  structured, 45
'invisible university', 48

job-related learning projects, 41
The Junto, 92–3
Junto School, Philadelphia, 92–3

Kellog Foundation, 71–2

leaders
  of children's playgroups, 186
  in community, 132
Leadership Education Programme, 72
learner responsibility, 25, 26, 86
learning
  definition of, 11–12
  efficiency of, 2, 13, *see also* quality of learning
  professionally guided, 34
  purposeful, 14–15
  reasons for, 38, 42, 52
  settings for, 12–14, 18
  voluntary, 29–33
  see also adult learning, community learning, lifelong learning, self-planned learning
Learning Box Schemes (1930s), Australia, 5
learning contracts, 27, 155–6, 188–9
learning episode, 38
Learning Exchanges, 158, 162–7, 184
learning how to learn, *see* mathetics
learning projects, 38–9, 41–2, 157
learning resource, community as, 8, 74, 82, 85, 86, 87, 92, 182
liberal models of community education, 8, 66, 67–8, 70, 80, 101, 173
liberating models of community education, 8, 66, 68–70, 71, 74, 94, 101, 179
libraries, 93, 159–62, 164, 166, 186
Library Project, USA, 166
lifelong education, 1, 72

lifelong learning, 1, 2, 77
  interface with community education, 67
Liverpool Education Priority Area Project (EPA), 72, 117–25
Living Room Learning, 6, 96–7
local newspapers, as source for community survey, 132
local radio (Liverpool EPA), 123–4
lyceums, 4–5, 93

Malvern Hills College, 185–6, 193
'major learning effort', 39
mandatory continuing education (MCE), 30–2, 33
mass education, 48
mathetics, 154–5, 156, 190–1
Merlin Street Comunity Centre, 122, 123
methodological pluralism, 136
Michigan Community School Service, 71–2
Middletown, US, community power analysis, 63
Midwinter, E., 72
military education, 30
modes of adult education transactions, 10
Morris, H., 71, 72–3, 74
motives for education activists, 9
  see also reasons for learning
motivational orientation to learning, 35, 36
Mott, C. S., 71, 77
Mott Foundation, US, 8, 71
multi-transactional education, 11

National Association for Voluntary Learning (NAVL), 31
National Extension College (NEC), Britain, 184
National Housewives Register (NHR), 191–3
natural societal setting, of adult learning in community, 12–13, 14, 15
needs, educational, 60–1, 67–8, 72, 76, 84, 85, 129, 130
neighbourhood community, 62, 63–6
neighbourhood schools, in urban conurbations, 72

neighbourhood self-help, 113
networks
  in community, 65–6
  of informal learning, 53–4
  of professional contacts, 201
New York State Study Circle Consortium, 184
non-institutional learning, 2, 25–6, 32–3, 48
  see also independent learning
non-vocational education, 29

objectives, *see* goals
open learning system, 5
Open University, 6, 27, 94, 188
oral tradition, in dissemination of skills/knowledge, 54
orientation to learning, 35, 36
origins of learning, 52
outreach, 86, 183, 186
outreach workers, 201

parental encouragement, role of, 52
participatory research, 141–4
paternalism, 75, 94, 132
'Parallel Educational Universe', 48, 56–7, 131, 145
peer acclaim
  as measure of success, 50–1
  ways of expressing, 55
peer groups, 46–7
peer matching, 163–4
'People Talking Back' programmes, Canada, 6
political apathy, 178
political dimension
  of community adult education, 9, 68, 69–70, 81–2, 175, 179
  to role as adult educator, 202
political issues, and study circle, 184
portfolio of experiential learning, 168–9, 170, 171
power analysis, community, 63
praxis, 69, 110, 115
prescribed needs, 129–30
prescriptive adult education, 88
pressure groups, 105
problems, of independent learners, 56

problem-solving, community, 79, 101–4
'process', 78–82, 183
'programme', 67, 78–82
programme planning, 65, 85, 199
programmed instruction, 39
projects, *see* learning projects
psychology
of adult learning, 149
training sessions, 160
psychomotor skills, 12, 39
purposeful learning, 14–15

qualifications, *see* credentials
qualitative modes of research, 134–7
quality of learning, 13, 19, 45–6, 47
quantitative modes of research, 134–7
questionnaires, for community surveys, 131

radio, 5, 6, 55–6, 97–8, 123–4
reasons for learning, 38, 52
see also orientation to learning
recognition, of independent scholarship, 48
recreational learning projects, 41
recreational role of adult education, 119
reforms, proposed to help independent scholars, 49
Regional Educational Opportunity Center (REOC), Massachusetts, 158
research
of adult education, 3
of Adult Learning Iceberg, 43–7
into older age groups, 42
and opposition to MCE, 31, 32–3
participatory, 7, 141–4
qualitative and quantitative modes, 134–7
work of A. Tough, 36–40
see also Community Survey
researching adult learning within community, 6–7, 128
in individual mode, 34
example of, 144–8
research reports, Adult Learning Iceberg, 40–3

research sample, of successful independent learners, 50–2
residents' groups, 119
resource location, adult educator's skills, 84
resources for learning, *see* learning resources
responsibility, *see* learner responsibility
retraining, 29
Return to Study Programme, 190–1
'revolutionary organizer', 179
role
of adult educators, 84, 176–9
of community and education workers, 65–6
of expert, in independent learning, 33
of informal community groups, 4–5
of Informal Educator, ambiguity of, 200–3
of institutions in adult education, 1–2
rural community, needs, 72
rural community studies, 64
Russell Report (HMSO 1973), 185

sample composition, 44–5, 50–1
Schemes in Neighbourhood Action and Participation (SNAP), 77
scholarship, independent, *see* independent learning
'Second Chance Education', 124
SEED programme, Western Massachussetts, 77
'self-actualisation', 79, 150
see also individual growth
self-assessment, 37–8, 40
self-deprecation, of intentional changers, 40
self-directed learning, 10, 19, 23, 27, 43, 157, 169
see also self-learning, self-planned learning
self-fulfilment, as reason for learning, 42
self-help groups, 11, 47, 113, 121
self-learning, historical analysis, 2, 91
self-planned learning, 4, 34, 39

self-planned learning projects, national survey of, 41–2
self-teaching, 26, 36–8
settings for learning, 12–14, 18
Settlement Centres, 93–4
Shelter Neighbourhood Action Project (SNAP), 121
Sidney Stringer School and Community College, 74–5, 78
simulation and growing exercises, 194–195
skill exchange, 162–3, 164, 166
  see also learning exchanges
'skill models', 36, 54
skills, types of, 12, 39
  see also independent learning skills
Smithdown Mothers Club, 122–3
social action, and adult education, 69, 105, 121
social change
  and community development, 76, 106
  as educational aim, 9, 69–70, 174–76
  and Free Universities, 183
  and Highland Folk School, 116
  and Sidney Stringer School, 76
social class
  in Community Survey, 186
  research sample, 39, 41, 44
social context to independent learning, 46–7
social development, process as, 80–1
social work volunteers, training, 187
socio-economic status, 41
  see also social class
societies, 50, 53–4
spouse, role in encouragement of independent learning, 37, 52, 148
structured interviews, 45
Study Circles, 183–4
study groups, 5, 6, 94–9, 184
success
  evaluated in terms of community change, 116, 117
  in competitions, 55, 57
  criteria of, 55–6
successful independent learners, 49–57

successful independent learning, 47, 55–6
supporting adult learners in the community, 84
  a case study, 185–93
  the group mode, 173, 176
  the individual mode, 152–4, 157, 162
  proposed reforms in formal educational system, 49
  see also assistance
supporting autonomous adult learning group, 191–3
survey, *see* Community Survey

tasks, of self-teaching, 36–7, 43
'teacher', definition, 24–5
teaching skills, 151, 181
technological change, implications of, 28
The Learning Exchange (TLE), Evanston, Illinois, 164–6
Third World countries, 89, 96, 143
Tough, A.,
  work of, 34, 35, 36–40
  influence of, 145
Toynbee Hall, London, 93
training
  of community adult educators, 193–7
  in service programmes, 29
  for library staff, 160–1
  for professional adult educators, 29–30
  for social work volunteers, 187
transactional modes, 10, 11
Tuesday Club (Liverpool EPA), 122
typology of community practice of adult education, 84–9

ubiquity of adult learning, 1–4, 43–4, 198
urban community studies, 63, 64
urban conurbations, and neighbourhood schools, 72

value choices
  and contextual variables, 198–200

implicit, 174 – 5
value judgements, 182
value systems, 68, 69 – 70, 81, 85
Village Colleges, 71, 72 – 3
vocational practical learning, 38
voluntary learning, 29 – 33
voluntary organisations, 4 – 5, 29, 54, 186

volunteer social work, 187

Workers Educational Association (WEA), 29, 107, 124
workshops, Highlander, 114, 116, 117
written product, of independent learning project, 48